[PAGE FRIGHT]

Harry Bruce

Page Fright

FOIBLES

and

FETISHES

of

FAMOUS

WRITERS

⟦A DOUGLAS GIBSON BOOK⟧

McClelland & Stewart

Library and Archives Canada Cataloguing in Publication

Bruce, Harry, 1934–
Page fright : foibles and fetishes of famous writers / Harry Bruce.

ISBN 978-0-7710-1712-4

1. Authorship – Anecdotes. 2. Authors – Biography.
3. Writing – Materials and instruments – History. I. Title.

PN165.B78 2009   808'.02   C2009-901778-4

We acknowledge the financial support of the Government of Canada through the
Book Publishing Industry Development Program and that of the Government of
Ontario through the Ontario Media Development Corporation's Ontario Book
Initiative. We further acknowledge the support of the Canada Council for the Arts
and the Ontario Arts Council for our publishing program.

Typeset in Dante by M&S, Toronto
Printed and bound in Canada

ANCIENT FOREST
FRIENDLY

McClelland & Stewart Ltd.
75 Sherbourne Street
Toronto, Ontario
M5A 2P9
www.mcclelland.com

1 2 3 4 5   13 12 11 10 09

TO PENNY

[CONTENTS]

Whenever the British actor, playwright, and novelist Stephen Fry answers questions from an audience, someone asks, "Do you write in longhand or on a computer?"

If longhand: "With pencil, ballpoint, or old-fashioned ink pen?"

If computer: "PC or Mac? Which font do you prefer?"

All successful writers field such questions, Fry says, and therefore know this simple rule: "Readers are more interested in process than in product."

But process, which is what this book is all about, includes not only tools but the rooms in which writers work; the number of hours, in each day or night, that they imprison themselves in those rooms; and the number of words, in each day or night, that they've sworn to write.

It includes the way they try to satisfy the world's loneliest calling while sitting down, standing up, lying flat on their backs, or soaking in bathtubs; while wearing pyjamas, "lucky" sweaters, favourite shirts, dirty jeans, immaculate business suits, or no clothing at all; and while surrounding themselves with cheap statuettes, faded photographs, quirky ornaments, and sentimental bric-a-brac.

For many writers, the process involves coping with mood disorders, emotional turmoil, and suicidal urges. Since cigarettes, booze, narcotics, hallucinogens, and stimulants have not only ambushed literary creation but fuelled it, they, too, are part of the story. And so are healthier addictions: hiking, jogging, exercising, and listening to great music.

Indeed, process is *everything* that creative writers do to make themselves as receptive as they possibly can be to what so many of them see as dictation from a forever-unknowable source. It arms them to overcome their eternal foe: writer's block.

Through painful trial and error, the more successful writers at last find a process that, more often than not, does work for them. They are reluctant ever to change it. For some, the very idea of replacing their fountain pens with PCs is preposterous.

"Oh, I use a Mac, by the way," Fry reveals. "Times Roman, 14 point. Very traditional."

And very coincidental. I, too, use Times Roman, 14 point, and will never switch to any other typeface.

Harry Bruce

ONE

"Speaking to the Eyes": Beginnings

In the early 1840s, William Bacon Stevens, a young historian and devout Christian in Savannah, Georgia, beheld with awe a manuscript roughly a thousand years old. A ninth-century copy of *Moralia in Job*, which Pope Gregory I wrote in the sixth century, it was the oldest of the exceedingly rare treasures that plantation and slave owner Alexander Augustus Smets kept among the five thousand books in the library at his brick mansion in the city.

Worms had chewed the volume's thick covers, but the brass clasps and studs were in good shape. The double columns of Latin words on vellum pages were remarkably neat and highly legible, and Stevens marvelled "that the hand which traced those lines in all their beauty has a thousand years since moulded into dust – that the mighty waves of more than thirty generations have risen, rolled onward, and died upon the writer's grave. . . . The little characters inscribed on that parchment . . . have enclosed for ten centuries, the thoughts of the illustrious dead, *speaking* to the eye now, as [they] did a thousand years back, the same sentiments of piety and truth; while the name, the habitation, the tomb even of the writer have, for ages, been buried in oblivion! How wonderful is the power of letters! We enjoy hourly their benefit, we seldom reflect upon their worth. Their origin is lost in the remotest antiquity. . . ."

Stevens then presented verse by a writer he identified only as Breboeuf:

Whence did the wond'rous mystic art arise,
Of painting SPEECH, and speaking to the eyes?
That we, by tracing magic lines, are taught
How both to colour and embody THOUGHT?

In 1803, thirty-seven years before Stevens thus praised the miracle of handwriting – already so routine among the literate they thought about it little more than about breathing – Thomas Astle, keeper of records in the Tower of London, declared, "The noblest acquisition of mankind is SPEECH, and the most useful art is WRITING. The first eminently distinguishes MAN from the brute creation; the second from uncivilized savages." After quoting those same lines by "Monsieur Breboeuf," Astle took a 240-page stab at explaining whence the mystic art arose and how it was that, over thousands of years, it had reached a state of such excellence that, with goose quill in hand and inkpot at the ready, he could race his linked and slanted letters across paper made from boiled shreds of rags. That paper, he enthused, "surpasses all other materials for ease and convenience of writing upon."

But it was upon stone that humans left the earliest known evidence of their compulsion to express themselves – and to do so in ways that would one day speak to the eyes of those who walked on the moon, performed open-heart surgery, defeated computers at chess, and gossiped on cellphones. On shadowy walls roughly thirty thousand years ago, cave dwellers engraved and painted graceful images of lions, bears, bulls, bison, wild oxen, reindeer, horses, and fuzzy rhinoceroses. No one knows for sure why they did this, but in 1970 handwriting historian Alfred J. Fairbank declared, "The beginnings of writing are in simple pictures. . . . Picture-writing was used to help memory or identify possessions or to make records of transactions, but its link with language was the key to civilization."

For the Indians, Mexicans, Phoenicians, Hittites, Babylonians, Assyrians, Ethiopians, Etruscans, and, indeed, virtually all the ancient civilizations, hieroglyphic scripts – in which pictures of people, animals, birds, tools, and other familiar things each stood for the sound of a word or syllable – were the pioneers of written language. Roughly nine thousand years ago, when the population of the world was no more than five million, the Middle East and Far East knew so little about each other they might as well have been in different galaxies. Yet the peoples of the Tigris and Euphrates basins and those of the Peiligang culture in what is now Henan province in northern China were both raising farm animals, growing grain, making pottery, and relying on their own systems of visual symbols, usually carved or scratched into hard surfaces, to record and convey information they could not trust their memories to preserve.

Among the human remains in twenty-four of the graves that archaeologists recently unearthed in Henan were tortoise shells that bore sixteen different inscriptions. These are anywhere from 8,200 to 8,600 years old. Since they include markings that resemble the characters of "eye," "sun," "day," "window," and numbers in certain Chinese writing of more than five thousand years later, some scholars see them as proof that, eons before any other civilization, the Chinese invented writing. Others argue that the inscriptions are little more than a bunch of prehistoric pictures.

No expert will ever nail down, to every other expert's satisfaction, exactly when the sophistication of real writing emerged from the crudeness of prehistoric proto-writing, but *Encyclopedia Britannica* identifies T'sang Chieh as the "legendary inventor" of

Chinese writing, and it was in the mid-2500s BC that he served the Yellow Emperor as official recorder.

"At night, hearing the ghosts wail for the creation of writing, T'sang Chieh looked up with his four eyes at the pointed rays of the star Wen Chang, Lord of Literature," a Chinese historian wrote in AD 847. "Inspired, T'sang Chieh looked down to see the footprints of the birds and animals. He watched the shadows cast by trees and vegetation. . . . Observing the forms of nature, T'sang Chieh copied them by scratching onto sticks of smoothed bamboo. These were the first Chinese pictograms."

AND LO! THERE CAME UNTO THE WORLD THE ALPHABET

"Sumerian was the first language to be written, and it is largely monosyllabic," Fairbank said. "The writing began as simple pictures and some can be traced to about 3100 BC." Sumer lay in that small "cradle of civilization" between the Tigris and Euphrates rivers in what is now Iraq, and by 2500 BC its ingenious people had a complete system of writing that contained as many as a thousand symbols. Nowhere, however, were hieroglyphics more beautiful and enduring than in Egypt. More than five thousand years ago, Egyptian priests used them to carve sacred inscriptions into stone and to paint them on temple walls. In hieratic writing, a shortening of hieroglyphics, scribes joined letter to letter. Around 1000 BC there finally emerged in Egypt the demotic script, a more colloquial and popular descendant of hieroglyphics.

But how wonderful is the power of letters! The alphabet, in which each letter represents its own sound within a word, remains one of civilization's foremost innovations. Its origins, however, are obscure. Experts on the ancient world long believed that, between 1730 and 1580 BC, the first alphabet arose among Semitic peoples in their homelands in Syria and Palestine. Egyptologists, however, recently discovered evidence that, centuries earlier, Semites who lived deep inside Egypt were already using an ancestor of our alphabet. West of the Nile, on the track of a desert road that soldiers, merchants, and traders used some 3,800 years ago, the scholars found inscriptions carved into limestone cliffs. The writing was Semitic, with Egyptian influences – and it was alphabetic.

Masters of hieroglyphics were professionals who had to know hundreds of pictographs; the alphabet, with fewer than thirty symbols, emerged as a kind of shorthand. The discoveries at the cliffs, the *New York Times* reported in 1999, supported "the idea of the alphabet as an invention by workaday people that simplified and democratized writing, freeing it from the elite hands of official scribes." Thus, alphabetic writing was "revolutionary in a sense comparable to the invention of the printing press much later." While becoming the mightiest trading and naval power on the Mediterranean, the Phoenicians improved the alphabet, and roughly three thousand years ago passed it on to the Greeks. The Greeks further improved it, and then the idea of the alphabet spread to the Etruscans, the Romans, and throughout Western culture.

First Baked Muck, Then Papyrus

Writing was so important to the ancients that they painted, inked, scratched, or engraved it on stone, bronze, brass, bark, linen, silk, camel bones, tortoise shells, pottery shards, limestone fragments, bare wood, plaster-coated and wax-coated wood, parchment, and vellum. The Sumerians wrote on clots of muck and baked them in the Middle Eastern sun. Much of their land was marshy, flood-prone, irrigated, and rich in alluvial silt. Pressing the triangular-shaped cut end of a reed into a cushion of damp clay, the writer produced wedge-shaped strokes in patterns that added up to strings of words. Later, the Babylonians, Assyrians, Hittites, and Persians also wrote in *cuneiform* (from the Latin *cuneus*, for wedge), and thousands of their inscribed tablets remain legible to this day.

The earliest surviving cuneiform writings of the Sumerians are financial accounts and supply lists of priests. Among other ancient peoples as well, the first known writings were not imaginative. They were official, ceremonial, and religious, or simply asserted ownership, preserved legal settlements, and recorded transactions. Around 2000 BC, however, certain scribes offered a series of myths and poems that evolved into *The Epic of Gilgamesh*. In all likelihood, Gilgamesh was a real king who, between 2700 and 2500 BC, ruled from one of the world's first walled cities, Uruk. Over centuries, as Sumerian, Hittite, Babylonian, and Assyrian scribes immortalized him on clay, he emerged in a long epic poem as a demigod with superhuman powers. He kills a gigantic ogre, crosses the Waters of Death, overcomes monstrous hardships, tangles with gods and goddesses, agonizes over the death of his closest friend, seeks wisdom and life everlasting and, like lesser Sumerians, comes to know grief, joy, failure, and triumph. He is a Mesopotamian precursor of Hercules.

The Epic of Gilgamesh may well be the oldest written story on Earth, and we owe its best-preserved and most complete rendition to the first author whose name has come down to us. He was Sin-liqe-unninni. He lived in Babylonia between 1300 and 1000 BC and wrote the "standard" version of the poem on twelve clay tablets. We know next to nothing about him, but can we possibly doubt his dedication to writing? One English translation of his *Gilgamesh* in Babylonian runs to more than seventeen thousand words. Yet Sin-liqe-unninni set out his entire epic by poking reeds into clumps of mud. His Muse must have immunized him against both writer's block and writer's cramp.

By his time, Egyptians had been making papyrus for roughly 2,500 years. A tall reed that grew abundantly in the shallower waters of the Nile and its delta, *Cyperus papyrus* was a godsend to the locals, and perhaps to the baby Moses. Some believe that it was this plant, not bulrushes, that his mother used to make the floating cradle in which she hid him at the edge of the Nile. The Egyptians turned some parts of *Cyperus papyrus* into food and fuel, and others into utensils, cloth, rope, sandals, skiffs, and garlands for shrines. But nothing the people of the Nile made from the hugely plentiful reed was anywhere near as important as papyrus. Upon this light, flexible ancestor of paper, scribes wrote quickly with ink they made from soot, gum and water, and pens they fashioned from hollow reeds. For a thousand years or more, papyrus was the most popular writing surface not only among the Egyptians, but among the Greeks, Romans, and other peoples who imported it from them.

The very pains the Egyptians took to manufacture it proved how indispensable it was. Papyrus makers split the stem, extracted strips of pith, laid them side by side to form a layer, placed shorter pieces over them at right angles, bonded the two crossways layers with paste or muddy Nile water, and then pressed, pounded, and hammered the sheet. Finally, they dried it in the sun. Using ivory, shells, or pumice, workers then polished one side until it was fit to receive writing. For purposes of shipment and book-length compositions, they pasted sheets end to end until they had a long strip, which they rolled up on wooden rods. Some rolls were 150 feet long, but most of those bound for Greece and Rome were thirty to thirty-five feet by nine or ten inches. They were tough enough to survive centuries of rolling and unrolling. Roman encyclopedist Pliny the Elder wrote, "Well-made papyrus can be more supple than linen."

Its production was no mere cottage industry. Egyptians produced it not in small workshops but in factories. They exported it to Mesopotamia – the Assyrians called it "the reed of Egypt" – and ports all around the Mediterranean. Rome had several papyrus dealers, and at stationery shops buyers had their choice of half a dozen grades and widths. They used papyrus not only for works of literature, but for correspondence, everyday business, and legal documents. In Rome, the government owned a cavernous warehouse for the papyrus its bureaucrats used in their offices. During the reign of Tiberius (AD 14 to 37), the failure of the papyrus crop made the "paper" so hard to get that, according to the *Encyclopedia Britannica* (1910), "there was a danger of the ordinary business of life being deranged." Two thousand years later, it would take power failures to cause that sort of crisis.

Estimates of the holdings in antiquity's biggest library and first research institute indicate how enormous the production of papyrus was. Built early in the third century BC, during the Hellenistic era that began in Egypt after the vast conquests of Alexander the Great, the Royal Library in Alexandria was still in its infancy when a bibliographical survey revealed it housed ninety thousand rolls. In the 1980 television series *Cosmos: A Personal Voyage*, astronomer Carl Sagan said that "the intellectual venture that has led us into space" actually began at this very library, and he claimed it housed nearly a million scrolls. That was an exaggeration but even if the total was only half that, and the average length of the scrolls was thirty-five feet, the papyrus there was more than 3,300 miles long. And that was only in Alexandria. Heaven only knows how many more miles of papyrus documents sat in the dusty libraries of ancient Greece, Rome, and Mesopotamia.

On Papyrus, the New Testament. And Sex Manuals

With due respect to *Gilgamesh*, it was papyrus, not clay, that allowed the arrival of literature in the world; encouraged its blossoming during what Edgar Allan Poe called "the glory that was Greece, the grandeur that was Rome"; and preserved it for the printing presses and websites of inconceivably distant times. Stone and metal were fine for inscribing laws, edicts, commandments, and dedications, but not for writing literature. British Egyptologist and author Amelia Edwards (1831–1892) once challenged her readers to imagine Sappho, Martial and Horace "laboriously scratching" their poems on bronze or stone. "How the perfume of the roses and the sting of the epigrams and the aroma of the Sabine wine would have evaporated under such a process!" Thus it was on papyrus that not only the New Testament survived, but also the writings of Homer, Aesop, Plato, Aristotle, Plutarch, Euripides, Marcus Aurelius, Tacitus, Cicero, Lucretius, and dozens of others. It was on papyrus that *The Aeneid* by Virgil (70–19 BC) travelled, in his own lifetime, all the way to Britain.

As recently as 2005, researchers at Oxford University employed a new technology called "multi-spectral imaging" to read papyrus fragments that had been illegible for more than two thousand years. Bills, wills, horoscopes, tax assessments, and private letters were among the suddenly readable documents, but so were works by giants of Greek classical literature. Dirk Obbink, director of the research, said the hoard contained "a complete slice of life – everything from Sophocles and Homer to sex manuals and steamy novels."

Even before the Greeks and Romans, however, the Egyptians had an extensive literature of their own, and in the Victorian era Amelia Edwards wrote about it as though it were the Eighth Wonder of the Ancient World:

> The Egyptians were the first people . . . who wrote books, and read books; who possessed books, and loved them. And their literature, which grew, and flourished and decayed with the language in which it was written, was of the most varied character, scientific, secular, and religious. It comprised moral and educational treatises; state papers; works on geometry, medicine, astronomy, and magic; travels, tales, fables, heroic poems, love-songs, and essays in the form of letters; hymns, dirges, rituals; and last, not least, that extraordinary collection of prayers, invocations, and religious formulae known as The Book of the Dead. Some of these writings

are older than the pyramids; some are as recent as the time when Egypt had fallen from her high estate and become a Roman province. Between these two extremes lie more than 5000 years. Of this immense body of literature we possess only the scattered wrecks – mere "flotsam and jetsam," left stranded on the shores of Time.

Since papyrus was expensive, the Romans also wrote on wax. They spread green or black beeswax on white sheets of wood and inscribed words on it with a stylus. This needle-like tool had a blunt end for corrections. Writers erased outdated inscriptions simply by smoothing the wax and using it again and again. Handy for casual jottings, keeping accounts, dashing off unimportant letters, and working on poetry or prose until it was good enough to transfer to papyrus, the tablets were the notebooks of the Roman Empire.

Like nineteenth-century schoolchildren with portable slates, Roman schoolboys wrote exercises on these waxed boards. Their teachers often tied tablets together to form primitive books, at least one of which grew dangerously heavy. "For in Plautus," Thomas Astle wrote in his 1803 history of handwriting, "a school boy of seven years old is represented breaking his master's head with a table book." The iron stylus could also be lethal. The historian Suetonius claimed that the sadistic despot Caligula (AD 14 to 41) incited a Roman mob to murder a senator with their stylli. Moreover, Astle continued, "Prudontius very emphatically describes the tortures which Cassianus [a schoolteacher] was put to by his scholars, who killed him with their *pugillares* (table books) and styles." The Romans eventually thought it best to outlaw iron stylli in favour of those fashioned from ivory or bone, a ruling that every teacher in the empire doubtless applauded.

FROM CHINA TO ENGLAND OVER
FIFTEEN CENTURIES: PAPER MILLS

The paper that the world now uses owes its origin to China. Paper first appeared there at least a century before the birth of Christ but, according to the British manufacturer of fine art paper, Inveresk PLC, "traditional Chinese records give the credit for its development to one T'sai Lun (about 105 AD), who was even deified as the god of papermakers." He taught them to pound and grind bark, rags, and fishing nets, and to mix the result with water to make a mushy pulp. With fine mesh screens, they turned the stuff into sheets of intertwined fibre, which they then pressed and dried. "This method of papermaking," the Ontario Science Centre asserts, "has not changed in 2,000 years."

China knew it was on to a good thing. It foiled whatever industrial espionage foreigners attempted and kept its papermaking formula a secret, even from nearby Korea and Japan, for at least five centuries. In 751, however, Arab forces defeated a Chinese army in a historic battle near the Taras River in central Asia, and among the prisoners they took were papermakers. The Arabs promptly forced them into paper production in Samarkand, and by 794 Baghdad, too, had a mill. Paper slowly spread westward in the Arab world, to Damascus, Egypt, Morocco, and, in the 1150s, Spain. Still later, mills emerged throughout continental Europe and finally arrived in England in the late 1400s. That was a good fifteen hundred years after the first sheets of paper, somewhere in China, began to accept ink.

The quality of early Chinese paper, Inveresk reports, was superb. Indeed, it was "comparable even with that of hand-made rag paper today." Chinese calligraphers have never been able to settle for anything less. Choosing from quivers of assorted brushes, they stroke ink onto this fine paper to express meanings that are literary, to be sure, but also visual. How they write is every bit as important as what they write and, unlike handwriting in the Western world, Oriental calligraphy is itself an art. Museums exhibit it as they do paintings, and the Chinese still treasure it as more valuable than paintings and sculpture. As a means of self-expression, they rank it alongside poetry. To connoisseurs of this Oriental art, the unique style of each calligrapher's creation reflects his character, emotions, culture, and appreciation of beauty. It thus reveals to the reader-viewer the very soul of the artist.

Chinese calligraphers preferred rabbit-hair brushes for small characters and sheep-hair brushes for bolder strokes, but also used ones made from the hairs of goats, weasels, wolves, tigers, and gorillas, and even the whiskers of mice. The ink consisted of lamp-black baked with a glutinous substance, and the finest grades were delicately perfumed. Perhaps the scent made it easier for the artist to convey not only the language of thought but what calligraphy authority Jean Long calls "the artistic beauty of the thought."

No Paper? Try Sheepskin

In the Roman Empire during the fourth century AD, slaughtered animals overtook aquatic plants as the raw material for the most popular forebear of writing paper. Made from the skins of sheep or goats, parchment was a bit coarse. But vellum – the treated skins of kids, lambs, and calves – was thin, firm, crisp, smooth, and glossy. Newly born or stillborn animals provided vellum's *crème de la crème*. The earliest users of the best vellum undoubtedly appreciated its beautiful writing surface, but probably failed to grasp how amazingly durable it was. While rot has destroyed all the ancient papyrus documents except those found in the dry heat of Egypt, thousands of vellum documents have survived the march of centuries. Vellum had a further advantage; it was reusable. Scribes could erase writings from it and use it repeatedly. That was important. The stuff was so expensive that, for routine work, they wrote in tiny letters.

"The ordinary modern process of preparing the skins," *Encyclopedia Britannica* reported in 1910, "is by washing, liming, unhairing, scraping, washing a second time, stretching evenly on a frame, scraping a second time and paring down inequalities, dusting with sifted chalk and rubbing with pumice. Similar methods . . . must have been employed from the first."

The finished product, however, more than justified the painstaking labour. While the several rolls of papyrus required to contain a whole book were awkward to handle and tricky to keep in proper order, just one volume of parchment or vellum pages could hold all of Homer, Virgil, or the Bible. As early as the first century AD, the expert writer of epigrams in Latin, Martial, touted the wonderful advantages of the ancient manuscript in book form that we now call the codex. "You want to take my poems wherever you go, as companions, say, on a trip to some distant land?" he wrote. "Buy this. It's packed tight into parchment pages, so leave your rolls at home, for this takes just one hand!"

Thus, the vellum codex ousted papyrus and dominated publishing right down to the arrival of paper mills and printing presses at the end of the Middle Ages. (While the history of printing is undoubtedly fascinating, this book deals only with the tools, materials, and habits that have helped creative writers fill the blank pages that confronted them.)

After barbarian hordes conquered the Roman Empire and plunged Europe into the Dark Ages, deeply religious men holed up for centuries in a chain of castle-like monasteries that stretched across the continent. Working in silence and, for fear of fire, with no light but the sun's, they preserved on vellum not only the Bible and other supreme texts of Christendom, but the works of medicine, science, history, philosophy, and literature that have travelled all the way from classical Greece and Rome to readers in the twenty-first century. An article at booksellerworld.com reports that the pages for one copy of the Bible required the slaughter of

210 to 225 sheep and "from the first fifty years of the ninth century we have records of forty-six large Bibles and eighteen Gospels produced at Tours. A sure cure for insomnia."

If making vellum was troublesome, making ink was doubly so. In the eleventh century, an Italian monk named Theophilus began to make what Samuel Johnson, some seven centuries later, would call "the black liquor with which men write," by cutting hawthorn branches before they produced blossoms or leaves in the early spring. He laid them in a shady spot for up to eight weeks until they dried out, pounded them with mallets, and peeled off their bark. He put the bark in barrels of water for eight days to allow the water to draw off the sap, then he dumped the water into a big cauldron, heated it over a fire, threw in more bark, boiled the liquid down to a third of its original volume, transferred it to a smaller container, and heated it again until it turned black and began to thicken. "When you see it become thick," he concluded, "add a third part of pure wine, put it in two or three new pots and continue to heat it until you see that it develops a kind of skin at the top."

Around the time that Theophilus wrote his ink-making instructions, an unknown writer, in scrupulously neat Old English, transcribed the epic saga *Beowulf*. Set in the fifth and sixth centuries and possibly composed as early as the seventh, the poem describes in eloquent and gory detail the struggles of the Scandinavian hero, Beowulf, against the bloodthirsty, man-eating monster, Grendel; the horrifying, revenge-seeking mother of the felled Grendel; and a dragon. The sole surviving manuscript sits in the British Library. Some of the poem's admirers now call it "England's national epic." Yet it would never have come to light if it weren't for the anonymous scribe who, a thousand years ago, copied all of its 3,183 lines onto the skins of animals – with the feathers of a bird. For centuries, the quill pen had been the writing instrument of choice throughout Europe, and it would remain so for centuries to come.

TWO

The Feather Is Mightier Than the Sword

About the works of Shakespeare, Hollywood producer Samuel Goldwyn is reputed to have said, "Fantastic! And it was all done with a feather!" Since quill pens wore out in about a week, it was actually done with hundreds of feathers, but each required so much maintenance that "fantastic" hardly exaggerated the bard's effort.

Writing in the seventh century AD, St. Isadore of Seville, theologian and encyclopedist, mentioned a quill pen, but it was probably well before then that the scribes who'd holed up in fortified Christian sanctuaries replaced their reed pens with doctored feathers of birds. They shaped and split the pointed ends of the horny and hollow barrels of strong wing feathers. Thus, when the greatest poets and novelists of the nineteenth century were young, the quill pen had been ruling handwriting in Europe for more than twelve hundred years.

In 731, the Anglo-Saxon monk and scholar known as the Venerable Bede wrote his *Ecclesiastical History of the English People* with a quill pen, and in 1809, Lord Byron, wielding essentially the same instrument, opened a satiric attack on Britain's literary establishment with these couplets:

O nature's noblest gift – my grey goose-quill!
Slave of my thoughts, obedient to my will,
Torn from thy parent bird to form a pen
That mighty instrument of little men!

For fine work, the stiff-spined feathers came from the wings of ravens and crows. Jane Austen, as a teenager in 1792, used a crow quill to write a poem in tiny letters on a slip of paper that she tucked into a needle-case and gave to a friend. Writers also employed the feathers of swans, peacocks, turkeys, eagles, hawks, owls, and vultures, but they mostly fashioned pens from goose quills. They sharpened them to make smaller letters than anyone could write with a reed pen. Goose quills were sturdy, flexible, and plentiful.

After cattle had eaten all their winter feed, farmers slaughtered them, but geese squawked, waddled, and gobbled year-round. "When it is recollected that every cottage keeps [them], and every green swarms with them, the number of geese in England must be very great," one Isaac Taylor wrote in 1823. "This is seen in a curious way, when large flocks, of eight or ten thousand, are driven to London. A piece of red rag, on a long stick, scares them on. They travel about eight miles a day." Writers, however, were so prolific they needed more quills than even all of Britain could supply. According to one BBC website, goose farms thrived throughout Europe, and, "at one point, St. Petersburg in Russia was sending to Britain no fewer than 27 million quills a year." In all likelihood, the founding fathers of the new republic on the far side of the Atlantic signed its constitution with Russian quills. Half a century later, in 1829, records show that thirty-nine ships sailed into Boston Harbor with millions of them. Thomas Jefferson wrote roughly twenty thousand letters in his lifetime and, to guarantee his quill supply, raised his own geese.

In the spring, when a goose grew quickly, as many as five of the outer feathers were yanked from each wing. To harden and strengthen a freshly plucked feather, and also to render membrane easy to scrape off, the pen maker usually buried it in hot sand. In 1754, however, *The Dictionary of Arts and Sciences* recommended that you stir it in hot ashes, press it almost flat on your knee with the back of a penknife, "and afterwards reduce it to a roundnefs with your fingers." To harden several quills at once, you held their barrels for one minute in a mixture of boiling water and alum. Ancient pictures show monks and evangelists at work with feathery quills, but many writers preferred to strip the barrel naked. The pen then looked like a skinny stick.

Every writer owned a special knife to turn feathers into pens (hence, "penknife"). It had a square wooden handle, a short steel blade with a thick back, and – owing to its owner's regular use of oil, water, whetstones, and a leather strap – a cutting edge as sharp as a razor's. Having selected a feather, the writer trimmed it, sliced off the point with a sloping cut, turned the cut side face up, inserted his knife into the freshly exposed hollow, and made a slit. He then whittled off the corners on either side of the slit and shaped the nib to suit his handwriting style. The nib was supple so, for ease and control of handwriting, the pen was far superior to the stiff reeds of ancient times.

If making a pen required skill and patience, however, so did looking after it. Since dried-out quills produced faint and ragged letters, writers stored them with the nibs in water and washed them after every use. Old ink blocked the flow of new ink, but after a quill was submersed in warm, soapy water, rinsed, and dried, it sprang back into its original shape. That, however, did not prevent ink from dripping, splattering, and smearing. Before the invention of blotting paper, writers kept a pot of powder handy to dry ink and prevent its spreading. Other problems interrupted their flow of thought. The barrel held so little ink that, after every few words, they had to dip the nib again. The point snapped off so easily that, after every couple of pages, they had to reshape and sharpen it.

That task wasn't easy for everyone. In a scene that Charlotte Brontë wrote in *Vilette* (1853), Paul Emanuel, a schoolmaster with whom the secretive teacher Lucy Snowe falls in love, chases Sylvie, a spaniel, into a classroom. There, he finds Lucy reading at a desk. He gazes at her so intently that, to hide her confusion, she starts to repair her pens.

> I knew that my action would give a turn to his mood. He never liked to see me mend pens; my knife was always dull-edged – my hand, too, was unskillful; I hacked and chipped. On this occasion I cut my own finger – half on purpose. I wanted to . . . set him at ease, to get him to chide.
>
> "Maladroit!" he cried at last, "She will make mincemeat of her hands." He put Sylvie down . . . and, depriving me of the pens and my penknife, proceeded to slice, nib, and point with the accuracy and celerity of a machine.

MIGHTY TRIUMPHS OF THE HUMBLE QUILL

In various lodgings near the theatres of London four centuries ago, Shakespeare used exactly such equipment – unimaginably cumbersome in comparison with today's writing tools – to churn out his immortal poetry and plays. Fantastic, indeed! Seated in a standard, panel-backed chair at a table that bore a book rest for his research, he wrote by daylight and candlelight on both sides of thick, coarse, folio-sized paper. At furious speed. Three centuries after his death, one analyst of his signature wrote, "The firm control of the pen in forming the sweeping curves in the surname is indeed remarkable . . . a free and rapid, though careless, hand."

Shakespeare wrote so fast with feathers that Fyodor Dostoevsky thought his work was not just careless, but slapdash. "A thing that has been written all at once cannot be ripe," Fyodor wrote to his brother, M.M. Dostoevsky. "They say there was not a blot on Shakespeare's manuscripts. That is why there are so many enormities and so much bad taste in him; he would have done much better if he had worked harder." Shakespeare wrote so fast that Virginia Woolf, who had dip pens, fountain pens, pencils, mechanical pencils, and typewriters at her disposal, confessed, "I never knew how amazing his stretch & speed and word-coining power is, until I felt it utterly outpace & outrace my own . . . even the less known & worser plays are written at a speed that is quicker than anybody else's quickest; & the words drop so fast one can't pick them up." Shakespeare wrote so fast he couldn't stop to insert punctuation. The speed of his hand fuelled the magic of his creation. Samuel Coleridge, no slouch himself at writing with feathers, marvelled that, as Shakespeare's sentences dashed after one another, "he goes on kindling like a meteor through the dark atmosphere."

More than 220 years after Shakespeare died, young Charles Dickens, while writing *Oliver Twist* (1837–39) and *Nicholas Nickleby* (1838–39), hit his own amazing stride with quill pens. "As Dickens writes," said Peter Ackroyd, one of his modern biographers, "he rarely pauses to correct; his handwriting is large and firm, springing from him with extraordinary speed. . . . He used a goose-quill pen with blue ink. He wrote on blue-grey slips of paper, eight and three quarter inches by seven and one quarter inches. On an ordinary day he would complete approximately two thousand words . . . but when he was writing in a furious vein he might complete almost four thousand words." Fast? Writing a century later with hard, clean pencils, handy erasers, and a typewriter, Hemingway was content if, on an ordinary day, "you put down properly 422 words as you wanted them to be. And days of 1,200 were something that made you happier than you could believe."

It was not only Shakespeare's and Dickens's characters that came to life at the nibs of quills but also Tamburlaine, the Faerie Queen, Lemuel Gulliver, Robinson Crusoe, Fanny Hill, Tom Jones, Elizabeth Bennett, Ivanhoe, the Frankenstein monster, the last of the Mohicans, the Lady of Shalott, Becky Sharpe, Jane Eyre, Heathcliff, Hester Prynne, Moby Dick, and Silas Marner; fields of golden daffodils; thou deep and dark blue ocean; the fruit of that forbidden tree; the house of Usher; Xanadu, where Kubla Kahn a stately pleasure-dome did decree; and indeed – from *The Canterbury Tales* to *Leaves of Grass* – every thought, scene, and invention in the literature of the English-speaking world during an entire millennium.

WITH QUILL IN HAND, BALZAC WAS UNBEATABLE

And not just of the English-speaking world.

In *Dead Souls* by Nikolai Gogol (1809–1852), a character enters "a splendid, shining hall" in which "legions of handsome gentlemen of the quill-driving profession make loud scratchings with pens." In *War and Peace*, an old man "went on writing so that his quill pen spluttered and squeaked," and in *Madame Bovary* the quill of the obnoxious Homais "kept squeaking along on the paper." Not in fiction, however, but in real England in the early 1600s, the quill pens of forty-seven biblical scholars and linguists scratched, spluttered, and squeaked for seven years. The men were translating the Bible from Hebrew and Greek to create the King James Version.

Year after year in the early 1300s, Dante Alighieri, the first important author ever to write in Italian, used quill pens while composing the fourteen thousand lines of *The Divine Comedy*. Five years after the Black Death in 1348, Giovanni Boccaccio laid aside his quill after completing *The Decameron*. A collection of one hundred tales, it influenced writers throughout Europe for centuries and earned him a deathless reputation as the inventor of the short-story form in literature. With quill pens, Boccaccio's chum Petrarch wrote such superb poetry that in 1341, during a ceremony that Rome had not seen in more than a thousand years, he was crowned with the coveted laurel.

An international celebrity and, in some eyes, the first modern lyric poet, Petrarch was also a powerful force in the emergence of the Renaissance. Like Boccaccio and a host of lesser writers, he passionately believed in unearthing and preserving the greatest literature of classical Greece and Rome. Out of the feverish copying of ancient Latin texts in the 1400s and 1500s, there came a new and speedy kind of handwriting. Without lifting their pens, the copiers now sloped their letters and joined many of them. They introduced upstrokes and straight-edged capital letters like those they could still see engraved on monuments of the Roman Empire. Since the Italian Renaissance, the longhand of the whole Western world has been a descendant of this cursive and "italic" style.

Between the mid-twelfth century, when the epic poem *La Chanson de Roland* emerged as the earliest major work of French literature, and the mid-nineteenth century, when Flaubert agonized over finding *le mot juste* while writing *Madame Bovary* (1856), every French creator of immortal literature used pens made from the wing feathers of one big bird or another. But none of them – not Rabelais or Ronsard, Villon or Voltaire, Montaigne or Molière, not Stendhal, Dumas, Hugo, George Sand, or any of the others who helped France achieve the cultural leadership of Europe – was so enslaved by the quill pen as the hugely prolific Honoré de Balzac (1799–1850).

He was short, fat, and lusty. A dandy and sybarite, he bought absurd treats for himself. "When he could add no more to the sumptuous magnificence of his [two] houses, his dinners, his carriage, and his servants[,]" British novelist Wilkie Collins wrote in 1863, "when he had filled his rooms with every species of expensive knickknack; when he had lavished money on all the known extravagances which extravagant Paris can supply to the spendthrift's inventory; he hit on the entirely new idea of providing himself with such a walking stick as the world had never yet beheld. . . . With this cane, nearly as big as a drum major's staff, and all ablaze at the top with rubies, diamonds, emeralds and sapphires, Balzac exhibited himself in a rapture of satisfied vanity at the theatres and public promenades."

Balzac spent enormous sums on champagne, paintings, fashionable clothes, magnificent furniture, and silver cutlery engraved with a coat of arms that featured a young cock and a naked woman. His footmen wore the liveries of a noble family to which he insisted, without offering a jot of proof, he was related. A groom looked after his horses and carriage and, dressed up in a showy uniform, drove him to the opera houses where Balzac had boxes of his own. The carriage rug was violet and bore a pretentious coronet. At a fashionable restaurant in Paris, publisher Edmond Werdet watched in awe as the novelist, barely five feet tall, gobbled one hundred oysters, twelve mutton cutlets, two roast partridges, one duck with turnips, one Normandy sole, and a dozen pears.

Balzac complicated his writing life with a never-ending load of crushing debts and a never-ending series of love affairs. The last, longest, and most passionate of these was with the wealthy Evelyne de Hanska, the Russian wife of a Polish nobleman. Only a few months before Balzac died, she finally consented to marry him. During his forties, novelist C.P. Snow wrote, his distractions included "schemes for wiping out those debts! And then becoming rich! Property deals! A new magazine! Plays! New lawyers, new contracts with publishers! Letters to Madame Hanska, far away at Wierzchownia [in the Ukraine]! New houses with back entrances so that he could slip away from the duns! Trips abroad with other women."

Yet this seemingly irresponsible and unfocused sensualist, who lived only fifty-one years, wrote more than ninety novellas and novels. In *La Comédie humaine*, which ran to forty-seven volumes, he attempted to reproduce all of French society and created more than two thousand characters from every profession and class. "Unquestionably he ranks as one of the few great geniuses who appear by one or twos, in century after century of authorship," Collins wrote, "and who leave their mark ineffaceably on the literature of their age." Forty-two years later, no less a writer than Henry James declared Balzac the greatest novelist of all time.

Describing the young Parisian's life as he churned out pot-boilers in a Paris garret, V.S. Pritchett wrote, "He could write as fast as he talked and this was very fast indeed. He wrote a novelette in two or three weeks, working in long timeless stretches; he boasted that he could wear out ten crow-feather pens in three days, in his rapid hand that dashed like black rain across the uncorrected pages."

After Balzac resolved to write not trash but lasting literature, he imposed upon himself a ritual of work so ruthless it probably shortened his life. While writing, Snow said, Balzac put in "a working day, a real working day, pen close to the paper, of about thirteen hours a day. No modern professional could endure anything like such labour, and it wouldn't be good for anyone to try."

Balzac went to bed at eight p.m., and his valet awakened him at midnight. He donned a white cashmere robe, like those worn by Dominican monks, and secured it around his waist with a gold chain, from which dangled tiny scissors and pliers, also gold. He stepped into white Turkish trousers, pulled on red leather slippers embroidered with more gold, sat down at a small table, grabbed a quill pen, and, by the light of four candles, began to work. Pritchett wrote:

To say that he worked is inadequate; he seemed to have a cease-less engine in his brain. . . . He wrote hour after hour and when he flagged and his head seemed to burst, he went to the coffee-pot and brewed the strongest black coffee he could find, made from the beans of Bourbon, Martinique and Mocha. He was resorting to a slow course of coffee poisoning and it has been estimated that in his life he drank 50,000 cups of it. When dawn came he stopped writing and, imitating Napoleon, lay for an hour in a hot bath. At nine messengers brought him proofs from the printers and he began the enormous task of altering almost everything he had written and in that handwriting that drove printers mad.

For lunch, he ate an egg or a sandwich and then spent the whole afternoon doctoring more proofs and writing letters. After five he chatted with friends. He ate dinner and, sharp at eight, climbed back into bed.

Taking quill pens to the proofs of his books, Balzac attacked his own writing with such gusto printers saw him as a madman. Collins offered this vivid description of Balzac's rewriting entire books on proofs:

He now covered with fresh corrections, fresh alterations, fresh expansions of this passage, and fresh abridgments of that, not only the margins of the proofs all round, but even the little intervals of white space between the paragraphs. Lines crossing each other in indescribable confusion were supposed to show the bewildered printer the various places at which the multitude of new insertions were to be slipped in. Illegible as Balzac's original manuscripts were, his corrected proofs were more puzzling still. The picked men in the office, to whom alone they could be intrusted, shud-dered at the very name of Balzac, and relieved each other at inter-vals of an hour, beyond which time no one printer could be got to continue at work on the universally execrated and universally unintelligible proofs. . . . He was literally the terror of all printers and editors; and he himself described his process of work as a misfortune. . . . "I toil sixteen hours out of the twenty-four," he said, "over the elaboration of my unhappy style, and I am never satisfied myself when all is done."

YOUNG MRS. TOLSTOY GETS DOWN TO WORK

If any one author launched the golden age of Russian literature (which could not help but be a golden age of the quill pen, as well), it was the playwright, poet, novelist, and short-story writer Aleksandr Pushkin (1799–1837). His best work powerfully influenced later Russian literature, and long after he died he had the stature in Russia that Shakespeare had in England. Pushkin showed the way for Turgenev, Dostoevsky, Tolstoy, and Chekhov. Of these, only Tolstoy (1828–1910) lived long enough to use quill pens, dip pens with steel nibs, fountain pens, and a typewriter.

It took him six years to write the nearly eight hundred thousand words of *War and Peace* (1865–69). His handwriting was at least as bad as Balzac's, and in 1863, at thirty-five, he assigned his nineteen-year-old wife, Sonya, the job of making a clean, legible copy of every page he wrote. At Yasnaya Polyana (Clear Glade), the 4,000-acre Tolstoy estate 130 miles southeast of Moscow, they lived in a rough, white, wooden manor house, surrounded by dense forest. Count Tolstoy was an aristocrat, but his furniture was crude, his serfs dirty and sometimes drunk, and his house, which had no running water, infested with cockroaches and lice. It was here that he'd been born and that Sonya, with little help from him, reared their thirteen children. In view of her crushing load of domestic responsibilities – and his fanatical revising of everything he wrote – her copying services verged on the superhuman.

Wearing a grey smock and slurping tea, he worked alone in an ample ground-floor study, but Sonya completed his monumental copying assignments while seated at a small table in a corner of the family drawing room. It was there that she wrote shopping lists and dinner menus and, as the Tolstoys' son Ilya remembered, "often sat over her 'copying' till three or four o'clock in the morning." Ilya believed she wrote out *War and Peace* no fewer than eight times, and "probably made even more copies of *Anna Karenina*." Since Sonya copied her husband's prose not only during "every free moment," but within full sight of her children, they thought she worked harder than he did. Daughter Tatyana remembered:

> We had scarcely finished wishing her goodnight before that pretty head, its hair so black and smooth, was already bent over the table again, her shortsighted eyes peering to decipher my father's manuscript, those pages crammed with writing, scrawled with erasures, the lines of script sometimes crisscrossing in every direction. In the morning my father would find the sheets back on his desk, plus a neat and legible fair copy, which he then proceeded to work over again, adding whole new pages, black with his vast, illegible scrawl, sometimes deleting other pages completely with a single stroke of the pen.

Since Tolstoy did not suffer interruptions to his work gladly, Sonya hated to disturb him. Occasionally, however, she had no choice but to show him a piece of his longhand and ask him what it said. "[Tolstoy] would read the passage impatiently until he reached the part in question," Louise Smoluchowski wrote in *Lev and Sonya* (1987), "but then often he, too, stumbled and hesitated and finally had to guess at his own intention." At such moments, the man whom many still see as the greatest novelist of all time could not read his own handwriting.

"To write legibly is civil and logical," handwriting historian Alfred J. Fairbank asserted in 1970. "To write with grace is friendly and generous, and adds a little to the virtue of civilized life." But

Balzac, Tolstoy, and countless other creative writers had more urgent things on their minds than mere legibility and civility. Their longhand resembled that of the English clergyman and essayist Sydney Smith (1771–1845), whom an admirer called "the wisest of witty men, and the wittiest of wise men." To a gentleman who asked to borrow one of his sermons, Smith mailed a letter in which he confessed, "I would send it to you with pleasure, but my writing is as if a swarm of ants, escaping from an ink bottle, had walked over a sheet of paper without wiping their legs." It was, of course, with the pointed shafts of feathers that Smith made all his ant tracks.

THREE

Inkwells, Steel Nibs, Billions of Ballpoints

T he quill, Ambrose Bierce wrote in his *Devil's Dictionary* (1911), is "an implement of torture yielded by a goose and commonly wielded by an ass. This use of the quill is now obsolete, but its modern equivalent, the steel pen, is wielded by the same everlasting presence."

The search for a more durable and maintenance-free pen than the quill had continued for centuries. Before the mass production of steel, metal nibs were too stiff and too vulnerable to rust and corrosion. By the 1830s, however, factories in the Jewellery Quarter of Birmingham had begun to produce steel nibs for general use. Though they were scratchy and still too rigid, one manufacturer bragged in 1838 that his had "the elasticity of the quill combined with the superior durability and uniformity in the appearance of the writing that a metallic instrument, when properly made, must always pre-eminently possess over the perishable yielding substance of the quill."

But it wasn't until the 1850s that the steel nib really began to shove aside the quill. Birmingham manufacturers improved the quality of their nibs by tipping them with hard alloys. Joseph Gillot's factory added slits to the "shoulders" on either side of the centre slit of each nib, and cross-ground the point. His nibs thus gained unprecedented flexibility, and the Gillot plant soon boasted 450 workers, churned out five tons of nibs a week, and enabled Joseph, once a mere grinder of knife blades, to become one of England's richest collectors of magnificent paintings. More than half the world's production of steel nibs soon came from Birmingham factories. The industry employed thousands, a great many of whom were girls and young women. From rolled sheets of the best Swedish steel, the most efficient workers each cut nearly thirty thousand nib blanks per day.

Some of the nib holders were ivory, ebony, glass, bone, silver, or gold but the most, by far, were wooden. Once the simplest handles had become as commonplace as buttons, few recognized the nibs as the miracle they were. "Nibs of dip pens cost very little, yet had to be so efficient they'd channel a steady stream of ink down a slit no wider than a human hair," handwriting historian Alfred J. Fairbank wrote. "Gravity, capillary attraction, the surface tension of the liquid, and the hand's pressure on the split parts of the nib all influenced the ink's performance."

In Lahore, India, when Rudyard Kipling was a twenty-year-old sub-editor of the *Civil and Military Gazette*, which he later called "my first and most true love," his sheer energy influenced the ink's per-formance. Another young man who worked there, Kay Robinson, said Kipling dipped his pen "frequently and deep into his ink-pot, and as all his movements were abrupt, almost jerky, the ink used to fly." By the end of each working day, Kipling, whose trousers and vest were made of white cotton, looked like "a Dalmatian dog."

Late in the Victorian era, one pen manufacturer found names for its products in the works of Dickens, Edward Lear, and Sir Walter Scott, and its posters at British railway platforms boasted, "They come as a boon and a blessing to men, the Pickwick, the Owl and the Waverley pen." It wasn't only to men, however, that steel nibs came as a blessing. They were so cheap that, for the first time, poor people of both sexes could afford pens. Moreover, as free education for children spread throughout the Western world, steel nibs helped hundreds of millions of youngsters learn to write, read, and become future book buyers.

In the late nineteenth century and much of the twentieth, the schoolchildren of Britain and North America worked at desktops that, in the upper right-hand corner, held a china or glass inkwell. A mischievous boy might dip into his ink not only his nib but the pigtail of any girl unlucky enough to be seated directly in front of him. Often, Joyce Irene Whalley wrote in 1975, schoolroom ink was "horrid." It "spread where it was not wanted, running down the shaft of the pen to the fingers and dropping blots on a newly written exercise." Yet the dip pen, along with its indispensable accessory, blotting paper, survived in schools, banks, and post offices until the mid-twentieth century.

DIP PENS OBSOLETE? SO WHAT? THEY STILL WORKED

Long after most authors switched to fountain pens and type-writers, a few continued to write with dip pens. They did not reject light bulbs in favour of candles or wear frock coats and celluloid collars but, even though the dip pen was a messy throwback to the days of Dickens, they refused to abandon it. If they threw out the tool they'd always used to produce work, might they not find they'd also thrown out the very *ability* to produce work?

Herein lies a pivotal theme of this book. With respect not only to dip pens, but to all the other tools that writers use to put words on paper – and to the hours and surroundings in which they choose to work – they tend to be slaves of habit. They do not understand the magical force that enables them to keep on "painting speech, and speaking to the eyes," but dread the day they'll wake up to find it gone forever. They therefore have good reason to tell themselves, "If it ain't broke, don't fix it." In short, many writers find writing so excruciatingly difficult they don't dare change how they do it.

As Pulitzer Prize–winning novelist John Hersey said in 1985, "Every writer becomes habituated to a way of working that may matter to him a great deal. Disturbing the rituals surrounding writing may be very confusing, very difficult." John Cheever, who won a Pulitzer in 1978 for his collected short stories, said, "There is nothing more painful for a writer than an inability to work."

Again and again, while discussing how they feel about their calling, writers use words like "terror" and "dread." The Canadian novelist and poet Margaret Atwood has earned so many literary prizes and exuded such self-confidence that one would never suspect that, as she approached her typewriter, she endured even a twinge of apprehension. She once said, however, "Blank pages inspire me with terror." Novelist John Barth, winner of the U.S. National Book Award for *Chimera* (1973), said that a writer at work experiences "a combination of an almost obscene self-confidence and an ongoing terror." John Steinbeck confessed, "I suffer as always from the fear of putting down the first line. It is amazing, the terrors, the magics, the prayers, the straightening shyness that assails one."

"I write in terror," said the American essayist, novelist, and short-story writer Cynthia Ozick. "I have to talk myself into bravery with every sentence, sometimes every syllable." She compared writers like herself to "a beast howling inside a coal-furnace, heaping the coals on itself to increase the fire." For novelist and journalist Joan Didion, writing fiction was "an occasion of dread for at least the first half of the novel." *One Hundred Years of Solitude* by Colombia-born Gabriel García Márquez sold thirty million copies, earned him comparisons with Tolstoy and Cervantes, and was the key to his winning a Nobel Prize. Could such a writer, a genius in many eyes, ever have feared the blank page? "All my life," he confessed, "I've been frightened at the moment I sit down to write."

"It's really scary just getting to the desk," said New York humorist Fran Lebowitz. "We're talking now five hours. My mouth gets dry, my heart beats fast. I react psychologically the way other people react when the plane loses an engine." For George Orwell, "Writing a book is a horrible, exhausting struggle, like a long bout of some painful illness."

Among the countless would-be-writers who failed to overcome the terror, none was a more shameless plagiarist than "Monsieur Willy." That was the pen name of Henri Gauthier-Villars, a degenerate, a philanderer, and the first husband of Colette, who wrote more than fifty novels. She vengefully wrote, "I've often imagined that M. Willy . . . had a neurotic horror of the blank page. . . . I imagine that he must have reckoned, in the throes of a pathological blackout, the courage, the solemn constancy it takes to sit down without despair at the edge of a virgin meadow . . . the raw, irresponsible, blinding, ravenous, and ungrateful white page. . . . There must have been a time when he could still believe that he was ready to write, that he was going to write, that he was writing. . . . The pen between his fingers, a pause, the swooning of his will deprived him of his illusion."

Enter the Fountain Pen

Though superior to the quill, the dip pen, for most writers, was far from ideal. The dip, dip, dipping interrupted their train of thought. If they were on the move, they had to carry their ink in leak-proof containers. By the 1870s, the demand for a more convenient tool had grown so strong that manufacturers produced a variety of portable "reservoir" pens. These supposedly enabled writers to scribble all day without stopping to reload the nib. Men kept them in their pockets, and women in their purses. Trouble was, these primitive fountain pens sometimes refused to release any ink at all, and at other times spat out fat blobs. As Joseph

Bourque wrote in his *History of the Waterman Pen*, "Dip pens needed a bulky protective case as well as an ink bottle with ominous spill potential, and the newfangled reservoir pens that carried the ink supply more efficiently in the barrel had an unpredictable tendency to gurgle puddles of that ink onto the paper. Neither was satisfactory."

Along came Lewis Waterman. A forty-year-old insurance broker in New York City in 1883, he chose to celebrate the signing of a big contract by using not his old dip pen and inkwell, but one of the more stylish of the new fountain pens. He laid out the contract for his client and handed him the pen he'd just bought. At first, it wouldn't write. Waterman then watched, horrified, as it burped ink all over the document. The disgusted client gave his business to a rival broker.

Vowing never to endure such humiliation again, Waterman used his brother's one-room workshop in Manhattan to invent a system that fed a smooth, even flow of ink from the barrel to the nib to the paper. "For the first time," Bourque wrote, "it became practical to carry around in a pocket a single, slim, reliable, affordable and graceful writing instrument." As late as 1893, however, some pens still leaked so badly that a joke in the *New York Times* read, "I would never trust him. He is as treacherous as a fountain pen." Still, the annual sales of Waterman's pens rose from the 500 that he sold from a New York cigar shop in 1884 to 350,000 in 1901. Seeing a marketing opportunity in the 1909 centennial of Abraham Lincoln's birth, the Waterman Company introduced the Lincoln Fountain Pen, which guaranteed "the emancipation of millions of slaves to the ink bottle."

DIP-PEN LOYALISTS: CONRAD, GRAVES, TOLKIEN, ET AL.

Even after dozens of companies churned out tens of thousands of reliable fountain pens per month and sold them in a brutally competitive marketplace, Joseph Conrad stuck to his old dip pen with a steel nib. Although he told a friend the sight of an inkwell and pen filled him with "anger and horror," the thought of switching to a fountain pen must have filled him with even more anger and horror. Few great novelists suffered such agonizing writer's blocks as he did. Never knowing when this dreadful paralysis would descend on his creativity, he simply could not give up the type of pen he best knew. "Conrad wrote with a common steel pen," his biographer, Jeffrey Meyers, reported, "which he sometimes saved, after it had worn out, for sentimental reasons."

As late as 1923, the British critic and literary scholar John Middleton Murry not only used a dip pen, but imagined a magic one. "The pen of my dream," he wrote, "is a golden pen; it glides over a great sheet of white paper like crisp parchment; it is dipped into a crystal well of ink blacker than a raven's breast; and the lines it traces are as fine as those which Indian artists draw with an elephant's hair. And it seems to me that if all these things were mine, the thoughts of my brain would be as clean and fine and definite as they. An idea would rise before my mind like a bubble. I should only have to trace the outline. The bubble would break, the dust of its rainbow colouring would float down, settle on my ink before it was dry, and be imprisoned in it for ever."

A deeply conservative professor at Oxford, J.R.R. Tolkien disliked industrialization, automobiles, machines, and, indeed, much of the modern world. Decades after fountain pens and typewriters had proved themselves to countless authors, Tolkien, who worked in snatches between ten at night and two in the morning, spent a dozen years writing *The Lord of the Rings* (1954) – with a dip pen. Since his salary was meagre, he scribbled much of the story on the backs of old exam papers. His closest friend for years was the novelist and literary scholar C.S. Lewis. Like Tolkien, Lewis continued to use the dip pen when most people saw it as an anachronism. His stepson Douglas Gresham, who co-produced the 2005 movie based on Lewis's classic series of books for children, *The Chronicles of Narnia* (1949–54), once remembered his stepfather writing four or five words, pausing, dipping his pen, writing four or five more, pausing, dipping his pen. . . .

"I think it's a wonderful way to write," Gresham said, "if you have the patience."

The English poet, novelist, translator, memoirist, and literary scholar Robert Graves had the patience. He wrote at least 140 books and swore by his trusty dip pen. After he read some of his poems to an audience in New York in 1966, a woman asked if he used a typewriter, and he replied, "No, madam, I have never learned to use a typewriter, and I have warned my daughters against learning to use this machine. I do not, as a matter of fact, favour a fountain pen, either. I use the old steel nib that has to be dipped in a pot of ink, and I find that a good nib takes me nicely through four thousand pages of manuscript before it has to be changed."

Shelby Foote also had the patience. A novelist from Mississippi, he began in 1954 to write a history of the Civil War. He worked on his three-volume, 2,934-page *The Civil War: A Narrative* for twenty years. It ran to nearly 1.5 million words – every one of which he wrote with dip pens. As late as 1999, when only the elderly among North Americans could recall using them as schoolchildren, Foote still wrote with one. At eighty-two, he said, "I avoid [computers] at all costs. I don't want anything to do with anything mechanical to come between me and the paper. I use an old-fashioned dip pen. . . . It makes me take my time, and I feel comfortable doing it, whereas the clatter of a typewriter, or to turn the drum back to make a correction, all that's a kind of interruption I can't stand. And I'm a slow writer. Five, six hundred words is a good day."

FOUNTAIN-PEN LOYALISTS:
THOMAS MANN, MURIEL SPARK, ET AL.

James M. Cain, who wrote *The Postman Always Rings Twice* (1934) and *Double Indemnity* (1936), believed his boyhood fascination with early fountain pens was a sign he would become a writer. At eighty-six, while remembering himself as a ten-year-old, he said, "My father smoked Turkish Trophy cigarettes. . . . Each pack was in a black and red box; they were oval cigarettes with coupons in each pack. For seventy of these things you could get a fountain pen. I would send off seventy of these things and got a succession of fountain pens. You know how you filled fountain pens at the time? You unscrewed them and filled it with an eyedropper. Today, whenever I take out the clinical thermometer to take my temperature, I think of those pens and the eyedroppers. So the succession of fountain pens may have been an omen."

The fountain pen became both a status symbol and, for personal and business correspondence, indispensable to tens of millions of people. Many writers simply could not work with any other writing instrument and grew deeply attached to it. The winner of the Nobel Prize for literature in 1929 and one of the greatest German-language novelists, Thomas Mann, said he had to have "fluid ink and a new smooth-flowing pen." But he kept his *old* smooth-flowing pens. A website about his house near Zurich, where he died in 1955, said that among the bric-a-brac that still crowded his mahogany desktop were "several fountain pens."

More than a century after the first good fountain pens went on sale, best-selling American author Mary Gordon wrote that, whenever she wielded her black, enamel, gold-trimmed Waterman's, with its extra-fine point, "I feel as if I'm wearing a perfectly tailored suit, and my hair is flawlessly pulled back into a chignon. . . . My pen is elegant, even if I'm wearing the terry robe whose frayed state suggests a fashion statement from a gulag." She normally used Waterman's ink, black. When she tried blue-black for a few weeks, it made her feel like "a punitive headmistress."

About one of Stephen King's roughly fifty best-selling horror novels, *Dreamcatcher* (2001), he wrote, "This book was written with the world's finest word processor, a Waterman cartridge fountain pen." As recently as December 2006, *The Hindu*, "India's National Newspaper," reported that "the creative exercise" for Anita Nair, whose novels in English had been translated into twenty-one languages, was about "her Parker gold fountain pen, and 'the pleasure of seeing the ink flow onto the page.'" Muriel Spark, whose *The Prime of Miss Jean Brodie* (1961) and nineteen other novels made her one of Britain's most admired writers, not only wrote with fountain pens but felt they were so personal she would never use one that anyone else had touched.

THE BALLPOINT WARS. THE UBIQUITOUS BIRO

In the late 1930s, Hungarian newspaperman Laszlo Biro decided that filling his fountain pen was a nuisance and enlisted the help of his brother George, a chemist, to invent a pen that held a year's supply of ink. To a small tube they fitted a conical point that had a tiny ball bearing at its tip, and loaded the tube with a jelly-like ink, similar to the printer's ink at the newspaper. Laszlo patented the pen in 1938 but in 1940, as nation after nation fell to the Nazi juggernaut, he and George fled Hungary and settled in Argentina. There, in 1943, he got a fresh patent for the pen. His ballpoint now became, if not quite a weapon, an instrument of war. Crews on Royal Air Force missions kept logs but, at high altitudes, their fountain pens leaked. Ballpoints did not.

As the war ended, the pens that had proved themselves in the sky were selling in Argentina, and the Eversharp and Eberhard-Faber companies got together to buy the right to make and market them in America. Then a hustler from Chicago, Milton Reynolds, visited Buenos Aires, returned to the United States with Biro pens, founded the Reynolds International Pen Company, ignored the Eversharp patent, and, at Gimbel's department store in Manhattan, beat Eversharp to the market. His Reynolds Rocket sold for US$12.50 (the equivalent of roughly $150.00 in 2009 currency). New Yorkers snapped up $100,000 worth of Rockets on the first day they went on sale.

After Eversharp sued Reynolds, legal battles helped sink both companies. Meanwhile, the first American ballpoints performed as treacherously as the first fountain pens had. "A feeding frenzy erupted, as dozens of companies rushed to market with outrageous claims, and shoddy, leaky and generally unreliable merchandise," a website about the history of pens reports. "Reynolds slipped away, pockets stuffed with money." Like Eversharp's product, his Rocket was a bust. By 1948, American ballpoints were selling for only fifty cents, and not well. They were so messy and unreliable that schools banned them from classrooms. Disgusted Americans briefly restored the supremacy of the fountain pen, but Biro's invention was too good to vanish.

The pen-history website claimed it "turned many a schoolboy's mouth blue, and destroyed the handwriting of generations of ordinary people," but once manufacturers debugged it, the ballpoint was unbeatable. Although handwriting historian Alfred J. Fairbank haughtily dismissed it as something "that might be thought of as no more than an inky pencil," it was handier, neater, cheaper, and more reliable than the fountain pen. As early as 1949, the 700 workers at the Miles Martin Pen Company in Reading, England, were turning out 550,000 ballpoints a week. Half a century later, the Bic pen company, which Marcel Bich founded in France in 1945 (adapting his name to suit the English-speaking marketplace), was selling 14 million of its Crystal ballpoints every day.

The first great writer to favour ballpoints was George Orwell. In 1946, shortly after they arrived in British shops, he began to write not with a disposable one, but with a refillable model. On Boxing Day, 1947, while he suffered in hospital from the tuberculosis that killed him two years later, he asked in a note to crime-fiction writer Julian Symons, "I wonder if you'd do me a great favour & buy me a Biro pen. Mine is just coming to an end – I can have it refilled but meanwhile I should have nothing to write with. I forget what they cost, but enclose 3 pounds." He later told Symons, "Thanks ever for sending the pen, which as you can see I'm using. My other was just on its last legs & you can't use [bottled] ink in bed." Nor could he use a typewriter in bed; he was too weak. As Orwell's tuberculosis worsened, and he at times suffered the hair-raising side effects of a prescribed drug, he hastened his own death by refusing to stop working on his masterpiece, *Nineteen Eighty-Four* (1949), at least some of which he wrote with a ballpoint.

Another convert to ballpoints was the American giant of literary and cultural criticism, Harold Bloom. "There cannot be a human being who has fewer thoughts on the whole question of word processing than I do," he said in 1990. "I've never even seen a word processor. I am hopelessly archaic." Asked if he thought word processors had affected students' papers, he said, "But for me the typewriter hasn't even been invented yet, so how can I speak to this matter. I protest! A man who has never learned to type is not going to be able to add anything to this debate. As far as I'm concerned, computers have as much to do with literature as space travel, perhaps much less. I can only write with a ballpoint pen, with a 'Rolling Writer,' they're called a black 'Rolling Writer,' on a lined yellow legal pad on a certain kind of clipboard. And then someone else types it."

It was with ballpoints, in "the more painterly hand-eye medium of longhand," that British author Martin Amis wrote the entire first drafts of his novels. "If I showed you a notebook of mine," he told an interviewer, "it would have lots of squiggles and trans-positions and lots of light crossings-out, so that you can see what the original was."

Like most of the world outside North America, he called ball-point pens Biros. Replying to a question about his writing super-stitions, he said, "I do sometimes feel tempted by computers until I realize what an amazing pleasure a new Biro is. . . . The pleasure you get from a new Biro that works. So you have the childish pleas-ure of paper and pen. New supplies. Superstitions."

Some writers, however, find pleasure in *old* supplies. Any number of superstitions walk hand-in-hand with The Muse.

FOUR

The Properly Pointed, Perfectly Portable Pencil

"The uprooting of a large oak tree during a storm led, it is said, to the discovery of the famous graphite mine of Borrowdale [in Cumberland] England," Clarence Fleming wrote in 1936 in a booklet for a pencil company. "This was in 1565, in the time of Queen Elizabeth. A wandering mountaineer, attracted by the particles of a strange black substance clinging to the roots of the fallen tree, soon had the people of the countryside excitedly discussing the mysterious mineral." Pure and solid, the graphite was the best in the world. Locals called it "wadd" and found it handy for marking sheep, but after they learned how good it was at marking paper, the pencil industry was born. (They thought graphite was a kind of lead, which pencils have never contained.) In *A History of Inventions and Discoveries* (1817) John Beckmann wrote that the lines a pencil makes "are durable, and do not readily fade; but when one chooses, they may be totally rubbed out." The pencil, therefore, could be used "with more convenience and speed than any coloured earth, charcoal, or even ink."

Keswick, a market town near the Borrowdale mine, became what the *Cumberland News* (April 5, 2007) called "the pencil capital of the world," and by the early 2000s, the Cumberland Pencil Company was manufacturing 60 million pencils a year and marketing them in seventy-four countries.

It was not in Britain, however, but in France that there occurred the most important technological breakthrough in the history of pencil manufacturing. During the Reign of Terror that followed the French Revolution, war broke out between France and Britain and cut off France's supply of pencils. "Since war, revolution, education and day-to-day commerce cannot get along easily without pencils," Henry Petroski wrote in *The Pencil* (1992), "the French Minister of War, Lazare Carnot, sought a substitute method to produce them in France." He hired inventor Nicolas-Jacques Conté to free France from its pencil crisis.

Conté removed the impurities from powdered graphite, mixed it with water and potter's clay, pressed the wet paste into long rectangular moulds, and, after the sticks dried, hardened them in a furnace. He then inserted them in grooves in wooden cases and glued strips of wood over them. By varying the proportions of graphite and clay, manufacturers could control the hardness or softness of their "lead." The principles of pencil manufacturing have remained the same ever since. Thus it was Conté who discovered the right way to make modern pencils.

STEINBECK WAS A DEMON FOR PENCILS

Among writers, the humble pencil has seldom received its due. Henry David Thoreau helped his father manufacture North America's best pencils and, to take notes and make sketches, carried one on all his wilderness forays. In a list of excursion equipment he compiled for other naturalists, however, he failed to include a pencil. This baffled Petroski. He could only speculate, "Perhaps the very object with which he may have been drafting his list was too close to him, too familiar a part of his own everyday outfit, too integral a part of his livelihood, too common a thing for him to think to mention."

Petroski suspected that John Middleton Murry used a pencil and "much rubbing with an eraser" to draft his eloquent gush about the golden pen of his dreams, and thought he should have acknowledged his debt to the cruder but handier tool. John Steinbeck certainly did. He wrote millions of words with pencils. About the characters in *East of Eden* (1952), he said, "They can't move until I pick up a pencil." Writing for six hours at a stretch, he used as many as sixty pencils per day. To avoid wasting time, he had an electric sharpener. Since the edges of hexagonal pencils cut his fingers during a long day's work, his pencils were round.

Steinbeck's mood and the weather often determined which pencils he chose to use; humidity influenced the performance of the graphite. "A pencil that is all right some days is no good another day," he wrote. "For example, yesterday I used a [Blackwing] soft and fine and it floated over the paper just wonderfully. So this morning I try the same kind. And they crack on me. Points break and all hell is let loose. This is the day that I am stabbing the paper. So today I need a harder pencil at least for a while. I am using some [Mongols] that are numbered 2⅜. I have my plastic tray you know and in it three kinds of pencils for hard writing days and soft writing days. Only sometimes it changes in the middle of the day. I also have some super soft pencils which I do not use very often because I must feel as delicate as a rose petal to use them."

Thomas Wolfe wrote his passionate, messy, and voluminous outpourings, including *Of Time and the River* (1935) and *Look Homeward Angel* (1939), by bearing down so hard on short, blunt pencils that he wore a groove in one of his fingers. Vladimir Nabokov, as disciplined as Wolfe was undisciplined, said, "I have rewritten – several times – every word I have ever published." Revealing his Tolstoy-like compulsion to revise his work, he added, "My pencils outlast their erasers."

Nor was F. Scott Fitzgerald reluctant to write, rewrite, and rewrite again – all with pencils. During periods when he swore off booze and mad escapades, America's literary darling of the Roaring Twenties often wrote for several weeks running, and with demonic energy. "He wrote in pencil with his left hand," his biographer Jeffrey Meyers reported, "and had a large, loopy hand that looked like a child's. He made several drafts, depending on the importance of his work, before sending it to a secretary to be typed."

"Wearing down seven Number Two pencils," Hemingway said, "is a good day's work." Writing with a pencil increased the intensity of his examination of his work-in-progress. It was his job "to convey every sensation, sight, feeling and place to the reader." Writing with a pencil gave him "three different sights" at his work to see if it contained absolutely everything he wanted the reader to get. "First, when you read it over; then when it is typed you get another chance to improve it, and again in the proof. Writing it first in pencil gives you one third more chance to improve it. That is .333, which is a damned good average for a hitter. It also keeps it fluid longer so that you can better it easier."

Until Georges Simenon reached his sixties, when he began to compose on a typewriter, he used pencils to dash off several novels a year in his tiny, neat longhand. Before each day's work, he sharpened four dozen pencils and lined them up on his desk. He then wrote at a furious pace, tossing out each pencil as its point wore down.

PENCIL-PUSHERS COULD WRITE JUST ABOUT ANYWHERE . . .

Pencils are supremely portable and, according to American humorist P.J. O'Rourke, the portability of writing has much to do with its artistic power. "Other creative types have strong string sections, naked artist's models and opera scenery that they must lug with them everywhere they go," he wrote. "Writers can grab a stub of pencil and the back of an envelope and dash off 'Lines Composed a Few Miles Above Tintern Abbey' any time Tintern Abbey happens to be a few miles away." William Wordsworth "wrote" immortal poems like "Tintern Abbey" entirely in his head, during long walks in the English countryside, and on such jaunts, O'Rourke insisted, "even the most compact laptop would be an encumbrance. And where would Wordsworth have plugged his battery recharger?"

It was the portability of pencils that enabled Hemingway to write at cafés in Paris, and sometimes just sharpening them put him in the mood for writing. All he needed, he wrote in *A Moveable Feast* (1964), were "the blue-backed notebooks, the two pencils and the pencil sharpener (a pocket knife was too wasteful), the marble-topped tables, the smell of early morning, sweeping out and mopping." When a girl he didn't know sat down in one of his hangouts, he continued, "I watched her whenever I looked up, or when I sharpened the pencil with a pencil sharpener with the shavings curling into the saucer under my drink." She somehow made him feel that "all Paris belongs to me and I belong to this notebook and this pencil."

But the handiness of pencils served no one better than his friend Fitzgerald. At twenty-one, while doing time as a useless officer in the U.S. army, Fitzgerald wrote fiction secretly. During evening study periods, with pencil and notebook hidden inside *Small Problems for Infantry*, he outlined twenty-two chapters of "a somewhat edited history of me and my imagination," and completed two. After his commander put an end to that stunt, Fitzgerald rushed to the Officer's Club at 1 p.m. every Saturday, when his duties were over for the week, and "there in a corner of a room full of smoke, conversation and rattling newspapers, I wrote a one-hundred-and-twenty-thousand-word novel on the consecutive weekends of three months." Two years later, his first published novel, *This Side of Paradise*, earned him instant fame.

Before Graham Greene became one of the best and most controversial novelists of the twentieth century, he lay in a British hospital and wrote with a pencil. In October 1926, at twenty-two, while recovering from the removal of his appendix, he worked on what would become his first novel, *The Man Within* (1929), and scribbled reviews for the *Glasgow Herald*. His future wife, Vivien Dayrell-Browning, typed the reviews and shipped them off to Glasgow. In November, he told her in a letter from Brighton, "I covered endless backs of envelopes with snippets for the novel." A dozen years and several novels later, he was finishing the thriller *Brighton Rock* (1938) and told his publisher, "The novel in its last 5,000 words has turned around and bit me. . . . So I'm going off to a country pub, I hope, tomorrow evening to finish it." With pencils.

In a dinky cargo ship that carried him in 1941 from Britain to West Africa, where he would serve Britain as a secret agent, he slammed a door on one of his thumbs. "The whole nail will go," Greene wrote in a letter home. "Bled a good deal and felt like hell. Luckily, my left. . . ." Luckily, because it was with his right hand that he clutched his pencil. Despite the pain in his thumb, the icy winter winds that lashed him while he stood watch, and violent seas that made him vomit, he wrote his usual five hundred words a day to complete a book called *British Dramatists* (1942). Six months after he arrived in Lagos, he had pencilled most of his seventy-thousand-word novel *Ministry of Fear* (1943).

. . . AND ON JUST ABOUT ANY SCRAP OF PAPER

For some, the beauty of the pencil lies in its enabling them to write not only wherever they happen to be but on whatever scrap of paper is handy when an idea hits them. One such writer is Mavis Gallant. A Canadian by birth and Parisian by choice since she moved there in 1950, she has published more than a hundred short stories, most of them in *The New Yorker*. "I begin in pencil," she said in 1988. "It's usually a visual image in a situation. . . . I start it in longhand. Then for the next few days there are bits of the story that come. . . . You get an accumulation of things. Written on buses. I'm not joking. Even on match covers. Once I had a story written on a metro ticket. A little bit of dialogue. Then I type it. Then I make all the corrections. . . . Once it's typed there's no doubt that that's the beginning and that's the end of it, and the story does this. Then I correct in pencil again and it's all around the edges. Then I type it all again to get it clean."

William Goyen, a Texas-born writer of fiction, non-fiction, and plays, said in 1975:

It's amazing how quickly something gets written. Now, when it comes, it can be on a bus, or in a store. I've stopped in Macy's and written on a drygoods counter and then suddenly had a whole piece of writing for myself that was accomplished. . . . When one's really engaged deeply in a piece of work, truly writing it, it takes over almost everything else and you find you're thinking about it constantly and it's part of everything that happens. Even the clerk in Macy's suddenly speaks out of the novel you are writing, it seems, or is a character in it. All the people in the world are suddenly characters in the novel you are writing. Everything contributes. . . . Therefore, I know that if I've been writing all morning and I've got to buy groceries at noon, I better take [a pencil and] paper with me, because I'm going to *keep* writing as I go down the street. You can write on the sack that your groceries come in, and I have!

It was with pencils that August Wilson did his teething as a creative writer, and with pencils that he later drafted plays on paper napkins. In the 1990s, Henry Louis Gates, Jr., the most celebrated black American intellectual then writing, called Wilson "the most celebrated American playwright now writing, and . . . certainly the most accomplished black playwright in this nation's history." Asked in 1999 if he wrote in bars and restaurants, Wilson recalled knowing a young painter who couldn't afford a tube of yellow paint. A twenty-year-old poet at the time, Wilson realized how lucky he was to require only a borrowed pencil to pursue his art. He wrote on napkins or paper bags and discovered poems wherever he walked. "Once, when I was writing on a paper napkin," he recalled, "the waitress asked, 'Do you write on napkins because it doesn't count?'"

The challenge to create literature that "counts" so intimidates some writers that they can't write. The cold, crisp, blank, and pure white page expects too much. But the writing they scribble on a napkin or a scrap of brown paper is like a limerick, doodle, or note to a friend. It doesn't count. Therefore it flows.

Remembering the waitress's insight, Wilson said, "It had never occurred to me that writing on a napkin frees me up. If I pull out a tablet, I'm saying, 'Now I'm writing,' and I became more conscious of being a writer. . . . That's why I like to write on napkins. Then I go home to another kind of work – taking what I've written on napkins in bars and restaurants and typing it up, rewriting."

In the twenty years before he died at sixty, August Wilson won two Pulitzer Prizes for drama, seven New York Drama Critics Circle Awards for best play, two Tony Awards for best play, and seven Tony Award nominations. Not bad for a fellow who wrote on napkins.

FIVE

The Long Reign of Longhand

Typewriters were scarce in post-war Britain, and George Orwell noticed "the astonishing badness of nearly everyone's handwriting." He wondered if there was any connection between neat handwriting and literary ability, but acknowledged, "The modern examples I am able to think of do not seem to prove much." Rebecca West and John Middleton Murry had "exquisite handwriting" but Osbert Sitwell, Stephen Spender, and Evelyn Waugh had "handwritings which, to put it as politely as possible, are not good. . . ." Arnold Bennett wrote a beautiful tiny hand over which he took immense pains. H.G. Wells had an attractive but untidy writing. Thomas Carlyle's was so bad that one compositor is said to have left Edinburgh in order to get away from the job of setting it up. George Bernard Shaw's was clear, small, and inelegant. And E.M. Forster's? "When I was at the B.B.C. and had the honour of putting him on the air once a month there was only one secretary in the whole department who could decipher his manuscripts."

Whether their handwriting was flowing, cramped, graceful, or abominable, many of the best writers refused even to try composing their work directly on a typewriter. They seemed to feel that the only way their creativity could freely flow from their brains to a sheet of paper was down one side of their neck, and through their shoulder, arm, and wrist to the digits that squeezed a pen or pencil. As late as 1963, W.H. Auden insisted, "Literary composition in the twentieth century AD is pretty much what it was in the twentieth century BC; everything still has to be done by hand. Most people enjoy the sight of their own handwriting as they enjoy the smell of their own farts."

The Paris Review offered intriguing proof that Auden was right, at least about handwriting. Since 1953 it has published more than three hundred interviews with novelists, short-story writers, poets, and playwrights from a dozen countries, and accompanied each transcript with a photograph of an early page of one of the author's manuscripts. The reproductions revealed that dozens of the finest novelists in the world wrote their first and most important drafts in longhand. Among them were Martin Amis, Julian Barnes, Jorge Luis Borges, Anthony Burgess, Truman Capote, Isak Dinesen, Lawrence Durrell, E.M. Forster, Carlos Fuentes, Joseph Heller, Mario Vargas Llosa, François Mauriac, John Mortimer, Vladimir Nabokov, V.S. Naipaul, Edna O'Brien, Cynthia Ozick, V.S. Pritchett, Jean Rhys, Isaac Bashevis Singer, William Styron, Gore Vidal, Evelyn Waugh, Thornton Wilder, and Angus Wilson. Although many poets chose to write directly on typewriters, five of the best – Joseph Brodsky, Ted Hughes, Philip Larkin, Archibald MacLeish, and Stephen Spender – were all longhand men. So were playwrights Tom Stoppard and Eugène Ionesco, and humorists Woody Allen and James Thurber.

"I choose to believe that there is some kind of mystic connection between the brain and the actual act of writing in longhand," said British playwright, screenwriter, and novelist Fay Weldon. A century after the arrival of efficient Underwoods and nineteen years after William Zinsser published his *Writing with a Word Processor*, American novelist Mary Gordon said the very laboriousness of writing by hand was a virtue. For it involved "flesh, blood, and the thingness of pen and paper," and these reminded writers that "however thoroughly we lose ourselves in the vortex of our invention, we inhabit a corporeal world." Like those who left on the walls of Paleolithic caves pictures of reindeer and rhinoceroses, the colour of dried blood, Gordon had to get her tool-bearing hand as close as she possibly could to the art she was creating for others to see.

Asked when he was sixty if he wrote with a typewriter or computer, Chinua Achebe, the prolific Nigerian novelist and "father of modern African literature," replied, "No! No, no – I'm very primitive; I write with a pen. A pen on paper is the ideal way for me. . . . Whenever I try to do anything on a typewriter, it's like having this machine between me and the words; what comes out is not quite what comes out if I were scribbling." About his chosen tool for writing, he concluded, "I am a preindustrial man."

For a million years and more, our ancestors used their hands to hunt, fish, pick fruit, and make tools, fire, and love. Anthropologist Bernard G. Campbell has argued that the hand "contributed as much as the eye to the making of man; together they gave him a new perception of his environment and, with his material culture, a new control of it." While stressing the importance to primitive tribes of gestural communication, ethnographer Lucien Lévy-Bruhl suggested that, among prehistoric peoples, hands were "so at one with the mind that they really formed part of it." More than two centuries ago, Immanuel Kant wrote that the hand was "the visible part of the brain." More than four centuries ago, Miguel de Cervantes wrote that the pen was "the tongue of the mind."

PICK UP THAT PEN, AND START DIGGING

Linking tongue and pen, the Kentucky writer and farmer Wendell Berry wrote, "Reading aloud what we have written – as we must do, if we are writing carefully – our language passes in at the eyes, out at the mouth, in at the ears; the words are immersed and steeped in the senses of the body before they make sense in the mind. They *cannot* make sense in the mind until they have made sense in the body. Does shaping one's words with one's own hand impart character and quality to them, as does speaking them with one's own tongue to the satisfaction of one's own ear? . . . I believe that it does." American novelist William Gass went further: "Writing by hand, mouthing by mouth: in each case you get a very strong physical sense of the emergence of language – squeezed out like a well-formed stool – what satisfaction! what bliss!"

Every handwritten word, said French literary theorist Roland Barthes, was "an enigmatic projection of our own bodies." Whenever he sat at his desk to think about what to write, he said, "I feel my hand move, join, dive and lift . . . thus constructing from the apparently functional lines of the letters a space that is quite simply that of a work of art. I am an artist . . . because in writing my body knows the joy of incising a virgin surface (its virginity representing the infinitely possible)."

American novelist Paul Auster said keyboards intimidated him. With his fingers hovering over one, he could not think clearly. His fountain pen was "a much more primitive instrument. You feel that the words are coming out of your body, and then you *dig* the words into the page. Writing has always had a tactile quality for me. It's a physical experience."

In "Digging," one of the best poems by one of the best Irish poets, Nobel laureate Seamus Heaney also likened writing by hand to stirring earth. For twenty-five beautiful lines, he marvelled over the skill with which his father and grandfather could wield a spade and then, at the end of the poem, said he had no spade to follow such men, and would do his digging with his pen.

Tracy Chevalier, an American in England, used a pen to write her best-selling *Girl with a Pearl Earring* (1999), which the *Wall Street*

Journal described as "a beautifully written tale that mirrors the elegance of the painting that inspired it." Asked about her writing habits, she said that, during the hours her young son was at school, she tried to write a thousand words in longhand, "and then I edit it and type it into the computer. Typing straight into the computer feels soulless. There's something tactile about touching the pen that touches the ink." Another novelist who disliked composing on a keyboard was Tom Robbins, whose bizarre plots, fantastic characters, and anti-establishment stance in the 1970s turned him into something of a cult hero among younger Americans. When he tried a typewriter, he said, "I missed the contact with the page. I like the idea of ink flowing out of my hand and saturating the page. There's something intimate about that."

"PENCIL, BALLPOINT, FELT TIP, FOUNTAIN PEN; THE MAGIC MOVES AROUND"

"As a poet, I know how words can occur to me with a pen in my hand," said Dan Gerber, an American poet, novelist, and essayist. "It's a little like the difference between having a direct relationship with the universe or with God, or having to go through 'an expert' or a priest." James Dickey's novel *Deliverance* earned him much money and fame, but at heart he never stopped being a poet. Writing by hand, he completed 150 to 175 drafts of his longer poems because "you are searching all the time for some kind of order. . . . Then, you are also trying to render it unforgettable." Dickey saw the writing of poetry "as quite a private matter between the poet, his hand, and the blazing white island of paper. . . ."

Pulitzer-winning poet Richard Wilbur wrote with a pencil, and laboriously, slowly, very slowly, line by line by line. He scrawled alternative words in his margins, but never reported to his typewriter "until the thing [was] completely done." He proceeded as Dylan Thomas told him he should. "It is a matter of going to one's study, or to the chair in the sun, and starting a new sheet of paper," Wilbur said. "On it you put what you've already got of a poem you are trying to write. Then you sit and stare at it, hoping that the impetus of writing out the lines you already have will get you a few lines farther before the day is done." During six hours of staring at the paper, pencil in hand, he often managed to write only two lines. For him, composition was "scarcely distinguishable from catatonia."

During the half-century that followed 1955, Donald Hall wrote more than a dozen books of such superior poetry that in 2006, when he was seventy-eight, the Library of Congress named him America's Poet Laureate. Long before that, he had revealed, "For thirty or thirty-five years, I've written in longhand – pencil, ballpoint, felt tip, fountain pen; the magic moves around. I used to work at poetry on a typewriter, but I tended to race on, to be glib, not to pause enough. Thirty years ago I gave up the keyboard, began writing in longhand, and hired other people to type for me. . . ."

He now began each poem with a hunch that a loose association of images inside his head contained something that *wanted* to become a poem. "I write out first drafts in a prosaic language – flat, no excitement," he explained. "Then very slowly, over hundreds of drafts, I begin to discover and exploit connections – between words, between images. Looking at the poem on the five hundredth day, I will take out one word and put in another." Always with a pen or pencil. "Three days later I will discover that the new word connects with another word that joined the manuscript a year back." His inspiration came "in the discovery of a single word after three years of work. This process never stops."

It is impossible to imagine any poet working quite like that with a keyboard. Pablo Neruda also gave up the typewriter for the pen. His ink was green, the colour of hope. Another giant of modern Spanish literature, Gabriel García Márquez, called Neruda the greatest poet of the twentieth century in any language, and biographer Alastair Reid said he was the most widely read poet since Shakespeare. When Neruda returned to Chile after winning the Nobel Prize for Literature in 1971, seventy thousand people jammed the nation's biggest soccer stadium to hear him read his work. No poet, before or since, has drawn such a crowd.

"Ever since I had an accident in which I broke a finger and couldn't use the typewriter for a few months, I have followed the custom of my youth and gone back to writing by hand," Neruda said in 1970. "I discovered when my finger was better and I could type again that my poetry when written by hand was more sensitive; its plastic forms could change more easily. . . . The typewriter separated me from a deeper intimacy with my poetry, and my hand brought me closer to that intimacy again."

From Loop to Loop, This Connects to That

Though Shelby Foote was not a poet but a novelist and Civil War historian, he well knew that deeper intimacy that came only with longhand. He said that William Faulkner, better than any writer he knew, "could communicate sensations, the texture of things." Rubbing his fingertips on a tablecloth, Foote said Faulkner "could make you feel it by describing it. That's our job." As Joseph Conrad had said, he continued, "you have to communicate sensation, the belief in what life is, what it's about, and you do it through learning how to handle a pen. That's why I have always felt uncomfortable having some piece of machinery between me and the paper – even a typewriter, let alone a computer, which just gives me the horrors!"

Foote's hero, Faulkner – whose handwriting Orwell, putting it as politely as possible, would have called "not good" – said, "I've got to feel the pencil and see the words at the end of the pencil." John O'Hara, who regarded Faulkner not merely as a genius but as "the only genius," marvelled, "Faulkner writes practically on the head of a pin; his calligraphy is so small he could write one of his long chapters on a single piece of copy paper."

American philosopher Sidney Hook had to *weigh* the words at the end of the pen. "The gravity of my thoughts seems to me to be in correlations with the pressure I put on my pen," he said. "When I type something, I always feel it's superficial because it seems to come off the top of my mind."

John Barth said that, like his Baltimore neighbour and fellow novelist Anne Tyler, he could not write fiction with anything other than a fountain pen. "She made the remark that there's something about the muscular movement of putting down script on paper that gets her imagination back in the track where it was," Barth said. "I feel that, too. . . . My sentences tend to go on a while before they stop: I trace that to the cursiveness of the pen. The idea of typing out first drafts, where each letter is physically separated by a little space from the next letter, I find a paralyzing notion. Good old script, which connects this letter to that, and this line to that – well, that's how good plots work, right? When this loops around and connects to that."

"I do not go near a word processor, or even a typewriter," said the Irish-born novelist Iris Murdoch. "I cannot imagine how thinking can take place on these awkward machines. There is no substitute for ink and I do not even like Biros. . . . For real *thinking*, as in philosophy or writing a poem or novel, one must use a notebook or paper which can be turned over, a pen which scratches out, opposite pages on which variants can be placed, and so on."

"My memory is certainly in my hands," novelist and historian Rebecca West said in 1981. At eighty-eight, she was still reviewing books. "I can remember things only if I have a pencil," she continued, "and I can write with it and play with it." When she was younger, she'd write a rough draft in longhand and another on a typewriter, but she now wrote only by hand. With a pencil?

"When anything important has to be written, yes. I think your hand concentrates for you. I don't know why it should be."

Many writers who compose their first drafts on keyboards know a time will come when they can't do without a pen or pencil. Believing that "you're in love with the truth when you discover it at the point of a pencil," Norman Mailer said he switched to long-hand "as soon as I found myself blocked on the typewriter." Fiction writer and memoirist Robert Stone said, "I've got to have a pen in my hand when I'm not actually typing." He composed his work on a typewriter, but only until "something becomes elusive." Then, to gain precision, he turned to longhand. "On a typewriter or word processor," he explained, "you can rush something that shouldn't be rushed – you can lose nuance, richness, lucidity.

"The pen compels lucidity."

SIX

"First, I Write by Hand. . . ."

Some critics regarded D.H. Lawrence as the greatest of modern English novelists, while others dismissed him as a bore and a blowhard, but it's indisputable that, among writers in longhand, he demonstrated phenomenal endurance. Remembering his writing for eighteen hours a day, Aldous Huxley said, "It was very extraordinary to see him work. It was a sort of possession; he would rush on with it, his hand moving at a tremendous rate. And he never corrected anything; because if he was dissatisfied with anything he would start again at the beginning." Lawrence believed his writing must "spring direct from the mysterious, irrational force within him," Huxley explained, and therefore refused to let his conscious intellect "come in and impose, after the event, its abstract pattern of perfection." Thus, he rewrote *Lady Chatterley's Lover* (1928) three times, from start to finish.

If Lawrence rushed ahead like a tidal wave, other longhand writers proceeded like caterpillars. American novelist and screenwriter Richard Price said, "What I'll do is write a page, reread it, edit it, write a half page more, and then I'll go back to the first thing I wrote that morning. It's like the nursery rhyme 'The House That Jack Built,' where you go back to the first line, and go all the way through, adding a line each time, and then back to the first. So I don't know whether I'm editing, re-editing, or writing something new, but it's a kind of creeping, incremental style of writing. I always sort of half-know where I'm going."

"Scribble, Scribble, Scribble"

Although Raymond Carver endured poverty, alcoholism, and a broken marriage, and died of lung cancer at fifty, he published ten books of prose and poetry; helped revitalize the American short story in the 1980s; and, in the opinion of Pulitzer Prize–winning novelist Marilynne Robinson, not only stood "squarely in the line of descent of American realism," but deserved fame "for the conceptual beauty of his best stories." Born in a small town in Oregon, Carver was the son of a sawmill worker and a waitress. He wrote about hard-up, hard-pressed, down-and-out, blue-collar workers. He himself had been a janitor, farmhand, deliveryman, and, as he said shortly before he died, "a paid-in-full member of the working poor."

He and English novelist Henry Green could scarcely have been less alike. The son of a wealthy industrialist from the West Midlands, Green was educated at Eton and Magdalen College, Oxford. His real name was Henry Vincent Yorke, but he ran his family's engineering firm and did not want business associates to know he was, gasp, a novelist. He therefore used a pseudonym and refused to be photographed. "He dedicated himself to business interests," said a website about the literary heritage of the West Midlands, "while quietly publishing a series of carefully crafted masterpieces that were much admired by such authors as W.H. Auden, Christopher Isherwood and John Updike." His writing style was subtle, enigmatic, and highly distinctive. American novelist Terry Southern, who interviewed him in 1958, called him not merely a writer's writer, but "a writer's writer's writer."

So Carver was a working stiff from the American West, while Green was an upper-crust businessman with a house in Knightsbridge, London, one of the world's most expensive and fashionable neighbourhoods. But they had one important thing in common: they wrote in longhand. Carver wrote his first drafts at top speed. Scribble, scribble, scribble. He filled up page after page after page just as fast as he could. To maintain his torrid pace, he left some scenes unfinished and others unwritten. In "a kind of personal shorthand," he jotted down asides to remind himself what to do later. "With the first draft it's a question of getting down the outline, the scaffolding of the story," he said. "Then on subsequent revisions I'll see to the rest of it."

Working at night, Green wrote draft after draft. After Southern observed that, on one page, he had done his rewriting not in words or phrases but in entire sentences, Green replied, "Yes, because I copy everything out afresh. I make alterations in the manuscript and then copy them out. And in copying out, I make further alterations." He rewrote "the first twenty pages over and over again – because in my idea you have to get everything into them. So as I go along and the book develops, I have to go back to that beginning again and again. Otherwise, I rewrite only when I read where I've got to in the book and find something so bad I can't go on till I've put it right."

THE PROBLEM WITH TYPING: YOU GET AHEAD OF YOURSELF

Until Cairo novelist Naguib Mahfouz retired from the Egyptian civil service at sixty, he wrote only from 4 p.m. to 7 p.m., but he did this six days a week, published more than thirty novels, and in 1988 became the only Arab ever to win the Nobel Prize for Literature. His masterwork, *The Cairo Trilogy* (1957), followed the life of a middle-class Muslim family from 1917 to the overthrow of King Farouk in 1952. After its appearance in English, critics compared Mahfouz with Dickens and Tolstoy. At eighty, he explained, "I make frequent revisions. I cross out a lot. I write all over the pages, even on the backs. Often my revisions are major. After I revise, I rewrite the story and send it to the publisher. Then I tear up all the old reworkings and throw them away."

His interviewer pointed out that many authors kept every word they'd ever written, but Mahfouz said that simply wasn't part of his culture. "I have never heard of a writer preserving his early drafts," he continued. "I have to discard my revisions – otherwise my house would overflow with useless paper! Besides, I have terrible handwriting."

To Graham Greene, typewriters were merely a necessary evil for the preparation of manuscripts for publishers, but writing, real writing, was forever "tied up with the hand, almost with a special nerve." It was with pens and pencils that he wrote the millions upon millions of words in his twenty-six novels and dozens of other books. When novelist and travel writer Paul Theroux was born in 1941, Greene, at thirty-eight, had already written *Brighton Rock* (1938), *The Power and the Glory* (1940), and other best-sellers, but Theroux would grow up sharing both his distrust of typewriters and addiction to longhand. After he'd begun to write his own best-sellers, he said, "It's fatal to get ahead of yourself. Typing, you can take a wrong turn. But if you do it slowly, writing a foolscap page or two a day, in a year you are all done. . . . You can't rush it."

Susan Sontag also liked the pace of longhand work. *The New York Observer* called her "a better writer, sentence for sentence, than anyone who now wears the tag 'intellectual,'" and the *Baltimore Sun* described her novel *In America* (1999) as "a magical accomplishment." With a felt-tip pen or sometimes a pencil, Sontag wrote her first drafts at a low marble table in the living room of her Manhattan apartment. "I like the slowness of writing by hand," she said in 1994. "Then I type it up and scrawl all over that. And keep on retyping it, each time making corrections both by hand and directly on the typewriter until I don't see how to make it any better."

Peruvian novelist Mario Vargas Llosa handwrote his way into the ranks of such luminaries of the Latin American literary boom as Gabriel García Márquez and Carlos Fuentes. "First, I write by hand," he said in 1990. "I always work in the morning, and in the early hours of the day. I always write by hand. Those are my most creative hours. I never work more than two hours like this – my hand gets cramped. Then I start typing what I've written, making changes as I go along." Switching between longhand and his type-writer, he spent nearly two years of mornings to finish just the first draft of *The War of the End of the World* (1981). That done, he at last knew that the novel lay somewhere within the "absolute chaos" of what he'd written. The fun could now begin. "I think what I love is not the writing itself, but the rewriting, the editing, the correcting."

WITH NAZIS OUTSIDE, THEY HANDWROTE TOGETHER

No writer ever had a better reason to switch from longhand to a typewriter than James Thurber. By the summer of 1941, at thirty-six, he was the celebrated creator of both wildly original cartoons and wildly funny prose for *The New Yorker*, but he was also so close to being blind that his wife, Helen, in a letter to friends, said, "Jamie cannot get out alone, has to be led around, except indoors, where he is very agile. And the worst is that he cannot read or draw. He writes in longhand on yellow paper, but cannot see what he writes, and you know his painstaking method of writing and rewriting. He felt at a great loss, and still does." Thousands of blind people had learned to touch-type, but not Thurber. Fourteen years after Helen described his misery, he said, "I still write occa-sionally – in the proper sense of the word – using black crayon on

yellow paper and getting perhaps twenty words to the page."
Below nineteen scraggly words, in which some of his awkward
letters were an inch tall, *The Paris Review* explained, "An example,
considerably reduced, of a Thurber manuscript page."

The fiction of James Graham Ballard, which includes *The
Atrocity Exhibition* (1969) and *Crash* (1973), is so unlike any other
writer's that *Collins English Dictionary* has a word for it: "Ballardian."
It means "resembling or suggestive of the conditions described in
J.G. Ballard's novels and stories. Especially dystopian modernity,
bleak man-made landscapes and the psychological effects of technological, social or environmental developments." If utopia is
heaven on earth, dystopia is hell; bad things happen to Ballard's
characters. He composed his nightmarish tales, however, under
the most benign conditions.

In the pretty Thameside village of Shepperton, where he had
lived for almost half a century, he wrote between 10 a.m. and
1 p.m. "in my sitting room – on a large table, popular with my
neighbour's cats." He was a widower. His children had grown up
and moved away. Working alone, he tried to write "about a thousand words a day in longhand, and then edit it very carefully later,
before I type it out." By 2004, he'd written nineteen novels and
twenty collections of short stories, without once experimenting
with a word processor. "I was already too old by the time they
came in," he said, "and I don't like staring at a screen." He was
seventy-four. Three years later, he said, "I distrust the whole PC
thing. I don't think a great book yet has been written on a typewriter." Among the better novelists of the early twenty-first
century, the voice of the Luddite was never more emphatic.

For fifty years, the novelist, playwright, critic, and philosopher
Jean-Paul Sartre and the novelist and essayist Simone de Beauvoir
maintained both an intimate friendship and a professional association. They were so close they often shared a room while he
wrote one book in longhand, and she another. During the Nazi

occupation of Paris, their favourite place to write was the Café de Flore on Boulevard Saint-Germain. It had red leather chairs, plenty of mahogany and mirrors, and a decidedly art deco look. Unsung in those days, it would later be famous as the hangout where Sartre, Beauvoir, and other leftist intellectuals launched the existentialist movement. They liked the Flore because German soldiers rarely showed up there and, in the fierce winters that tortured Paris during the Occupation, the proprietor burned black-market coal in a fat, pot-bellied stove.

Beauvoir and Sartre worked in the afternoon, and on the second floor. "They sat at opposite ends of the room so they would not be tempted to talk," Hazel Rowley wrote in *Tête-à-Tête* (2005), "and – in the fug of tobacco fumes, amid the jangle of coffee cups, the hubbub of conversation, and the distraction of people making their way to the toilet or phone – they wrote. Both used fountain pens. Sartre's handwriting was small, neat, and professional. Beauvoir's jagged calligraphy was almost impossible to decipher. Even Sartre complained about it."

While Sartre and Beauvoir were writing together in the heart of wartime Paris, Malcolm Lowry and Margerie Bonner were writing together at a fisherman's shack in a great fiord inland from Vancouver. Once a leading lady in silent films, Bonner now wrote mystery novels, and Lowry wrestled with what critics would eventually recognize as one of the strangest masterpieces of the twentieth century, *Under the Volcano* (1947). The couple loved the shack. Nearby, Lowry wrote to a friend, was "a fine wet ruin of a forest full of snakes and snails and terrific trees blasted with hail and fire. We dive from our front porch into a wild sea troughing with whales and seals. We have a boat, now diving at anchor. Everywhere there is a good smell of sea and timber and life and death and crabs."

He wrote *Under the Volcano* with a pencil and, to make it legible, Bonner typed it for him. His cramped and twisted handwriting was as tortured as his mind. Here was an alcoholic Englishman disintegrating in British Columbia, and he was writing a novel about an alcoholic Englishman disintegrating in Mexico. In the first chapter, a character finds a letter written by the protagonist and, according to Sherrill E. Grace, editor of the collected letters of Lowry, the handwriting of the fictional Englishman bore an uncanny resemblance to that of the real one. It was, Lowry wrote in the novel, "half crabbed, half generous, and wholly drunken . . . the Greek e's, flying buttresses of d's, the t's like lonely wayside crosses save where they crucified the entire word, the words themselves slanting steeply downhill, though the individual characters seemed as if resisting the descent, braced, climbing the other way."

AND AN OLD DOG LEARNS AN OLD TRICK

Joyce Carol Oates wrote her earliest novels entirely on a typewriter, but it mysteriously turned into "a rather alien thing – a thing of formality and impersonality." Nominated three times for the Nobel Prize in Literature, winner of two National Book Awards and three Pulitzers, and the author of more than a hundred books, Oates wrote in 2001, "I don't use a word processor but write in longhand, at considerable length. (Again, I know: writers are crazy.)"

P.G. Wodehouse took a little longer to decide he preferred longhand to typewriters. Set in a silly society, frozen forever in an England of leisured classes and their servants, his novels about the addlepated Bertie Wooster and the unflappable Jeeves have delighted millions of readers. At ninety-one, Wodehouse had written eighteen plays, lyrics for thirty-three musical comedies, and more than ninety novels, and still worked seven days a week. He confessed, however, that he no longer wrote as fast as he once did. "I used to write about two thousand words [per day]," he said. "Now I suppose I do about one thousand."

On a typewriter or in longhand?

"I used to work entirely on the typewriter. But this last book I did sitting in a lawn chair and writing by hand. Then I typed it out. Much slower, of course. But I think it's a pretty good method. It does pretty well."

SEVEN

The Almighty Typewriter.
Can You Hear the Rhythm?

While visiting Boston in 1874, Mark Twain got his hands on one of the world's first typewriters, which printed only capital letters, and used it to write an error-riddled note to fellow author William Dean Howells: "YOU NEEDNT ANSWER THIS; I AM ONLY PRACTICING TO GET THREE; ANOTHER SLIP-UP THERE; ONLY PRACITI?NG TI GET THE HANG OF THE THING. I NOTICE I MISS FIRE & GET IN A GOOD MANY UNNEC-ESSARY LETTERS & PUNCTUATION MARKS. I AM SIMPLY USING YOU FOR A TARGET TO BANG AT. BLAME MY CATS, BUT THIS THING REQUIRES GENIUS IN ORDER TO WORK IT JUST RIGHT."

Twain also told his brother Orion in Hartford, Connecticut, "I AM TRYING TO GET THE HANG OF THIS NEW-FANGLED WRITING MACHINE, BUT AM NOT MAKING A SHINING SUCCESS OF IT. HOWEVER THIS IS THE FIRST ATTEMPT I HAVE EVER MADE. . . . I PERCEIVE THAT I SHALL SOON EASILY ACQUIRE A FINE FACILITY IN ITS USE. . . . I BELIEVE IT WILL PRINT FASTER THAN I CAN WRITE. ONE MAY LEAN BACK IN HIS CHAIR AND WORK IT. IT PILES AN AWFUL STACK OF WORDS ON ONE PAGE."

His enthusiasm quickly turned to disgust. He got so many letters asking him to describe not only the typewriter but his progress as a typist that he denounced the contraption as his "curiosity-breeding little joker." If the flood of inquiries was a nuisance, so was the machine itself. Like most early American typewriters, it was clumsy, balky, and infuriating. Twain soon dumped it. Since he hired a woman to copy "a considerable part" of *The Adventures of Tom Sawyer* (1876) on a typewriter, however, he claimed to be "the first person in the world to apply the type-machine to literature."

The first great writer in the world to apply the type-machine to literature with his own fingers, however, was Friedrich Nietzsche. Were it not for the Malling-Hansen Writing Ball, a beautiful, handcrafted typewriter from Denmark that looked like an oversized pincushion, Nietzsche could never have written *Thus Spake Zarathustra* (1883–35), *Beyond Good and Evil* (1886), or any of the other revolutionary treatises that made him the most influential philosopher of the modern era.

Since his boyhood in Saxony, he'd suffered migraine headaches, violent stomach attacks, and spells of near-blindness. While serving as a medical orderly in the Franco-Prussian War (1870–71), he was felled by both diphtheria and dysentery. Now, in 1882, he was still only thirty-seven, but could not keep his eyes focused on a page without enduring exhaustion, pain, and blinding headaches. Fearing his promising career as a writer might be over, he bought one of the writing balls that artisans had been improving ever since Rasmus Malling-Hansen, principal of a Danish institute for deaf mutes, had invented the prototype in 1865. Nietzsche mastered touch-typing and, with his eyes closed against the intolerable glare of his paper, wrote as he'd never written before.

A composer who knew him noticed that his prose was now tighter, terser, and more telegraphic than the earlier work he'd written by hand. In his own work, the composer continued, his "thoughts" in both music and language often depended on the quality of his pen and paper. Yes, Nietzsche replied, "our writing equipment takes part in the forming of our thoughts." Once he was completely comfortable with his writing ball, media theorist Friedrich A. Kittler wrote, his prose changed from "arguments to aphorisms, from thoughts to puns, from rhetoric to telegram style."

GOOD ONLY FOR "A LEARNED PIG"

In 1904, Twain still remembered the typewriter he'd first reviled in 1874. "That early machine was full of caprices, full of defects – devilish ones," he wrote. "It had as many immoralities as the machine of today has virtues. After a year or two I found that it was degrading my character, so I thought I would give it to Howells. He was reluctant, for he was suspicious of novelties and unfriendly toward them, and he remains so to this day. But I persuaded him. He had great confidence in me, and I got him to believe things about the machine that I did not believe myself. He took it home to Boston, and my morals began to improve, but his have never recovered."

Remington & Sons Co., manufacturers of firearms, made the typewriter that Twain learned to hate. With its flower decals and foot pedal to advance the paper, it looked like another Remington product, the household sewing machine. In the early 1890s, hundreds of companies were churning out typewriters in North America, but Remington's No. 2 model dominated the marketplace. Then the Wagner Typewriter Co. (later Underwood) produced a machine that enabled the typist to see the letters as they appeared on the paper. That was, in many respects, the first modern typewriter. Shortly after the turn of the century, the company was producing hundreds of them every week.

By definition in those days, a "manuscript" was handwritten but the authors' longhand was often so execrable that, once editors began to receive typewritten submissions, they refused to consider anything else. In Jack London's somewhat autobiographical novel *Martin Eden*, the hero, a would-be writer, endured the rejection of all his stories until he rented a typewriter, mastered it in one day, and began to type not only his new work but "his earlier manuscripts as fast as they were returned to him."

By 1909, when *Martin Eden* first appeared, the arrival of typewriters had swelled to an overwhelming invasion. Many writers, however, abhorred them. They remained loyal to their scratchy dip pens, leaky fountain pens, the sweep of their writing arm, and the feel of their wrist against the grain of paper.

Typewriters, some warned, would sabotage the writing skills of all who used them.

Decades later, even as tens of millions of people welcomed into their homes the low hum and blinking screen of the personal computer, countless writers stuck with either their beloved electric typewriters or the clackety-clacking, slam-banging, bell-ringing, ribbon-spinning manual antiques they'd been using all their lives.

Computers, some warned, would sabotage the writing skills of all who used them.

At the dawn of the typewriter age, James Russell Lowell (1819–91), the Massachusetts-born poet, humorist, editor, professor, and diplomat, wrote, "I could never say what I would if I had to pick out my letters like a learned pig." Later, when Underwood was selling millions of its legendary No. 5 models, literary critic Edmund Wilson said, "I believe that composing on the typewriter has probably done more than anything else to deteriorate English prose."

Pencil-wielder Graham Greene, while applying his reviewer's stiletto to J.B. Priestley's autobiography *Midnight on the Desert* in 1937, linked his victim's rotten prose to the typewriter. "'Tap-tap away': the sound of the typewriter is mesmeric, and I can well believe that a great part of Mr. Priestley's work is done under its spell," Greene wrote. "The huge vague cosmic words pour out: 'cold hell,' 'eternal zero,' 'freezing universe,' 'flashes of lightning into the inmost recesses of the human heart.' . . . Tap, tap, tap, out it pours from the machine: graceless sentences: (It is one of Mr. Priestley's illusions that he has a 'professional trick of rather easy and pleasant exposition'). Tap, tap, tap: too fast for the elementary courtesy of quoting a contemporary poet correctly; too fast for grace or exactitude; too fast, much too fast, for ideas."

A year later, an editorial in the *New York Times* pointed out, disapprovingly, that the typewriter was driving out "writing with one's own hand."

No one at mid-century, however, hated the typewriter more than German philosopher Martin Heidegger. To him, it symbolized everything that was soul-destroying about mass society, big industry, and modern technology. It was only through language, he believed, that one could come to an understanding of Being, and the typewriter was busily destroying the only true way to write language. The hand, the word, and writing shared a holy relationship. The hand entrusted to the word "the relation of Being to Man," but the typewriter ripped writing away from the "essential realm of the hand, i.e. the realm of the word." It turned the word into something merely "typed" and degraded it into nothing more than a "means of communication." Thus it transformed that whole relation of Being to Man – and certainly not for the better.

As late as 1985, British poet Philip Larkin feared the electric typewriter as others feared computers. To Anthony Powell, he wrote, "How very bold of you to buy an electric typewriter; the only time I tried one I was scared to death, as it seemed to be running away with me. I felt as if I had been put at the controls of a Concorde after five minutes' tuition."

On the Road, All 120 Feet of It

"The typewriter," Darren Wershler-Henry wrote in *The Iron Whim: A Fragmented History of Typewriting* (2005), "has become the symbol of a non-existent sepia-toned era when people typed passionately late into the night under the flickering light of a single naked bulb, sleeves rolled up, suspenders hanging down, lighting each new cigarette off the smouldering butt of the last, occasionally taking a pull from a bottle of bourbon in the bottom drawer of the filing cabinet."

Sinclair Lewis alone, however, proved that the era, sepia-toned or not, wasn't exactly "non-existent." The first American to win the Nobel Prize for Literature (1930), Lewis was a both a spectacular drunkard and a Herculean worker. John Updike said he was "able to rise, in whatever unhomey shelter his wanderlust had brought him to, through whatever grisly thickness of hangover, and go to his typewriter and pound out his daily five thousand words." Quite possibly, with his suspenders hanging down and, as he grew older, with protective tape wrapped around his two forefingers. Those were his typing fingers, and his typing passionately late into the night had made them extremely sensitive.

"My father had one of those great big old-fashioned Underwoods," Erskine Caldwell remembered when he was seventy-nine, "and the first thing I ever wrote was on that typewriter. Since then I've always had to see what I'm working on right here before me." Readers in forty languages had purchased eighty million of his books. "In the old days in New York you could rent a room very cheaply," he continued, "and I wrote several books in rented rooms because I had no distractions whatsoever. I could put a typewriter on the bed, sit opposite it in a chair, and write that way all day and night if I wanted to."

Christopher Isherwood, the British-born, Santa Monica–based novelist and screenwriter, said that, when he was young, "I was absolutely fanatical. I wrote in longhand, and I couldn't bear for there to be any erasures on the paper, and since this was before all these wonderful breakthroughs with Liquid Paper, etc., I used to scratch words out with a razor and then polish the paper with my thumbnail and write it in again. It was terrible! I wasted so much energy fussing." The typewriter freed him from all that: "Now I go through the first time in a very slapdash way, and if I get into some nonsense or digressions, I write through to the end and come out on the other side. I'm not at all perfectionist at first. I do all the polishing in the last draft. . . . What I tend to do is not so much pick at a thing but sit down and rewrite it completely." He wrote three entire drafts of some novels. "I've found that's much better than patching and amputating things."

"Here I am at last with my typewriter," Jack Kerouac, nineteen, wrote in 1941. "America is sick as a dog, I tell you. That's why, with my new typewriter and a lot of yellow paper, I am grown dead serious about my letters, my work, my stuff, my writing." He could type a hundred words a minute and, ten years later, in only three weeks, he banged out on a roll of paper a single-spaced paragraph that stretched for 120 feet: the first complete draft of *On the Road*. Wershler-Henry thought Kerouac saw the typewriter "not only as an instrument for the production of truth, but also as a means of channeling and disciplining the relentless flow of images and ideas through his head."

At forty-four, John Irving had written the best-selling *The World According to Garp* (1978), *The Hotel New Hampshire* (1981), and *The Cider House Rules* (1985) and well knew that, at the beginning and end of his writing any novel, he could work at his blue IBM typewriter for no more than two or three painful hours per day. "Then there's the middle of a book," he said. "I can work eight, nine, twelve hours then, seven days a week – if my children let me; they usually don't. One luxury of making enough money to support myself as a writer is that I can afford to have those eight-, nine-, and twelve-hour days. . . . Ask a doctor to be a doctor two hours a day. An eight-hour day at the typewriter is easy; and two hours of reading over material in the evening, too."

When Alan Cheuse, at thirty-eight, abandoned his teaching career to become a writer, he did not begin in longhand. "In the half-finished basement room of a starter house on the outskirts of Knoxville, Tennessee," he recalled, "I set my manual Kmart portable typewriter on a Kmart picnic bench and placed that bench under the basement's only window, with a view out under the house's rear deck toward some young redbud trees. . . . I started typing. When I looked up from my work, those redbud trees had burst into blossom, and I had written . . . a short story that after a couple of revisions I sold to *The New Yorker*, which published it less than a month before my fortieth birthday." He was now off and typing as a writer who would inspire reviewers to rave about his "startling talent," "immense gifts," and "brilliant creations."

Once Typed, It's Cold, Bare . . .
"As Though Someone Else Had Written It"

Just as some writers had to have pen in hand to think clearly, others had to start typing. Flannery O'Connor, while succumbing to a painful and exhausting disease called lupus, told a friend in May 1964, "I have got so I think on the typewriter (and almost nowhere else)." One of the finest of the many fine women writers who emerged from the American South, O'Connor died at thirty-nine but, in the second half of her short life, wrote two novels and two collections of short stories. "It takes great energy to typewrite something," she wrote, as her days dwindled down. "When I typewrite something the critical instinct operates automatically and that slows me. When I write it by hand I don't pay much attention to it."

She had the unusual notion that since a writer used ten digits to type but only three to push a pen, the typewriter was "the more personal instrument." Five weeks before she died, her typewriter sat on a table beside her bed, and, she wrote, "I get out of the bed into the typewriter, so to speak, and every day I am able to do a little more." She'd had four blood transfusions in the previous month, but she declared, "As long as I can get at that typewriter, I have enough." On July 28, 1964, she ended a letter to a friend with "Don't know when I'll send those stories. I've felt too bad to type them." Six days later she was gone. The stories were published the following year in *Everything That Rises Must Converge*.

The handwriting of Robertson Davies, the Canadian whose magical novels moved an American critic to call him "the white-bearded magus of the North," was neat, elegant, and supremely legible but, while composing fiction, he used a typewriter. "I type because writing by hand I find to be a very great betrayer," he said in 1989. "If you try to write [by hand] legibly, as I do, you finish a page and think, *That's a handsome page.* This is absolutely wrong. Also, you can only write so long with a pen before your hand becomes tired, and then your invention begins to tire. If you type . . . you have what you've written there before you – cold and bare. Then you can go over it, and it is as though someone else had written it and you can edit it with great severity."

Explaining why he liked a manual typewriter, Don DeLillo, whom literary critic Harold Bloom named as one of four major American novelists of his time (along with Cormac McCarthy, Philip Roth, and Thomas Pynchon), said, "There's a rhythm I hear that drives me through a sentence. And the words typed on the white paper have a sculptural quality. They form odd correspondences. They match up not just through meaning but through sound and look."

He liked to see words and letters as they "came off the hammers onto the page – finished, printed, beautifully formed." While working on his eighth novel, *The Names* (1982), DeLillo decided to type every paragraph, no matter how short, on a fresh page of its own. "No crowded pages," he explained. "This enabled me to see a given set of sentences more clearly. It made rewriting easier and more effective. The white space on the page helped me concentrate more deeply on what I'd written."

Historian and biographer David McCullough, winner of two Pulitzers and two National Book Awards, said his refusing to abandon his manual Royal, a 1940 model, for a computer was no affectation. He, too, enjoyed seeing keys rise and slam letters on paper. "I like rolling the paper and pushing the lever at the end of the line," he said. "I like the bell that rings like an old train. It's a great piece of machinery. I even like crumpling up pages that don't work. One of our kids used to call them my 'wrong pages.' I don't like the idea that technology might fail me, and I don't like the idea that the words are really not *on* anything."

Eudora Welty, the Mississippian whom the *Columbia Encyclopedia* called "one of the finest short-story writers of any time or place," said in 1972, "My ideal way to write a short story is to write the whole first draft [with a typewriter] in one sitting, then work as long as it takes on revisions, and then the final version all in one." The typewriter, she continued, "helps give me the feeling of making my work objective. I can correct better if I can see it in typescript."

Martin Amis wrote his first draft in longhand, then attacked it with his typewriter. Having finished a novel, he said, he always thought that whether or not it won him a literary prize, he certainly deserved one for typing it. "The Booker Prize is for typing," he said. "Even going from second draft to final draft, hardly a page survives without being totally rewritten. . . . The very act of retyping will involve you in thirty or forty little improvements per page. If you don't retype, you are denying that page those improvements."

Auden loathed the typewriter but wrote, "I must admit that it is a help in self-criticism. Typescript is so impersonal and hideous to look at that, if I type out a poem, I immediately see defects which I missed when I looked through it in manuscript."

HOW THE TYPEWRITER SPAWNED A POETRY ALL ITS OWN

To Charles Olson, a six-foot-eight-inch poet who enjoyed fishing by hand for halibut off Gloucester, Massachusetts, the typewriter was neither an aid to editing nor just a tool for putting words on paper. It was the *only* way to compose poetry. He believed the act of converting handwritten pages to printed pages destroyed the poet's presence in the finished work, but that writing directly into the typewriter preserved it. In the words of Marshall McLuhan, Olson saw the machine as "the personal and instantaneous recorder of the poet's work."

"It is the advantage of the typewriter," Olson wrote in *Projective Verse* (1950), "that, due to its rigidity and its space precisions, it can, for a poet, indicate exactly the breath, the pause, the suspensions even of syllables, the juxtapositions even of parts of phrases, which he intends. For the first time the poet has the stave and the bar a musician has had. For the first time he can, without the convention of rime and meter, record the listening he has done to his own speech and by that one act indicate how he would want any reader, silently or otherwise, to voice his work."

Thus the birth of the typewriter led to the birth of typewriter poetry.

Twenty-three years after *Projective Verse* appeared, Marjorie G. Perloff, an American professor of English, said it seemed "safely enshrined as a cornerstone of avant-garde poetics, perhaps the key theoretical statement in defense of the 'new poetry.'" Beloved for his encouragement of younger writers, Olson was a bridge between the time of Ezra Pound and William Carlos Williams and some of the best American poets of the 1950s, 1960s, and 1970s. Long after Olson's death in 1970, there was no shortage of

American poets who liked typewriters. Anthony Hecht, whose *The Hard Hours* won a Pulitzer Prize in 1968, said twenty years later that, at the Library of Congress, he'd attended a sherry party with seven or eight fellow poets, "and I was more shocked than I can easily say to find that I was the only poet in the room who did *not* compose on a typewriter."

MAY I INTRODUCE MY DEAR FRIEND, IBM SELECTRIC?

Many writers found the sound of a typewriter both comforting and stimulating.

Not for them the light, feathery pit-a-pat of fingertips gently tickling a computer keyboard. They wanted to see, hear, and make keys noisily hit paper; to slam back the carriage return, and thereby signal the completion of one more line; and to roll a fresh sheet of paper into the machine, and signal the completion of one more page. The action, the racket, the sweat: these told certain writers they really were writing.

They often felt a deep, personal attachment to their Underwoods, Olivettis, Royals, etc. "I love my old typewriter," David McCullough said. "There's nothing wrong with it. It works perfectly after forty years of steady, heavy service."

"I loved the golden hum of my first electric typewriter," poet and novelist Paul West wrote, "the twinkle of its red spot, the way it made the music-weather channel tremble on the screen when I rolled its knurled knob back and forth." And now? In 1996? "My [Smith Corona] De Ville 470s serve me well enough; I am hardly aware of what my fingers touch, and I often look away. Sometimes I think I am playing piano, which I cannot do, but I hear rhythms in my tapping and sometimes, Glenn Gould-like, I chant as I go to remind myself of what's coming in the next few lines."

Other writers saw their typewriters as friends, collaborators, or father confessors. Wright Morris, whose twenty novels included winners of a National Book Award and the American Book Award for Fiction, found his electric typewriter companionable. Urging Saul Bellow to get one, he said, "When I'm not writing, I listen to the electricity. It keeps me company. We have conversations." After an interviewer asked Henry Miller if "something is going on between you and the machine," he said, "Yes. In a way the machine acts as a stimulus; it's a cooperative thing."

Isaac Asimov, who bragged of "having reached 451 books," felt the same loyalty to his elderly IBM Selectric that some men felt for their best hunting dogs. World famous for his science fiction, he distrusted that triumph of science reality, the computer. "I heard many stories about people getting word processors and then never using their typewriters again," he wrote. "I simply wasn't going to do that to my typewriter, so I hardened my heart against the growing clamour all about me to the effect that I *must* get a word processor."

He succumbed in 1981, but not completely. "Short pieces of up to 2,000 words or so, I do directly on the word processor, I admit," he wrote. Admit? Did he feel guilty about taking even that amount of work away from his typewriter? "In the case of anything longer, however, I write my first draft on my typewriter and then transfer it into a word processor. . . ." Until he died in 1991, despite all the conveniences the word processor offered, he kept right on composing the first drafts of his books on his good old IBM Selectric.

Humorist P.J. O'Rourke understood. Without his forty-pound Selectric, he confessed in 2003, he was "compositionally helpless." Since it was so old that having it repaired was no longer easy, he was happy to accept other Selectrics as gifts from friends who'd bought computers, which he reviled. New York author Alan Furst, whose spy novels earned comparison to those of Graham Greene and Eric Ambler, wrote, "I work on a descendant of the magnificent IBM Selectric, using a typeface that has a sort of 1940s look to it, and I write 1940s-style novels about the 1940s." Furst called his typewriter "a writer's machine, if ever there was one" and revealed he'd once discovered an "IBM Selectric underground" at an office supply store in Paris. The owner led him to a basement, then to a lower basement, and down a long corridor to a padlocked door. With a key on a chain attached to his belt, the Frenchman opened the door and switched on a light. *Voilà!* On metal shelves, a dozen old Selectrics.

"I keep them around," he said. "There's always somebody who wants one."

CALLING ALL UNDERWOODS. CALLING ALL UNDERWOODS

When Hugh MacLennan was in his seventies and completing his last novel, *Voices in Time*, his elderly Underwood died of old age and overwork. With that black, noisy, anachronistic, typewriting contraption – whose shape was as familiar to the elderly as Model T Fords had once been – MacLennan had earned his reputation as Canada's first internationally acclaimed novelist and had written no fewer than five winners of Governor General's Awards. Now, the machine was just a mess of keys, spools, wheels, and other useless parts. It was too old to repair or replace, and he was too old to switch to another brand. How could he possibly finish *Voices in Time*?

His alarmed publisher, Douglas Gibson, asked Peter Gzowski, the host of CBC Radio's "This Country in the Morning," to appeal to his listeners for old Underwoods in working order. Gzowski was the most popular on-air personality in the country. He was "Mr. Canada," and, to enable a pioneer of modern Canadian literature to finish his last novel, dozens of Gzowski's fans now rummaged through their attics for dusty Underwoods of a certain age. MacLennan accepted the machine that best suited him and, sure enough, *Voices in Time* reached bookstores in 1980. The author's biographer, Elspeth Cameron, declared it "MacLennan's greatest novel."

Without Gibson, Gzowski, and the Canadians who answered their request, this story could never have had its satisfying ending. They recognized the breakdown of a certain old man's certain old typewriter as a national emergency.

EIGHT

Hail the Conquering Word Processor

A s early as 1972, John Hersey used "a huge and very versatile typewriter" to revise the longhand draft of his novel *My Petition for More Space* (1974). The machine was the heart of the Yale Editor, a program under development at the Yale School of Art, and it worked much like the computer-driven word processors of the future. Curious about its usefulness among creative writers, the programmers asked Hersey if he'd like to try it, and in 1985 he recalled:

> I found it just wonderfully convenient. It could remember what I'd done, and help me find mistakes. If I used an out-of-the-way word and had a dim memory of having used it a hundred pages earlier, I could simply type the word and ask the machine to find it, and there it would be, in its context, right away, instead of my having to riffle through a hundred pages and spend two or three hours looking for it. It was simply a time-saver. It took about a month to get used to looking at words on a screen, almost as if in a new language; but once that was past, it seemed just like using a new typewriter. So when these badly named machines – processor! God! – came on the market some years later, I was really eager to find one.

Revising on a typewriter was such a nuisance that, even when Hersey knew he should change a page, he was reluctant to retype it. Once he had his word processor, however, revision was so pleasurable he spent more time and care on it than ever before. Theories about how computers corrupted and spoiled writers by distancing them from their work were, he said, simply "nonsense."

Like fanatical joggers in the early 1970s, many writers who turned to computers in the early 1980s resembled religious converts. Their eyes gleamed with the wonder of having finally found grace. Those who'd previously composed on typewriters swore that the word processor magically released the spontaneity of both their handwriting and their speech, and eased the translation into text of their imaginings. Some found the screen a better "listener" than any page in a typewriter, and others marvelled over the malleability of every paragraph they inserted in the computer's memory. Fluidity was next to godliness.

"God looked down at the writers," wrote novelist and memoirist Frank Conroy, director of the Writers' Workshop at the University of Iowa, "and said, 'I haven't done anything for these people for a long time, hundreds of years, so I'm going to make up for it.' The word processor saves so much time and drudgery in editing and rewriting."

Among writers who got together before the arrival of word processors, *New York Times* columnist Russell Baker wrote in 1985, "it was whine, whine, whine. How hard writing was. How they wished they'd gone into dry cleaning, stonecutting, anything less toilsome than writing. Then the word processor was invented, and a few pioneers switched from writing to processing words. They came back from the electronic frontier with glowing reports: 'Have seen the future and it works.' That sort of thing."

One pioneer was James Fallows, a writer and editor for *The Atlantic.* "For six months, I found it awkward to compose first drafts on the computer," he wrote in 1982. "Now I can hardly do it any other way." Since he no longer stopped at the end of each line to slam the carriage back into place, and at the end of each page to insert another sheet, he wrote faster than he ever did with a type-writer. "It is also more satisfying to the soul," he said, "because each maimed and misconceived passage can be made to vanish instantly, by the word or by the paragraph, leaving a pristine green field on which to make the next attempt."

None of the converts, however, was more enthusiastic about his new faith than the American writer about writing, William Zinsser. He had used typewriters to write nine good books of non-fiction and seemed an unlikely prospect for sellers of word processors. He admitted he was "a mechanical boob" and, like many writers, had "the humanist hang-up." Proud to appreciate art, music, and literature, he neither understood science and technology nor wanted to understand them. Moreover, he was deeply conservative about his work habits. Why change equip-ment that, for decades, had served him well? Why risk writing into a humming, winking box that, owing to one slip of one finger, might destroy his entire masterpiece-in-progress?

Yet Zinsser, the very first time he tried a word processor, fell madly in love with it. "Real sentences began to appear on the screen, one after another," he marvelled in 1983. "Then I had a real paragraph. Then I started another paragraph. Soon I had a second paragraph. I was *writing!* . . . The sentences on the screen were mine – I recognized the style. . . ."

As his writing gathered momentum, the touch of the keys and the speed and ease of his typing lifted from his fingers and shoul-ders "the weight of a lifetime." He loved the way paragraphs rearranged themselves as he cut, changed, or added words; seeing words reach the end of each line, and then automatically continue on the line below; playing with his writing on the screen until he got it right; and not having to print his story until it read as he wanted it to read.

"There's no kind of tinkering that you can't do – and undo – instantly," Zinsser wrote in the fourth edition of *On Writing Well* (1991). "When you finish your revisions, the machine will paginate your entire article and the printer will type it while you go and have a beer. Sweeter music could hardly be sung to a writer than the sound of his article being typed exactly the way he wants it – but not by him."

Zinsser was nearly sixty when he fell for word processors. Among heaven knows how many others who experienced similar late-life conversions was Canada's foremost cultural journalist, Robert Fulford. By 1982, at fifty, he'd been using manual typewriters since he was a teenager to bang out millions of words about books, movies, jazz, fine art, architecture, politics, and much else.

He'd been editor of *Saturday Night* magazine for a dozen years and had complained in private that after several of his contributors had switched to word processors their prose had markedly deteriorated. Fulford liked to tell a story about an American novelist who switched on his computer one morning and discovered to his horror that the fifty thousand words he'd spent months writing had simply vanished. When he tried to recover them, happy faces invaded his screen. Enraged, he punched a wall and broke his knuckles.

"While the electronic word processor is a wonderful machine, the rattler is also a wonderful snake," Russell Baker wrote, after a computer destroyed a piece he wrote in 1985, "but can you really trust either one to be a pal?"

Fulford, in those days, planned to remain among the Luddites of the writing world, thank you very much. In 1998, however, he told a friend, "I would now never write – except on a word processor." He had invented his own system:

First, I enter in a computer file all my research material: notes on the interviews I've done, all my scattered thoughts, quotations from articles and books, bits copied from my *Canadian Encyclo-pedia* on CD-ROM, and various stories I've found on the Internet. When I have what I imagine is all I need, I make a second copy of this file. If the subject is Jones then one file will be "Jones" and one "Jones-re," for research. Jones-re will never change and may end up being printed out for a magazine's checker. But the main Jones file will be slowly cut and reshaped and rethought. Eventually that file will turn into an article. How's this for pretension? It actually occurred to me that this is something like a sculptor "finding" (as they used to say) a work of art inside a raw piece of stone.

Another writer who was late but happy to switch to a word processor was Charles Bukowski, poet, novelist, boozer, and denizen of skid row in Los Angeles. At seventy-one, three years before he died in 1994, Bukowski said, "The writing's not bad for an old guy, I guess, and, yeah, maybe now I fear the loss of my soul. When I wrote my first computer poem I was anxious that I would be suffocated by these layers of consumerist suffering. Would old Dostoevsky have ever used one of these babies? I wondered, and then I said, 'Hell, yeah!'"

For Some, the Word Processor's an Insolent Bully

"Thus Bukowski voices one of the concerns about the 'technolo-gizing' of the writing process," American literary scholar David Stephen Calonne wrote in 2006. "Will the computer take away the 'sacred,' 'natural,' elemental aspect of writing, turning what used to be a profound solitary communion with one's soul into another sterile technocratic transaction?'"

Any writer who used a computer, Kentucky author Wendell Berry warned in 1990, risked a dangerous separation of mind and body. The words on both the screen and the printout had "a sterile, untouched, factory-made look." One's body simply did not work like that. "The body *characterizes* everything it touches. What it makes it traces over with the marks of its pulses and breathings, its excitements, hesitations, flaws and mistakes. . . . And to those of us who love and honour the life of the body in this world, these marks are precious things, necessities of life."

Some felt that the word processor not only banished from the act of writing a priceless intimacy, but also *used* the writer, rather than the other way around. "I didn't like the machine's insolence," American biographer Leon Edel said in 1988. "It tried to make me its slave." Tom Sharpe, the English writer of several bitingly satiric novels, had a similar reaction: "That bloody cursor blinking at me on the word processor screen is awful. I mean it's blink, blink, blink. Well, screw this bastard. It's telling me to get on." Irish novelist Josephine Hart said she had no trouble dominating a pen but "machines seem to have a mind of their own."

Zinsser declared, "I've never met a writer with a word processor who can even imagine going back to the way he or she wrote before," but he had not met Kent Haruf, the Colorado-born novelist whose *Plainsong* was a finalist for the National Book Award in 1999. Haruf wrote his first novel on a manual typewriter and his second on a computer, "but I never did like the way that felt." He missed the "visceral rightness" of working with paper and the clack-clack of the typewriter's keys. "Furthermore," he wrote in 2001, "unless you print out constantly, you lose parts of drafts, certain phrases and sentences, that you may later wish you had saved. So when I began to write *Plainsong*, my third novel, I knew I wanted to go back to using a typewriter, at least for my first draft. . . ."

Primo Levi, author of fiction, poetry, and memoirs, said the words he'd written with a computer were mere "shadows." Lacking "the reassuring support of the paper," they were "immaterial." Sharpe complained that, when he tried a word processor, his writing was "not even on a piece of paper. It's not an object, you see, it's simply an image. . . . With a screen, you switch it off, it's all gone. . . . A piece of paper is substantial. You can hold it, touch it. When you've written a lot of words on paper, you feel by God you've done something."

After conceding that word processors were tidy, Iris Murdoch asked in the early 1980s, "Why not use one's mind in the old way, with pens, paper, notebooks etc., instead of dazzling one's eyes staring at a glass square which separates one from one's thoughts and gives them a premature air of completeness?" A dozen years later, Martin Amis asserted, "It's all nonsense about how wonderful computers are because you can shift things around. Nothing compares with the fluidity of longhand. You shift things around without shifting them around – in that you merely indicate a possibility while your original thought is still there. The little cursor, or whatever it's called, that wobbles around the middle of the screen falsely gives you the impression that you're thinking. Even when you're not."

Kansas poet Albert Goldbarth, whose collection *Heaven and Earth* won the National Book Critics Circle Award, also spurned word processors. To write an essay for the anthology *Tolstoy's Dictaphone: Technology and the Muse* (1996), he used a Bic ballpoint and a one-dollar, spiral-bound notebook. He typed the piece on his IBM Selectramatic, had staff at a Kinko's run off half a dozen copies, and declared, "Although Tomorrow may be a compelling place, and all of Dickens may fit in a fiche smaller than a pepper grain, and be called to the fore by voice command, and come with a 3-D enhancement map of Dickens's gaslit London, and even if Dickens-simulation himself is pixel'ed-up to instruct me in whist . . . if it goes on a screen instead of a page, I'm sorry but the future stops *here*."

THAT "JUST ABOUT DOES IT THIS WEEK, SPACEWISE, FOLKS"

Some authors said the word processor made their work look so neat, clean, and *finished*, it encouraged them to under-edit, while others said it made revising so effortless it encouraged them to over-edit. They tinkered endlessly with their sentences. Critic Joan Acocella saw booby traps in the very ease with which users of word processors could erase or move blocks of text. A page produced on a typewriter was "like a record of the torture of thought" but the final text on a computer's screen buried "the evidence of our struggle" and asserted "that what we said was what we thought all along." Or, as Martin Amis put it, "The trouble with a computer is that what you come out with has no memory, no provenance, no history." Acocella also argued that messing about with scissors, glue, and tape made writers think twice, "and maybe it was wise for us to hesitate before changing the order in which our brains produced our thoughts." Was it a coincidence, she wondered, that accompanying the rise of the word processor was a rise in the amount of writing "that seemed to say, 'This paragraph is here because it seemed an O.K. place to shove it in'"?

An early complaint about word processors was that they seduced writers into not "speaking to the eyes," as Monsieur Breboeuf's verse put it centuries ago, but into endlessly babbling to the eyes. Frank Conroy may have seen the word processor as God's gift to writers but, as the head of a writers' workshop, he well knew that "the computer empowers bad writers to more easily churn out a lot of pages." In 1985, *New York Times* columnist Russell Baker spoofed this empowerment, beginning with the jubilant statement, "I switched to word processing, and – man alive! Talk about easy!" and ending with this:

What the great thing – really great thing – really and truly great thing is about processing words like this, which I am now doing, is that at the end, when you are finally finished, with the piece terminated and concluded, not to say ended, done and thoroughly completed to your own personal, idiosyncratic, individual, one-of-a-kind, distinctive taste which is unique to you as a human person,

male or female, adult or child, regardless of race, creed or colour
– at the end which I am now approaching on account of exhausting available paper space the processing has been so easy that I am
not feeling the least, smallest or even somewhat minuscule sensation of tired fatigue exhaustion, as was always felt in the old days
of writing when the mechanical machines, not to mention goose-
quill pens, were so cumbersomely difficult and hard to work that
people were constantly forever easing off on them, thus being
trapped into the time-wasting thinking process, which just about
does it this week, spacewise, folks.

Eighteen years later, American humorist P.J. O'Rourke insisted
that word processors still made it all too easy to save "a meandering prolixity," pretentious sentences, and silly metaphors. Far
better, he said, to sit at your IBM Selectric with your feet buried in
crumpled paper than have a digital memory neatly store your mistakes. Word processors lured writers into producing too much too
fast, and into stupidly hunting down facts. "Imagine *Gulliver's
Travels*," O'Rourke wrote, "if Jonathan Swift had known what was
on the other side of the world."

For O'Rourke, the most compelling reason for rejecting word
processors was his contempt for the whole culture of computers.
"I can't picture myself fiddling with wires and transistors and
geeky *Popular Electronics* hobby stuff like somebody who belonged
to the Ham Radio Club in high school," he wrote. "I became a
writer to have a cape buffalo head on my wall, not a mouse on
my plastic laminated Scooby-Do pad." He refused "to have some
pubescent twerp with his mom's earring in his tongue, who
combs his hair with Redi-Whip and has an Ani DiFranco tattoo on
his shin, come show me how a computer works. What does the
twerp know about Wordsworth and *Two Gentlemen of Verona* and
shooting a cape buffalo?"

FAREWELL TO THE GROSS TYPEWRITER

For Toronto poet, editor, and essayist Darren Wershler-Henry, however, who was young enough never to have used typewriters, there was only one way to work, and it wasn't with anything as ludicrously obsolete as one of them. In *The Iron Whim: A Fragmented History of Typewriting* (2005), he called himself "an unabashed techno-geek," who wrote on a machine "whose power and elegance make the bridge computers on the average TV starship look like they're cobbled together from old walkie-talkies, LC fish locators, and spray-painted Barbie purses. . . ." At the top of a staircase, sitting like "a statue in a shrine or a family photo on a piano," Wershler-Henry did keep a typewriter. It reminded him just how lucky he was never to have to use it.

Ralph Lombreglia, whose short stories appeared in *The New Yorker* and *The Atlantic Monthly*, loathed the typewriter. The racket it made sabotaged his ability to write, and even to think. Knowing that each page would come to an end, but not precisely when, was maddening. While engrossed in his work, he often failed to notice that the roller had spewed out a finished page, and he kept right on pounding away at the keys. All in all, the typewriter was a "grossly mechanical apparatus . . . an ever-present hostility." Lombreglia therefore wrote his fine stories with pencils. Then, however, a word processor entered his life.

"Today, even the clackiest personal computer keyboard is vastly quieter than a mechanical typewriter," Lombreglia wrote in 1996, "and on a computer, a writer's workspace is not chopped into small physical chunks that must be rolled in and out of a machine. Those differences were more than enough for me; I could make prose on one of those wonderful gizmos, and I started to."

The right way to respond to digital technology, he said, was "to embrace it as a new window on everything that's eternally human, and to use it with passion, wisdom, fearlessness and joy." He himself embraced it so heartily that he wrote columns about it for the on-line edition of *The Atlantic Monthly*, and yet he continued to wield a pen or pencil, on paper, to compose at least half the words in every piece he wrote for publication. "The desire for variety is not a character flaw," he explained. "When I grow tired of the keyboard and screen, I can go to my pen and paper. And then I can go back. I enjoy the mix. I feel refreshed by it." Human beings, after all, were organisms and "organisms like to be refreshed."

NINE

Pins, Paste, Scissors, Recorders.
The Right Paper, Please

"It's utterly irrational, but I love foolscap," George Steiner said. "In America it's called 'legal' size." A French-born American professor of comparative literature, whose achievements inspired Cambridge University to name him an Extraordinary Fellow, Steiner taught in three languages. He wrote poems, novels, and books of literary, cultural, and philosophical criticism and composed his work on "very old-fashioned typewriters." He said, "I tend to type single-space on those huge sheets, badly typed without any attention, often even to paragraphing. This is the first, naively typed, brute output. . . . So in a funny way, my rough draft is a single-spaced, typed scribble on foolscap. . . . I walk up and down the room like a deprived mother hen when I do not have that odd size of paper which somehow corresponds to the way I see a problem."

Susan Sontag wrote in longhand on yellow legal pads, which she called "that fetish of American writers." Blue lines cross the classic yellow legal pad. It has a margin or "down line" that's one and a quarter inch from the left side of each page, a red gummed top, and the undying loyalty of longhand writers as varied as American literary critic Harold Bloom; American novelist Nelson

DeMille, whose thrillers have sold more than thirty million copies; American writer of poems, essays, and novellas (*Legends of the Fall*, 1979) Jim Harrison; American author Beverly Cleary, whose thirty-odd books for children and young adults feature such beloved characters as Henry Huggins and Ramona Quimby; American novelist and Civil War historian Shelby Foote; the first African-American writer ever to win the Nobel Prize for Literature (1993), Toni Morrison; and the Kentucky poet and novelist whom the *New York Times* called "the prophet of rural America," Wendell Berry.

President Richard Nixon wasn't much of a writer, but it was on a yellow legal pad that in August 1974 he scrawled, "End career as a fighter." Five days later, on another one, he drafted his resignation speech. Gore Vidal, who *was* much of writer, then told an interviewer, "I write novels in longhand on yellow legal pads – exactly like the First Criminal Nixon."

On a wall in the corridor outside the Manhattan apartment of the Wall Street lawyer and novelist Louis Auchincloss, a mural by his wife showed the couple in the early 1950s as they sat on a bench in Central Park with their two boys. Auchincloss was bent over a yellow legal pad. By his ninety-first birthday, in 2008, he was enjoying what was shaping up as America's longest-running literary career, and still bending over yellow legal pads. It was on them, in longhand, that he'd written no fewer than forty-seven books of fiction and seventeen of non-fiction.

Margaret Mitchell spent ten years scribbling on yellow legal pads to write *Gone With the Wind* (1936). William Styron wrote on yellow legal pads and, when he lived at the Manhattan dwelling of non-fiction writer Gay Talese, habitually brought one to the dinner table. "And his penmanship was just beautiful," Talese recalled, "as was his prose, of course. It was so graceful and clear." It was with fountain pens, on yellow legal pads, that John Irving wrote eleven novels and two books of non-fiction.

Lawyer John Grisham wrote his first novel, *A Time to Kill* (1987), in longhand on yellow legal pads. Working on it in his spare time, often on the steps of the De Sota County courthouse in Mississippi, it took him three years to finish, but it launched him on a career that saw total sales of his novels, including *The Firm* (1991) and *The Pelican Brief* (1992), surpass sixty million copies.

Canadian-born Bruce McCall, whose humorous illustrations and prose frequently appear in *The New Yorker*, imagined a writer who, having been exposed as a plagiarist, concocted this not-guilty plea: "I was in my Amsterdam hotel room, writing in longhand on a yellow legal pad like so many other authors, when a sudden wind gust from North Africa – a sirocco, I think it's called – picked up several loose sheets and sent them scurrying. Only later, when they printed the side-by-side comparison of my writing with passages from that other book, did I realize what happened. Those pages I chased down had been blown through an open window from another writer's legal pad!"

For Some, a Grade-School Exercise Book Was Good Enough

While not insisting their paper be a legal pad, many writers did insist it be yellow. It unnerved them to face a sheet of white paper. It reminded them they were Writers, and Writers faced horrible blocks. Like paper napkins, cheap yellow paper was friendlier, less formal, and more inviting. "I preferred yellow paper because it's not so responsible looking," poet Conrad Aiken said. "I would just let fly [on a typewriter] and then put the thing away after it was written and not look at it until the next day. Then go to work on it with a pencil – chop and change, and then copy that off again on the yellow paper – and this would go on for days."

Kent Haruf typed first drafts on "the old pulpy yellow paper that was once used by newspaper reporters." The stuff was obsolete but the secretary of a university where he'd taught had stumbled on enough to last him a lifetime and offered it to him. "It was a great gift to me, like manna, like a propitious omen," he said. "I'm very frugal with this old yellow paper: I type on both sides."

Among those who wrote in longhand on yellow paper were humorist, actor, screenwriter, and film director Woody Allen; the author of more than forty western and crime novels, Elmore Leonard; the hugely prolific Isaac Asimov; the decidedly unprolific and frequently drunken Malcolm Lowry (*Under the Volcano*, 1947); the Scottish novelist Muriel Spark; and the African-American writer of six autobiographies, Maya Angelou.

Alexandre Dumas, père (1802–1870), the world's most widely read French author, wrote his poetry on yellow paper, his nonfiction on rose-coloured paper, and his enormously popular historical novels on blue paper. Wherever American novelist and biographer Mary Gordon went in the world, she bought notebooks:

In Orleans I bought notebooks of confectionery colours: lime, strawberry, lemon. *Calligraphie*, their black letters proclaim. These malleable darlings are best for travel writing or short stories. In a smoke shop near Trinity College, Dublin, I bought long notebooks in canary (long fiction, not novels) and square red ones (journalism). . . . Across from the British Museum I found hard notebooks covered in a burlaplike material in turquoise, maroon and orange (literary criticism). . . . There are some that are so pretty I use them as a consolation for the nauseating work of revision: soft pastels, sky blue, powder pink, with a Gray Art Deco design. . . . A secret of notebook lore is the treasure trove of Swedish notebooks, primary colours with neutral borders; fuchsia and mauve, peacock and dove-coloured. These seem so healthy, so sturdy, that I use them for my uncensored journals: they can take it; they will keep it to themselves; nothing can hurt them and mum's the word.

When Colette, twenty-seven in 1900, began to write her somewhat autobiographical novels about the young Claudine, which
launched her career as one of the leading French authors of the
twentieth century, she used small penmanship exercise books like
those she'd known as a schoolchild. "The heavy grey-ruled pages,
the vertical red line of margins, the black cover and its inset medallion and the ornamental title, *Le Calligraphie*," she remembered,
"reawakened the urge, a sort of itch in my fingers." Robert Frost,
who rejected desks in favour of writing boards and claimed he'd
even written some verse on the soles of his shoes, also used school
composition books and spiral notebooks.

To write the novel *No Great Mischief* (1999), one of the finest
novels ever written by a Canadian, Alistair MacLeod spent a dozen
years constructing sentences with ballpoint pens, scratching them
out, and rewriting them – all on the right-hand pages of cheap
scribblers that lay open before him. On the left-hand pages, he
wrote notes to remind himself to insert essential information and
to make sure certain things happened to his characters. Midway
through the writing of each of his short stories, its last sentence
would come to him, and he would scrawl that, too, on one of the
left-hand pages of a scribbler like those in which millions of children messed about with pencils, ballpoints, and crayons. MacLeod
never forgot those sentences. One afternoon, forty years after the
publication of his first short story, "The Boat," he rattled off its
ending as confidently as though he'd written it that morning:
"There was not much left of my father, physically, as he lay there
with the brass chains on his wrists and the seaweed in his hair."

Emily Dickinson, the reclusive Massachusetts spinster who
often dressed entirely in white and rivalled Walt Whitman as the
greatest American poet of the nineteenth century, composed
her first drafts on the backs of recipes, grocery lists, and used
envelopes. As for Edith Wharton, in her adolescence she wrote in

black ink on her mother's creamy vellum. Later, she used second sheets from her own stationery box and, later still, blue ink on pale blue paper that she found easy on her eyes.

ENVELOPES, INDEX CARDS, POST-IT NOTES – ANY SCRAP IN A STORM

While William Maxwell, fiction editor of *The New Yorker* for forty years, wrote his own fine fiction, he used glue to capture his best sentences. "I've gotten to the point where I seem to recognize a good sentence when I've written it on the typewriter," he said. "Often it's surrounded by junk. So I'm extremely careful. If a good sentence occurs in an otherwise boring paragraph, I cut it out, rubber-cement it to a sheet of typewriter paper, and put it in a folder."

Eudora Welty wrote on a typewriter, but revised her typescripts with scissors and pins. "Pasting is too slow, and you can't undo it," she said, "but with pins you can move things from anywhere to anywhere, and that's what I really love doing – putting things in their best and proper place, revealing things at the time when they matter most. Often I shift things from the very beginning to the very end. Small things – one fact, one word – but things important to me."

"I remember long ago seeing a large spread in *Life* about William Faulkner," Pulitzer-winning poet Anthony Hecht said in 1989. "He had covered one entire wall with aligned rows of typing paper on which he had outlined the various parts of the novel he was working on. The whole thing, in all its diversity and complexity, lay mapped out before him on the wall, and he could address any part of it at his convenience, always conscious of its relation to and place in the whole design. I can't tell you what freedom from anxiety this provides. . . . At the end of the day you can go to bed in peace, knowing where and how you can start up again."

While Joan Didion worked on her first novel, *Run River* (1963), she wrote scenes as they came to her, and not in any sequence. "When I finished a scene I would tape the pages together and pin the long strips of pages on the wall of my apartment," she said. "Maybe I wouldn't touch it for a month or two. Then I'd pick a scene off the wall and rewrite it." Kent Haruf taped brown wrapping paper to a wall and scrawled notes on it about the novel he was banging out on yellow paper.

Before Jack London drank himself to death at forty in 1916, he wrote more than twenty novels, two hundred short stories, and four hundred essays and articles. By his thirties, his biographer Alex Kershaw wrote, he'd invented a rudimentary system to help him write the thousand words per day that he demanded of himself: "Across his bed dangled a string, hung with notes scribbled anywhere and at any time. As he moved from scene to scene, so the stuff of fiction passed before him along a literary washing-line. Jack wrote as he often talked – in staccato bursts, shooting from the hip and never retracting a word." London was a damn-the-torpedoes writing machine.

Nabokov, by contrast, was the most meticulous of craftsmen. An uncompromising searcher for the perfect word, he wrote on index cards. He revised and expanded the writing on each card, and rearranged them, until they became novels. Asked if he jumped from one section of his plot to another or moved through it from beginning to end, he said, "The pattern of the thing precedes the thing. I fill in the gaps of the crossword at any spot I happen to choose. These bits I write on index cards until the novel is done. . . . I am rather particular about my instruments: lined bristol cards and well sharpened, not too hard, pencils capped with erasers."

What index cards were for Nabokov, tiny yellow Post-it notes are for British author Will Self. While writing one of his grotesque, satiric novels – reviewer Michael Bywater describes his *The Butt*

(2008) as "strange, misleading and horribly compelling" – Self sticks hundreds upon hundreds of Post-Its to the walls of his study. Arguing that all artists "fetishize" their working methods, he says, "I write ideas, tropes, images, observations, snippets of dialogue, themes, factoids, descriptions on these notes and put them in relevant zones on the wall. Then I reorganize them into scrapbooks, then I turn them into books. Then I write more ideas, etc. on Post-it notes. And so it goes on: the auto-cannibalization of the fictive world."

Simenon required seven-by-ten-inch manila envelopes to write novels. Although the detective stories that starred Inspector Maigret were his most famous creation, he also wrote novels that he felt were closer to being real literature, as well as diaries and autobiographical works. All in all, he wrote nearly 400 books and sold more than 550 million copies of them. Literary critic George Steiner called him "the most extraordinary fictive shaper . . . in our time." The shaping would start with an idea for a novel rising from Simenon's subconscious to his conscious thinking, and continue with his imagining, in detail, the story's opening setting. Then, he said, "little by little, a small world will come into my mind, with a few characters."

After two days of letting the story gel like this, he could no longer bear to not get something down on paper. On manila envelopes, he wrote the names and ages of his characters and of their family members. According to *Paris Match* (August 27, 1960), he always began with his hero:

> First, his name. To find it, Simenon copies from the telephone directory at least 300 surnames. These he repeats aloud until the moment when one of them comes to the fore. He writes it down on the back of a commercial format envelope. . . . After the name, he notes the age, the address, the telephone number. He wants to know everything about his character, even things he'll never use.

His father's age, and whether he's still alive, his mother, his children, his friends. If he has a bad liver or a strong heart. Simenon wants to have the plan of his house, to know the style of his furniture and what street the windows look out on. These elements united, Simenon opens a map of the city where the action will take place. He adds to the envelope the names of streets, distances. Everything is weighed, measured, timed.

Down with "Straightjacketing Keyboards"

In 1908, Thomas Edison, inventor of Dictaphones, sent one to Tolstoy as an eightieth-birthday gift. This may well have been the first time any great novelist received an electronic aid to writing, but Tolstoy rarely used it. He said it was "too dreadfully exciting." Some later writers, however, added tape recorders to their tools. They found it handy for organizing ideas or, while driving, to preserve whatever useful notions popped into their heads. To catch flaws in their work, others read it into a tape recorder and played it back.

Humorist S.J. Perelman recalled that Raymond Chandler, writer of hard-boiled detective fiction, used one while trying to conquer "the most bitter reluctance to commit anything to paper." To a tape recorder, Chandler "spoke the utmost nonsense – a stream of consciousness which was then transcribed by a secretary and which he then used as a basis for his first rough draft. Very laborious. He strongly advised me to do the same . . . in fact became so excited that he kept plying me with information for months about the machine that helped him."

Playwright Tom Stoppard wrote all his dialogue with a fountain pen, but not the stage directions. Thus his early manuscripts contained only the words his characters uttered. "Then I dictate the play," he said, "adlibbing all the stage directions into a tape machine, from which my secretary transcribes the first script."

British writer Catherine Cookson wrote the first sixteen of her ninety-odd novels in longhand, but then switched to a tape recorder. She wrote sagas about families in nineteenth-century England and, with the tape running, spoke in strong dialects, usually North Country, as she acted out the parts of her characters.

By January 2007, Richard Powers, whose ninth novel, *The Echo Maker* (2006), won a National Book Award, had tossed off half a million words of published fiction without having touched a keyboard, written in longhand on paper, or dictated to anyone other than himself.

"I write these words from bed, under the covers with my knees up, my head propped up and my three-pound tablet PC – just a shade heavier than a hardcover – resting in my lap," he told readers of the *New York Times*. "I speak untethered, without a headset, into the slate's microphone array. The words appear as fast as I speak, and they wait out my long pauses. I touch them up with a stylus, scribbling, or re-speaking as needed. Whole phrases die and revive, as quickly as I could have hit the backspace. I hear every sentence as it's made, testing what it will sound like, inside the mind's eye."

Powers argued that, once upon a time, all storytellers simply talked their tales, and "no technology caused more upheaval than the written word." According to Plato, he explained, the talkative Socrates warned that writing obscured authority, sabotaged memory, and distorted meaning. For centuries just about everyone who could read did so out loud. "Our passage into silent text came late and slow, and poets have resisted it all the way. From Homer to hip-hop, the hum is what counts."

It took Powers weeks to get accustomed to "auditioning myself in an empty room" and to trust the flow of his own speech, but once he was comfortable with what he was doing, he no longer had any use for "straightjacketing keyboards." He asked, "What could be less conducive to thought's cadences than stopping every time your short-term memory fills to pass those large-scale musical phrases through your fingers, one tedious letter at a time? You'd be hard-pressed to invent a greater barrier to cognitive flow." Having worked as a computer programmer and data processor, Powers was better prepared than most writers to use the newest electronic gadgetry to discover the forgotten virtues of the oldest way on Earth of telling stories.

TEN

Out of Their Mouths Popped Literature

Whether they use longhand, a keyboard, or both, most writers must *read* their work as it emerges from their heads. To those whose creative juices refused to flow, Guy de Maupassant urged, "Get black on white." Put some words down where you can scrutinize them. Mess with them. That's how writers write, and it's so hard to do it that American journalist, screenwriter, and playwright Gene Fowler once said, "Writing is easy. All you do is sit staring at a blank sheet of paper until the drops of blood form on your forehead." Thus it's inconceivable to nearly all creative writers (with the notable exception of Richard Powers) that they could ever just talk and have immortal literature dance out of their mouths.

That's why one can't help wondering if John Milton – the seventeenth-century Puritan whose *Paradise Lost* remains one of the greatest epic poems ever published in any language – weren't touched by one of those angels in whom he so fervently believed. For he dictated to amanuenses all of its 10,565 lines, and every one of its more than 85,000 words. When he began to "write" *Paradise Lost* in 1658, he was forty-nine and had been blind for six years.

To make matters worse, Oliver Cromwell died that year, his Commonwealth fell apart, and in due course Charles II became king of England. These events threatened Milton's very life. For he had backed the republican cause ever since the Civil War of the 1640s tore England apart. He had served it as the most learned and eloquent propagandist in British history and, after Cromwell came to power in 1649, he was the government's salaried secretary of foreign languages. Now he was a fugitive. London's hangman publicly burned some of his pro-republic writings, royalists issued a warrant for his arrest, and he dodged from neighbourhood to neighbourhood until his enemies nabbed him and threw him in jail. Owing perhaps to the influence of friends like his former assistant and fellow poet Andrew Marvell, a member of Parliament, his incarceration lasted only a few weeks. Marvell and others may have convinced the authorities that a blind, aging, unemployed, and embittered champion of a hopelessly lost cause couldn't possibly be a threat to the new order.

Milton's private life turned as sour as his public one. After his second wife died in 1658, he wrote a sonnet that sorrowfully began, "Methought I saw my late espoused saint." Five years later, at fifty-four, he married a twenty-four-year-old; one of his daughters by his first wife, long deceased, said his wedding was no news, but if she could only hear about his death "that would be something." By then, Milton had been losing himself in *Paradise Lost* for five years.

As a young man, he'd been a poet, but for two decades, as he churned out pamphlets and treatises for the republican movement, he scarcely wrote a line of verse. When the Commonwealth collapsed, his faith in English politics collapsed with it, and the urge to write poetry seized him once again. Three centuries after his death, the Argentinian writer Jorge Luis Borges, who also dictated his work after becoming blind, said, "He sacrificed his sight and then he remembered his first desire, that of being a poet."

In *Paradise Lost*, Milton sought "to justify the ways of God to man." He told the story of God's defeating the beautiful, intelligent, powerful but arrogant Satan and his gang of rebel angels, and hurling them all down to Hell; of Satan's vengefully tricking God's beloved creations, Adam and Eve, into eating from the Tree of Knowledge and thereby disobeying Him; and of His consequent expulsion of the couple from the Garden of Eden. Some have argued that Milton felt such sympathy for Satan that he made him too attractive. Both knew how failure felt and, while writing *Paradise Lost*, perhaps Milton subconsciously explored the losses that the downfall of the republic and restoration of the monarchy had inflicted on him.

His blindness may have intensified his sense of rhythm, memories of images, and sensitivity to the subtleties of sounds. The blank verse in *Paradise Lost* is so majestic and sonorous it has reminded some of the tones from a mighty pipe organ in a cathedral. Milton once explained that a divine spirit gave him verses at night and, the next day when he was ready "to be milked," he simply chanted them to an amanuensis.

In his last years, he also dictated not only *Paradise Regain'd* and the blank-verse drama *Samson Agonistes*, but several essays and treatises. It was *Paradise Lost*, however, that inspired his younger contemporary, the poet, playwright, and critic John Dryden, to call him a greater epic poet than either Homer, who may also have been blind, or Virgil.

Scott "Wrote" *Ivanhoe* While Screaming in Pain

In 1820, William Hazlitt wrote that Montesquieu, the eighteenth-century French philosopher and man of letters, admitted he "often lost an idea before he could find words for it: yet he dictated by way of saving time, to an amanuensis." Hazlitt called this "a vile method, and a solecism in authorship." In our own time, however, Cambridge anthropologist Alan Macfarlane argued that Montesquieu's talking out his ideas to secretaries helped make his writing admirably simple and direct: "It is a conversation between the author and the scribe, with the reader taking the place of the note-taker. As the spoken word was constantly revised Montesquieu made strenuous efforts to maintain the energy, lack of coherence, [and] spontaneity of the original speech. He woos and amuses the reader, creating deliberate confusions, surprises, a rushing to and fro as in the effort of a raconteur in a club to keep his audience."

Adam Smith dictated *The Wealth of Nations* (1776) to an amanuensis. "This gives his writing its peculiar interest and simple feel," Macfarlane continued. "He is again talking to one person, even if it is written down. He is desperate to communicate, hates handwriting, so pours out and elaborates the teeming thoughts to a paid listener." Macfarlane believed that while Smith dictated he strode back and forth in his study in the Scottish port of Kirkcaldy. But thirty-seven years after Smith's death in 1790, writer and publisher Robert Chambers wrote, "It was his habit to compose *standing*, and to dictate to an amanuensis. He usually stood with his back to the fire, and unconsciously, in the process of thought, used to make his head . . . rub sideways against the wall above the chimney piece. His head being dressed in the ordinary style of that period with pomatum [pomade], he did not fail to make a mark on the wall. That mark remained till lately, when, the room being painted anew, it was unfortunately destroyed."

When Sir Walter Scott was too sick to hold a quill he, too, dictated prose. A court clerk, judge, publisher, poet, novelist, biographer, translator, and the famously hospitable laird of his manor on the River Tweed in the Borders country of Scotland, he put himself under the most brutal pressure and, in his mid-forties, endured a series of mysterious cramps. They invaded his stomach with such force his neighbours could hear the screams that his agony wrenched from his lips. Opium gave him only temporary relief. His hair turned white, and his face yellow and haggard. He lost so much weight he shrank within his clothes and doubted he'd live much longer. Too weak to handle a pen, Scott now wrote four historical novels by dictating them to friends. They included *The Heart of Midlothian* (1818) and *Ivanhoe* (1819).

One of his amanuenses was John Ballantyne, his publishing partner in Edinburgh and, as Scott's biographer S. Fowler Wright wrote in 1932, "John said that he used to start in the morning with a dozen pens laid out for use, so that he should not risk having to pause to mend a quill when the narration was in full flow. Scott lay on a couch at this time, the sentences of dictation often broken with groans of pain, but there were times when he would forget his physical weakness in the excitement of climax, and pace rapidly up and down the room as he dictated, in the different voices of the characters, the conversation which he conceived." It was not for nothing his fans called him "the wizard of the North."

The attacks tortured Scott for more than two years but ended in 1820 as inexplicably as they'd begun. Owing in no small part to the books whose hundreds of thousands of words he'd declaimed to Ballantyne and others, and punctuated with moans and shrieks, he became the most popular writer in the world. His historical novels would influence Balzac and Tolstoy.

Stendhal, too, blurted his writings to amanuenses. He was a Napoleonic cavalryman, a spy, wit, dandy, diplomat, philanderer, Italophile, and, as a writer of French fiction, both a Romantic and a pioneer of Realism. At fifty-five in 1838 he holed up in Paris to write *The Charterhouse of Parma*. A historical yarn about the post-Napoleonic adventures of a young Italian noble, Fabrizio del Dongo, it won praise from Balzac as the most important novel of his time, and from André Gide as the greatest French novel anyone had ever written. It was roughly 300,000 words long and, as C.P. Snow wrote, "it was written at the rate of eight thousand to ten thousand words a day, which is the all-time speed record for a major novel."

Stendhal started *The Charterhouse* on November 4, jammed the manuscript into six big boxes on December 26, and sent them to a friend for delivery to a publisher. How did he write this classic so astoundingly fast? In *Stendhal* (1997), Jonathan Keates wrote, "In these fifty-two days, shutting out visitors and only allowing himself the occasional distraction of an evening at the opera and the Théâtre des Funambules or a call on the Montijos for a party and some Spanish songs, he followed the method employed with most of his other books, writing a rough draft of each section, then dictating a finished version to a copyist."

The method influenced the style. "From the very beginning," Yale professor Bernard Knox wrote in 1999, "the narrative takes the reader by storm with its fervid pace . . . and this speed lies at the base of another aspect of the narrative, its unpredictability."

A GIRL WITH A PENCIL SAVES DOSTOEVSKY'S BACON

In the mid-1860s, Fyodor Mikhailovich Dostoevsky was forty-five, spiritually crushed, and financially desperate. He had recently tended his wife Maria while she slowly succumbed to tuberculosis. His older brother Mikhail, whom he loved deeply, had also died. Fyodor tried to rekindle a turbulent affair he'd once endured with a young woman who'd both loved and loathed him, but she now spurned him. He was an epileptic and never knew when a fit would leave him writhing on the ground and foaming at the mouth.

By 1866, the literary journal that he and Mikhail published had gone out of business and, for two years, he'd been struggling to support both the impoverished family that Mikhail had left and the feckless son of Maria by an earlier marriage. Dostoevsky was bankrupt and so heavily in debt he agreed to a publishing deal that, if it weren't for a girl named Anna, would have enslaved him to a swindler. She was good with pencils, very good.

In a letter to a friend in June 1866, Dostoevsky explained, "I was in such dire straits that I was forced to sell the publication rights for an edition of all my previous writings – on a one-time basis – to a speculator named Stellovsky, a rather nasty man and a thoroughly incompetent publisher." The contract bound Dostoevsky to an outrageous concession. If he failed to deliver a new novel to the nasty man by November 1, Stellovsky would be "entitled to publish, over a nine-year period, at no cost and at his discretion, anything I may write, without paying me any remuneration whatsoever." For all this, Stellovsky gave him a measly three thousand rubles.

Dostoevsky used some of the money to pay debts, but blew much of it at roulette tables. By October 1, his creditors were hounding him, visions of debtors' prison tormented him, and, since he was still working on *Crime and Punishment* for another publisher, he had yet to write even one line of the novel he owed to Stellovsky just four weeks hence.

Could he possibly dictate an entire novel in one month? He had to try, and at 11:30 a.m., October 4, Anna Grigoryevna Snitkina, twenty, pretty, and nervous, showed up at his house in Moscow. She'd just bought plenty of pencils and "a small portfolio, which I felt would lend a more businesslike air to my youthful figure." She was fresh out of stenography school, and Helen Muchnic, an expert on Russian literature, has described her as "untried, unsure of her ability, wanting desperately to make good, and very much in awe of her prospective employer, over whose works she had wept since girlhood." Anna, however, instantly proved herself the epitome of efficiency and grace under pressure. "Every day for the next four weeks she took down Dostoevsky's dictation in short-hand," Muchnic wrote, "and transcribed it at home each night; thanks to her faithful perseverance, the novel was finished in the nick of time."

On her first day of work, Anna remembered, "I got out my notebook, and Fyodor Mikhailovich began pacing about the room in swift strides, diagonally from the door to the stove and back. Every time he reached the stove he would invariably knock against it twice. On top of this he smoked one cigarette after another, throwing his unsmoked stubs frequently into the ashtray lying at the corner of his desk. . . . [He] really did like to walk around the room while dictating, and in the difficult spots he used to pull his long hair."

"I have hired a stenographer now and, even though I read over and revise whatever I dictate three times, stenography practically doubles the speed of my work," Dostoevsky told a friend. "This was the only way I could finish writing the ten printer's sheets for Stellovsky in *one* month – I could not have written five otherwise."

"Our last dictation took place on the twenty-ninth of October," Anna remembered. "*The Gambler* was finished. From October 4 to 29, that is, in twenty-six days. . . . He was hugely pleased."

If escaping the clutches of Stellovsky hugely pleased him, so did Anna herself. No sooner had they finished *The Gambler* than he wanted her as his wife. He'd had little luck, however, with the women he'd previously loved and, as Muchnic wrote, "he hardly dared hope that his sensible and helpful young secretary would accept a sick, poor, ugly man who was twenty-five years older than herself." He need not have worried. "The eighth day of November, 1866," she wrote in her memoirs, "was one of the great days of my life. That was the day Fyodor Mikhailovich told me that he loved me and asked me to be his wife. Half a century has passed since then, and yet every detail is as sharp in my memory as if it had happened a month ago."

They married three months after he proposed to her but, even before their wedding, she helped him finish *Crime and Punishment*. At her urging, he worked on it alone, refusing to see visitors, from two to five every afternoon. Then, in the evenings, "I would sit down at the desk, he would seat himself next to me and the dictation would begin, punctuated with talk, jokes and laughter. The work progressed well, and the last installment of *Crime and Punishment*, comprising about a hundred and fifteen pages, was written in the space of four weeks. Fyodor Mikhailovich declared that his writing had never before come so easily to him and attributed his success to my collaboration."

Thanks to Anna, the last fourteen years of Dostoevsky's life were his best. She helped him negotiate with creditors and publishers, held him during his horrifying epileptic fits, and gave him joy in bed. As he flitted about western Europe – always in financial straits, and periodically indulging in calamitous gambling sprees – she stuck with him. Even when he gambled away money she'd raised by selling her own possessions, she forgave him. He so valued her judgment that, following her advice, he rewrote whole passages of his fiction. While he worked on *The Idiot* (1868), *The Eternal Husband* (1870), *The Possessed* (1871–72), *The Raw Youth* (1875), and *The Brothers Karamazov* (1879–80), his most intimate editorial consultant was his wife. He hadn't known it on October 4, 1866, but the nervous girl who rapped on his door that morning would be the amanuensis of his dreams.

MISS BOSANQUET, I'M READY. TAKE A NOVEL, PLEASE

By 1896, Henry James, a fifty-three-year-old American who'd settled in England twenty years earlier, had published *Washington Square*, *The Portrait of a Lady*, and *The Bostonians*; seven other novels; dozens of shorter works of fiction, including *Daisy Miller* and *The Aspern Papers*; and a raft of essays about poets, novelists, and parts of London and France that charmed him. Unlike other established authors, however, he now chose to revolutionize the way he strung his words together on paper. Since he suffered hand cramps while writing with pens, he began to dictate to typists not only his journalism and business correspondence but all his fiction.

From 1907 until he died in 1916, his amanuensis was Theodora Bosanquet. Upon hiring her, he told her to find a furnished flat as "a temple for the Remington and its priestess." She enjoyed her work. To conquer his mild stutter, he delivered his sentences to her in a stately manner and, she remembered, "once I was seated opposite him, the strong, slow stream of his deliberate speech played over me without ceasing." While dictating to her, he often sank into a trance; he heard neither wailing cats outside a nearby window nor the blaring automobile horns of unwelcome visitors outside the door. He heard only his own voice and the sound of the Remington.

Bosanquet later said that he always "found it more difficult to compose to the music of any other make. During a fortnight when the Remington was out of order he dictated to an Oliver type-writer with evident discomfort, and he found it almost impossibly disconcerting to speak to something that made no responsive sound at all." While dying in 1916, James asked that someone operate his Remington beside his bed. He wanted its music to waft him away. (For many years after he died, Bosanquet claimed he was still dictating to her, and that, thanks to her spirit medium, she knew that the dead authors George Meredith, Thomas Hardy, and John Galsworthy wanted her to take dictation from them as well.)

James once confided to Bosanquet that dictating was "more inspiring" than writing longhand, and "it all seems to be so much more effectively and unceasingly *pulled* out of me in speech than in writing." Dictating pulled out of him the most intricate, meandering, and, to some, infuriating sentences in modern literature. They seemed to amble in mazes, endlessly. Parenthetical remarks appeared at every bend in the path, and the more revisions he dictated the more flourishes he planted. "In the old days when he wrote in longhand, he was much briefer and crisper," his biographer Leon Edel said, "but now he luxuriated in fine phrases and he was exquisitely baroque. It's a grand style but not to everyone's taste."

While a writer types or works in longhand, his fingers and wrists may grow so tired he wants to put an end to a sentence. But, as American literary critic Joseph Epstein has pointed out, "talk rolls and flows, lasting quite as long as breath, and even the need for breath may be satisfied by a semi-colon stop, after which one may roll on and on. Although James frequently excused himself to his correspondents for writing in 'Remingtonese,' he doubtless greatly enjoyed dictating to a typist, for talking his writing gave full freedom to his impulse to qualify, his hyper-subtlety, his need for utmost clarity, and his endless pursuit of nuance." Moreover, James had an "abiding love of complexity *per se*" and "writing by dictation did not so much change Henry James's style as give full vent to it."

H.G. Wells loathed it. Reading James's later novels reminded him of "a magnificent but painful hippopotamus resolved at any cost, even at the cost of its dignity, upon picking up a pea." In 1978, American novelist and journalist Joan Didion told an interviewer that James's sentences were "perfect," but also "very indirect, very complicated. Sentences with sinkholes. You could drown in them."

Here, then, complete with sinkholes, is one sentence from the second paragraph of *The Ambassadors*, which James dictated shortly after the turn of the nineteenth century:

There were people on the ship with whom he had easily consorted – so far as ease could up to now be imputed to him – and who for the most part plunged straight into the current that set the landing-stage to London; there were others who had invited him to a tryst at the inn and had even invoked his aid for a "look round" at the beauties of Liverpool; but he had stolen away from every one alike, had kept no appointment and renewed no acquaintance, had been indifferently aware of the number of persons who esteemed themselves fortunate in being, unlike himself, "met," and had even independently, unsociably, alone, without encounter or relapse and by mere quiet evasion, given his afternoon and evening to the immediately sensible.

And three decades later, here is James Thurber having fun at James's expense:

Although I never met Henry James, I attended (or we'll say that I did) a party one time at which he told the plot of *The Bat*, the mystery play then very popular and attracting a great deal of attention. One was really not supposed to tell how the play "came out," for this would impair the pleasure of persons who had not yet seen it and who wanted to; I forget now whether it was also supposed to impair the pleasure of those who had not seen it and who had no intention of seeing it, but I suspect that it was; in those days, people's pleasure was pretty easily impaired. There were a few persons at the party who knew how the play came out but hadn't seen it, and a few others who had seen it and still didn't know how it came out. Most of us, however, had not seen it and didn't much care how it came out.

WHY SOME WRITE IN THEIR HEADS: THEY CAN'T SEE

If writer's cramp caused a middle-aged James to start dictating his fiction, the onset of blindness caused a middle-aged Thurber to start dictating pieces that confirmed his standing as the funniest American writer since Mark Twain. His memory was astounding, and he composed in his head every word of entire essays and short stories. In 1955, at sixty-one, he spent his mornings "turning over the text in my mind. Then in the afternoons, between two and five, I call in a secretary and dictate to her. I can do about two thousand words. It took me about ten years to learn." Having dictated the two thousand words, however, he'd barely left the starting line: "I rewrite everything all the way through from five to twenty times." After his wife read one of his first drafts, she said, "'Goddamn it, Thurber, that's high-school stuff.' I have to tell her to wait until the seventh draft, it'll work out all right."

Since he wrote in his head he was never quite sure when he was *not* writing. "Sometimes my wife comes up to me at a party and says, 'Dammit, Thurber, stop writing.' She usually catches me in the middle of a paragraph. Or my daughter will look up from the dinner table and ask, 'Is he sick?' 'No,' my wife says, 'he's writing something.'"

Ved Mehta, born in India and blind since he was four, dictated to amanuenses hundreds of magazine articles and short stories, and twenty-five books, many of them autobiographical. He was a staff writer at *The New Yorker* for thirty-three years. Back when he was a twenty-year-old at Pomona College in California – and a shy, achingly lonely Hindu whose home lay halfway around the world – he rode a train to Seattle, the hometown of his beautiful classmate, Joan Johnstone. There, he rented a one-room apartment and hired her as his amanuensis. "She had such a kind, bright voice," he wrote decades later, "that just to hear her greet me thrilled me." For eight hours a day, six days a week, he dictated to Joan the story of his young life.

"The dreamer in me imagined that if she came to know [my personal history] she might fall in love with me," he continued. "I fancied that even if I never ended up dating her, if she accepted my offer, then at least for a whole summer her voice would be in my ear and the breath of her presence would surround me. . . . Once I started dictating, the material arranged itself into episodes and scenes, conversations and reflections, if in a bare-boned way.

Joan wrote down everything in longhand with a fountain pen, forming my words with brisk strokes and scratches and little taps as she finished one line and started another." For a while, she was "my recording angel," but they drifted apart. She had not fallen in love with him, but if he had not loved her he might never have discovered how much he loved writing.

Then there was Lola. In 1966, when Mehta was thirty-two and researching his *Portrait of India* (1970), he spent months rising at dawn and travelling until eleven or twelve at night. Thoroughly exhausted, he impulsively invited Lola, his part-time secretary, to join him as he explored India. For five weeks, she criss-crossed the country with him. "She took down my conversations in short-hand," he said, "and even recorded her own impressions of the people we met." Soon, she was doing more than that. Her impressions were so much like his and their ideas and personalities meshed so tightly that "it was rather like discovering a double, and that of the opposite sex. . . . We became lovers. I thought if I could have seen, I would have seen what she was seeing. The experience was so intoxicating that I thought I would never be able to do reporting on my own again. I have told the story of our brief affair and breakup in *All for Love* (2001)."

ELEVEN

Keep Out! Writer at Work

Several years before Franz Kafka wrote his nightmarish novels *The Castle* (1930) and *The Trial* (1937), he told his fiancée in a letter, "I have often thought that the best mode of life for me would be to sit in the innermost room of a spacious locked cellar with my writing things and a lamp. Food would be brought and always put far away from my room, outside the cellar's outermost door. The walk to my food, in my dressing gown, through the vaulted cellars, would be my only exercise. I would then return to my table, eat slowly and with deliberation, then start writing again at once. And how I would write! From what depths I would drag it up!" And how he *did* write! Kafka was a Czech who worked in German, and no less a novelist than Nabokov called him "the greatest German writer of our time. Such poets as Rilke or novelists as Thomas Mann are dwarfs or plaster saints in comparison to him."

"The first thing that distinguishes a writer," Martin Amis said, "is that he is most fully alive when alone. . . . The most interesting things happen to you when you are alone." Scottish journalist Neal Ascherson said in 2006 that Philip Roth, Don DeLillo, and Aleksandr Solzhenitsyn all "live in seclusion, barricaded –

sometimes literally – against the casual visitor. Philip Roth lives alone in Connecticut, bound . . . to a routine as solitary as a monk's, as disciplined as a soldier's. He works all day, keeping himself in shape with exercise gear, and often works again at night. Don DeLillo does four hours of writing in the morning, then 'a few miles around a local high-school track,' then writes again until the evening." About Solzhenitsyn, the Russian diarist Lidiya Chukovskaya once wrote, "It was as if he had sentenced himself to imprisonment in some strict regime camp. . . . He was convict and guard rolled into one, and his own surveillance of himself was perhaps more relentless than that of the KGB." Ascherson decided the three novelists shared "a sort of Protestant fiction ethic, apparently sacrificing the pleasures of normal living in order to realize and fulfill every grain of their own potential."

American writer Robert Stone, whose dark and violent novels include National Book Award–winner *Dog Soldiers* (1974), said writing fiction was not only "goddamn hard" but also "very lonely." South African novelist and Booker Prize–winner Nadine Gordimer described the solitude of writing as "quite frightening" and "quite close sometimes to madness."

Writers have always holed up to work. More than four centuries have passed since the father of the personal essay, Montaigne, said that, in the library at his chateau in southwest France, "there is my seat, that is my throne. I endeavour to make my rule there absolute, and to sequester that only corner from the community of wife, of children, and of acquaintance. . . . Miserable in my mind is he who in his own home hath nowhere to be to himself." Cambridge anthropologist Alan Macfarlane wrote in 2002 that the eighteenth-century essayist, philosopher, and social commentator Montesquieu "retired into his moated castle [in Bordeaux], and if there were still too many distractions in the library withdrew into a tiny cell in the wall." Adam Smith "quietly worked in his house in Kirkcaldy, Scotland, full of contentment, and with a beautiful view and a garden down to the sea." Alexis de Tocqueville "retired to a garret in Paris [to write *Democracy in America*] and then later to a special room in the Norman countryside. All three found tranquility."

Thomas Carlyle (1795–1881) was not so fortunate. In the eyes of his contemporaries, the gloomy historian, biographer, critic, and philosopher was Britain's leading thinker, but he was also an irritable insomniac who suffered from gastric pains and an intense sensitivity to noise. In London, the whistles of steam engines, shouts of street vendors, rattle of carriage wheels, clip-clopping of hooves, blaring of barrel organs, barking of dogs, yowling of cats, and shrieking of a neighbour's chickens added up to a din that, for him, was sheer torture.

At the top of the narrow staircase to his Chelsea attic, he had a "soundless room" installed. Alas, the *London Observer* later reported, he forgot that "soundproof rooms are, like safes, absolutely incapable of ventilation. The room completed, he locked himself up in it, and smoked; and, being fortunately missed, was discovered by a housemaid senseless upon the floor." Whatever the cause of the stuffiness, however, it was not soundproofing. The room turned out to be the noisiest in the house, and Carlyle bitterly complained that the silence it promised was no more than "a flattering delusion of an ingenious needy builder."

In our own time, Nicholas Baker has a foolproof way of ensuring that "the chirping, barking, jingling cash-drawer of a world is out of reach, and therefore more precious." Earplugs. An American, Baker writes novels that are singular for what Toronto reviewer and magazine editor Jason McBride calls "their relentless attention to the obscure, the overlooked, the forgotten or the willfully ignored. If the devil is in the details, Baker might be Beelzebub himself." Here then are Baker's relentless details about his dirt-cheap solution to unwelcome noise:

"Some years ago I bought an industrial dispenser pack of two hundred pairs of Mack's earplugs from earplugstore.com. Most recently, though, I buy them from the drug store. Recently Mack's began offering them in orange, which is less disgusting than white. I can sit anywhere, in any loud place, and work. Everything becomes twenty feet farther away than it really is. . . ."

No Visitors, Please. Disconnect the Phone

Marcel Proust, whom Graham Greene declared "the greatest novelist of the twentieth century," found the silence and solitude he craved in an apartment in Paris that he had lined with cork and, to sharpen his remembrance of things past, filled with his late father's velvet armchair, his late mother's grand piano, and other furniture he'd inherited from them. André Maurois wrote, "It was thus within four walls padded with cork and proof against outside noise that he wrote his great work [the somewhat autobiographical, sixteen-volume, novel cycle, *À la recherche du temps perdu*]." Proust's asthma attacks were so severe he rarely left the apartment. He kept the windows shut, as well as the heavy drapes that covered them, and inhaled medicinal fumigations. As he worked, he lay under a royal blue spread on the lumpy mattress of a brass bed. Around him, Maurois continued, were "his school exercise books, covered in black . . . from which he cut passages here and there to paste into the final manuscript. The room was full of the yellow vapours of his fumigations and impregnated with their acrid smell. Through the fog one could distinguish Marcel, pale, a little puffy about the face, his eyes shining across the haze, dressed in a light shirt and innumerable threadbare and scorched pullovers one on top of the other."

"Every day I write," American novelist Marguerite Young said. "If there is ever an interruption, like an electric-meter man or a doorbell ringing, it drives me crazy. . . . I don't want anyone near me physically. I don't want to see anyone. I'm just absolutely closed in, and I get more so as the years go by, more and more loving of privacy." In as much solitude as she could possibly arrange for herself, she spent eighteen years writing the 1,200-page *Miss MacIntosh, My Darling* (1965). It inspired Kurt Vonnegut, Jr., to describe Young as "unquestionably a genius," and Norman Mailer to call her "a gentle Hercules in high heels."

"I prefer to get up very early in the morning and work," said Katherine Anne Porter, whose collected short stories (1965) won both the Pulitzer Prize and a National Book Award. "I don't want to speak to anybody or see anybody. Perfect silence. I work until the vein is out." While spending from three to five hours every day for nearly three years on writing part of *Ship of Fools* (1962), she lived alone in rural Connecticut and, she said, "I kept myself free for work: no telephone, no visitors – oh, I really lived like a hermit, everything but being fed through a grate!"

LEAVING HOME TO BE ALONE

Every weekday morning, Martin Amis left the house in London where he lived with his family and drove his Audi to a rented flat to write, in his words, "for as long as I can." Which wasn't long. He didn't return home until evening, but regarded two hours of concentrated writing as "a very good day's work." That left time for reading, making coffee, throwing darts, playing tennis or snooker, and such solitary activities as "picking your nose, trimming your fingernails, or staring at the ceiling." Only toward the end of a novel – when the compulsion to clear his desk of "this five years of preoccupation" injected him with hysterical energy – did he write for six or seven hours at a stretch.

Amis was scarcely the first writer who left home to work alone. At thirty-five, Graham Greene, who had published six novels, decided he could no longer bear writing in the stylish house in South London that he shared with his wife, Vivien, and their two children. Not that she hadn't tried to keep him happy there. "I was particularly impressed by Vivien's behaviour as the Protective Wife," writer Arthur Calder-Marshall recalled. "One could not telephone Graham in the morning, because he was writing. Messages would be taken and passed on at more convenient times." Living in an atmosphere of comfy domesticity, however, bored Greene almost to death. He thought about committing suicide. "He hated writing at home," Malcolm Muggeridge remembered. "He didn't like the life of an author, simply getting up in the morning and being all the time in the house." In 1939, Greene began to work in a studio he'd rented in Bloomsbury.

"I don't think he wanted to see the children much – that was why he found a workshop elsewhere – they were quite good and very small," Vivien said decades later.

"You don't want to hear doors opening and shutting," she added, "and to step out of your room for a minute and feel you are back in a domestic setting. You want to be quite separate."

When Alistair MacLeod's six children were young he made himself quite separate at Broad Cove on the west coast of Cape Breton Island by building a clifftop writing shed that overlooked the Gulf of St. Lawrence and, in the distance, Prince Edward Island. When he stepped out of his room for a minute, he knew he was not back in a domestic setting.

MacLeod spent most of his working life as a professor of English at the University of Windsor in southwestern Ontario, but it was here in Inverness County that he grew up. Summer after summer after summer, he returned to his family home at Broad Cove. It was Cape Breton and Cape Bretoners that he portrayed in such powerful fiction that, even though he published only sixteen short stories and one novel, *No Great Mischief* (1999), the *Globe and Mail* named him "the greatest living Canadian writer." Short-story writer Alice Munro, who certainly rivalled him for that distinction, said about *No Great Mischief,* "You will find scenes from this majestic novel burned into your mind forever."

MacLeod usually worked in his shed between 8 and 11 a.m., "before life begins to gnaw at me." The place had no running water, electricity, or phone but, to write, he needed only ballpoint pens, cheap scribblers, and "to be rested and alone." A little way inland, at the modest house that in his great-grandfather's day also had no running water, electricity, or phone, he explained that he had built his lofty hideout "purposely so people could not get to me." Now that he was seventy-three, he cheerfully added, "I can hardly get there myself."

"It's important to me to have a place to work outside of where I live," American novelist and screenwriter Richard Price explained in 1996. "So I have always found myself an office. I go off to work as if I had a clock to punch; at the end of the day I come home as if I had just gotten off the commuter train. I needed to impose a structure on myself. . . . I try to keep it as close to a nine-to-five job as I'm able, probably closer to ten to four."

Irish-American writer J.P. Donleavy lived in big cities while "germinating" his novels but, to write them, retreated to his estate in rural Ireland. There, he said, "you can control your environment. Interruptions annoy me and stop my writing. Isolation is a necessity, also an acute loneliness and a sense of slight rejection."

HOTEL ROOMS SUIT SOME.
OTHERS GO DOWN TO THE SEA IN SHIPS

For William S. Burroughs the perfect retreat for writing was a room in the elegant Chase Park Plaza Hotel in St. Louis. "There's not a sound in here," he said. "It's been very conducive to work. I've got a lot of room here to spread out all my pages in all these drawers and shelves. It's quiet. When I want something to eat, I pick up the phone. I can work right straight through. . . . To be completely alone in a room, to know there'll be no interruptions and I've got eight hours is just exactly what I want – yeah, just paradise."

"I have kept a hotel room in every town I've ever lived in," Maya Angelou told a Manhattan audience. "I rent a hotel room for a few months, leave my home at six and try to be at work by six-thirty. To write, I lie across the bed, so that this elbow is absolutely encrusted at the end, just so rough with callouses. . . . I stay until twelve-thirty or one-thirty in the afternoon, and then I go home and try to breathe."

She allowed hotel staff to empty wastebaskets in her room but, since she never slept there, not to change the bedsheets. "I insist that all things are taken off the walls," she continued. "I don't want anything in there. I go into the room, and I feel as if all my beliefs are suspended. Nothing holds me to anything. No milkmaids, no flowers, nothing. I just want to *feel* and then when I start to work I'll remember."

Susan Sontag wrote much of *The Volcano Lover* (1992) in Berlin and in a hotel in Milan. "I wasn't in my apartment in New York, with all my books, and I wasn't in the place that I was writing about either," she said. "That sort of double-distancing works very well for me." Later, back in New York, she had a hunch that, in "complete isolation," she could write a certain chapter in three days. "So I left my apartment and checked into [the Mayflower Hotel] with my typewriter and legal-sized pads and felt-tip pens, and ordered up BLTs until I was done."

As a young man, Erskine Caldwell travelled not to reach any particular destination, but to write. "I'd ride a bus, from Boston to Cleveland maybe, and get off at night once in a while to write. I'd do a story that way in about a week's time. Then, for a while, I took the night boats between Boston and New York. . . . The rhythm of the water might have helped my sentence structure a little. At least I thought it did."

Determined to escape the stream of uninvited visitors to his home in Sarasota while he worked on the last of his forty books, *Valley Forge* (1975), MacKinlay Kantor, on New Year's Day, 1974, boarded the luxurious ss *Monterey* in Los Angeles for a voyage to New Zealand, Australia, and islands in the South Pacific. At five every morning, he reported to the ship's library. There, in splendid solitude, he spread out his research, plugged in a Dictaphone, and, because he insisted on hearing how his work sounded before he committed it to paper, dictated his story. His seventieth birthday came and went, and he went ashore at ports of call, but he missed not one day of work. Back in the United States by April, he had his entire novel on dictabelts. All it required now was typing and polishing.

William Goyen, Texas-born writer of fiction and stage plays, wrote much of his first novel, *The House of Breath* (1950), aboard a U.S. aircraft carrier. "I found that there are many hidden places on an aircraft carrier where one can hide out and do secret work," he said. "And this was easily achieved. Also, on the night watches and so forth, there was a lot of time." Graham Greene and Jack London both wrote in cockroach-infested and rat-ridden shacks, and aboard ships that ploughed through storms.

"Can you write at sea?" an interviewer asked Hemingway.

"Perhaps better than anywhere else," he replied. "My boat, *The Pilar*, has no radio, no telephone and, since the war, no radio communications of any kind. You can anchor in the lee of some bay in the Gulf Stream and write on a writing board with no intrusions and you have no excuses if you fail to work well."

At thirty, Raymond Carver had endured a string of "crap jobs," spent years "raising kids and trying to write," gone bankrupt, and fallen into further debt and heavy boozing. "There was always a wagonload of frustration to deal with – wanting to write and not being able to find the time or the place for it," he said. "I used to go out and sit in the car and try to write something on a pad on my knee." He went on to write such powerful short stories that critic A.O. Scott decided he was "an international icon of traditional American literary values."

When Winnipeg novelist David Bergen was a young father he, too, wrote in his car. In 2005, he won the $40,000 Scotiabank Giller Prize for *The Time in Between*, but a couple of decades before that, whenever his children raised a ruckus at home, he fled to his 1981 Oldsmobile Cutlass to write, and also to an Aerostar that he parked in a Safeway lot. In 2002, the *Globe and Mail* described his "reminiscing about the joy of tilting the driver's seat and resting the coiled steno pad against the steering wheel."

TWELVE

To Hide Out, or Greet Life

S ome arranged their lives to guarantee they could write not only alone, but alone at home. From 9 a.m. until his two sons returned from school at 2 p.m., Gabriel García Márquez wrote in his house in Mexico City. "I can only work in surroundings that are familiar and have already been warmed up with my work," he said in 1981. "I cannot write in hotels or borrowed rooms or on borrowed typewriters. This creates problems because when I travel I can't work."

Tolstoy's children never dared enter his spacious study, which opened onto a terrace. He hung his hat on the stuffed head of a stag and decorated the room with antlers he'd brought back from the Caucasus Mountains, a bust made from the death mask of his brother Nikolai, and photographs of Dickens, Schopenhauer, and friends among Russian writers. In one of two areas separated by a partition of bookshelves, Tolstoy sat in a round-backed arm-chair and raced his pen across the paper on his desk. He had set up everything to suit himself perfectly. In 1875, however, he fell into a depression so deep that, as he later wrote, he feared he might hang himself "on the crossbeam of the bookshelves in the study where I undressed alone every night."

When Thomas Mann's four children were all under ten, they were unwelcome in his study. In strict command of his household and himself, he often seemed to them both remote and frightening. He never shouted, but they dreaded his ominous silences. Every morning he arose at precisely eight, drank one cup of coffee with his wife, Katia, shaved, bathed, dressed, and, at nine sharp, entered his study and closed its door. From then until noon, he took no phone calls, saw no visitors, tolerated no loud noises. If the children disturbed him, they'd hear him angrily clear his throat or, worse, see him charge out of his study.

One summer in the 1920s, little Janey Hard, a niece of Rudyard and Carrie Kipling, stayed at their secluded mansion under the Sussex Downs and, as she recalled eight decades later, "it hardly needs saying that Aunt Carrie, who guarded her husband like a benevolent dragon, would never have allowed us to disturb him while he was at work." Mrs. Kipling, an American, was less than popular among writers in England. Henry James called her "this hard, capable little person."

"I live in a suburban house [six thousand feet above sea level, in Johannesburg] where I have a small room where I work," said South African novelist Nadine Gordimer. "I have a door with direct access to the garden – a great luxury for me – so that I can get in and out without anybody bothering me or knowing where I am. Before I begin to work, I pull out the phone and it stays out until I'm ready to plug it in again."

A LAUNDRY ROOM OF HER OWN

For generations, however, women writers found it all but impossible to establish in their own homes the do-not-disturb conditions that countless men saw as their natural right. Virginia Woolf in 1928 famously declared, "A woman must have money and a room of her own if she is to write fiction." Well over a century earlier, however, it was with little money and no room of her own that Jane Austen did all her writing. "[She] had no separate study to retire to, and most of the work must have been done in the general sitting-room, subject to all kinds of casual interruptions," her nephew, J.E. Austen-Leigh, wrote in 1870. "She was careful that her occupation should not be suspected by servants, or visitors, or any persons beyond her own family party. She wrote upon small sheets of paper which could easily be put away, or covered with a piece of blotting paper. There was, between the front door and the office, a swing door which creaked when it was opened; but she objected to having this little inconvenience remedied, because it gave her notice when anyone was coming."

It was under these conditions that, in six years, Austen wrote six novels that readers would love, study, and discuss for two centuries.

As twentieth-century women earned fame as writers, some did get rooms of their own. But not all. In the 1950s and 1960s, Canadian short-story writer Alice Munro endured working quarters at least as makeshift as Austen's. She went on to win three Governor General's Awards; the W.H. Smith Award for the best book published in the United Kingdom; comparisons with Chekhov and Flaubert; and an acknowledgment in *The Times* of London that her short stories made "it difficult to remember why the novel was ever invented." In 2001, however, her first child, Sheila Munro, looked back to her own girlhood and recalled her mother writing *Lives of Girls and Women* (1971) in a laundry room. The typewriter competed for space with a washer, dryer, and ironing board. Sheila never knew where in the house she might stumble on her mother writing:

> I might find her reclining on the couch writing in one of her spiral notebooks when I came home from school, or scribbling away at the kitchen table when I came downstairs for breakfast. She'd always put the notebook away without skipping a beat, in the same

way that Jane Austen put her embroidery frame over her writing whenever someone came into the room. . . . After my father went off to work she mopped the floors and shook out the rugs and rinsed out the diapers. She washed and rinsed out the clothes and put them through the wringer and hung them out on the clothesline . . . and there would still be time for writing. She typed away while I busied myself exploring the yard, tearing the pages out of magazines in the living room, or rolling potatoes across the kitchen floor. And every afternoon after lunch I had a nap. She made sure of that.

The twin daughters of neurologist Alice W. Flaherty, who wrote *The Midnight Disease: Writer's Block and the Creative Brain* (2004), were premature and so small after their birth that, while she worked, they slept in one of her desk drawers. "Once in a while a little arm would come out and pat the screen," she wrote. "When they woke up, I could nurse one on my lap while I typed across her, simultaneously rocking her sister in an infant bouncy chair with one foot." When both babies fell asleep again, she put them in their crib and lay down beside them in her own bed. Then, while listening to their gentle breathing and using a book light, she continued to write, "in tiny, tiny writing on tiny, tiny Post-its, which I would stick to the wall and collect in the morning."

She was sure she wrote at her best when she could smell her daughters' hair "and hear the little grunts they make in their sleep. Even now that they are in pre-school, I love it when one sits on each knee as I write – although there admittedly is a problem seeing the computer screen over their heads." Flaherty thought it was better for children to have a mother who derived joy from her work, and shared the joy with them, than one who resented them for interfering with her calling. Not every mother who wrote, however, enjoyed working beside breathing, grunting babies.

"And no one who has tried both to mother and to write can honestly say they are not, at times, conflicting vocations," Judith Thurman wrote in her biography of Colette. After Colette had a daughter, she settled this conflict simply by refusing to take any responsibility for her. She chose writing over mothering. "My strain of virility," she wrote, "saved me from the danger which threatens the writer, elevated to a happy and tender parent, of becoming a mediocre author." Colette neglected the well-being of her daughter, whom Thurman called "a wild and lonely little girl," in favour of protecting "the well-being of a possibly precious part of myself."

Is Solitude Best "in the Midst of Multitudes"?

The creative juices of some writers have actually flowed well amid family hubbub. By the time Chekhov was a medical student in Moscow, his father, a grocer, was bankrupt, and the youth furiously wrote short stories to support his parents, a sister, and two of his four brothers. During the year he turned twenty-five, he wrote at a dining room table, with family and boarders bustling and talking away nearby, yet managed to write more than 120 articles, sketches, and short stories. In a nation whose people had so little use for privacy their language had no word for it, Chekhov grew up fast.

The American essayist and writer of children's books E.B. White said he worked well among the most routine household distractions.

> My house has a living room that is at the core of everything that goes on: it is a passageway to the cellar, to the kitchen, to the closet where the telephone lives. There's a lot of traffic. But it's a bright, cheerful room, and I often use it as a room to write in, despite the carnival that is going on all around me. A girl pushing

a carpet sweeper under my typewriter table has never annoyed me particularly, nor has it taken my mind off work, unless the girl was unusually pretty or unusually clumsy. My wife, thank God, has never been protective of me, as the wives of some writers are. In consequence, the members of my household never pay the slightest attention to my being a writing man. They make all the noise and fuss they want to. If I get sick of it, I have places I can go. A writer who waits for ideal conditions under which to work will die without putting a word on paper.

The Japanese Nobel Prize winner Kenzaburo Oe said in 2007 that he usually worked in his living room while his forty-four-year-old brain-damaged son, Hikari, listened to music nearby. Oe and his wife, Yakari, devoted much of their lives to the care of Hikari, whose condition was so severe that his blossoming as one of Japan's most gifted composers seemed nothing short of miraculous. Oe's best-known novel, *A Personal Matter* (1964), describes a father's slow acceptance of an infant son who was born with a wounded brain. Forty-three years later, Oe said that writing about Hikari had been "one of the pillars of my literary expression."

He had learned from him that in the creation of both music and literature lay "a healing power, a power to mend the heart." By now perhaps, nothing seemed more natural to Oe than to be writing fiction in the room in which Hikari was hearing music. Was his son not his muse?

"I can write with Hikari and my wife present because I revise many times," he said. "The novel is always incomplete and I know I will revise it completely. When I'm writing the first draft I don't have to write it by myself. When I'm revising, I already have a relationship with the text so I don't have to be alone. I have a study on the second floor. . . . [But] the only time I work there is when I'm finishing up a novel and need to concentrate – which is a nuisance to others."

At ninety, Louis Auchincloss had published more than sixty books. While writing in longhand on legal pads, he said, he'd been happy to share the living room of his Manhattan apartment with his rambunctious young children. "I don't remember any conflict coming up," he said. "I can't imagine what it would be. I didn't have any timetable on when a book was to be done. What difference would it make?"

As a young novelist, William Goyen worked alone in "hidden places," but the older he got the more he liked to participate in daily life. He had his writing hideaway in a spacious apartment in New York City, "yet all around me in the other rooms the life of a family goes on, and I like to know that. I also like to know that twelve flights down I can step into the midst of a lot of human beings and feel a part of those. . . . Maybe solitude is best had in the midst of multitudes."

SOME WROTE AT ANY TIME, IN ANY PLACE, IN ANY COMPANY

Isaac Bashevis Singer, the Nobel Prize winner whom one critic called "the magician of West 86th Street," wrote every day at a messy little desk in the living room of his apartment. His name was in the Manhattan telephone book and, even while hard at work, he answered calls from strangers who wanted to talk about a piece of his fiction they'd read. He invited many of them to his apartment for coffee, and some for lunch. "And I am interviewed, and I am all the time interrupted," he said in 1968. "Somehow I manage to keep on writing. I don't have to run away. Some writers say they can only write if they go to a far island. They would go to the moon to write not to be disturbed. I think that being disturbed is part of human life and sometimes it's useful to be disturbed because you interrupt your writing and while you rest, while you are busy with something else, your perspective changes or the horizon widens."

Asked where she wrote, London novelist Anita Brookner replied, "Anywhere. In my flat, or in my office [at the Courtauld Institute of Art]. I have even written on a bus. . . . I type what I've written at the office. I prefer working there because I *like* the interruptions – telephone calls, visitors. I am completely schizophrenic, as I can carry on a conversation in my head while another apparently sensible conversation is taking place with someone who has just come into the room. At home, the isolation wears on me. It is a terrible strain."

More than a century before Brookner's time, another Londoner knew he could write "anywhere." William Thackeray, his biographer D.J. Taylor wrote, ground out millions of words not only in clubs and inns, but "on chop-house dining tables, in stagecoaches, against deadlines with the printer's boy chafing in the hall, at leisure in the study at Palace Green." Writing in longhand on a portable desk, aboard a stagecoach that barged along washboard roads, was a trick no modern writer has had to learn.

When Ray Bradbury decided to write his classic science-fiction novel, *Fahrenheit 451*, the cries of his newborn daughter prevented him from writing at home, and he had no money to rent an office. While walking around the University of Los Angeles, however, he heard people typing in the basement of Powell Library. "I went to investigate and found a room with twelve typewriters that could be rented for ten cents a half-hour. So, exhilarated, I got a bag of dimes and settled into the room, and in nine days I spent $9.80 and wrote my story; in other words, it was a dime novel."

"I like living too much to be seated at a desk all day," said Chilean poet Pablo Neruda. "I like to put myself in the goings-on of life, of my house, of politics, and of nature. I am forever coming and going. But I write intensely whenever I can and wherever I am. It doesn't bother me that there may be a lot of people around." About Allen Ginsberg, fellow poet Robert Creeley said, "[He] can write poems anywhere – trains, planes, in any public place. He isn't the least self-conscious. In fact, he seems to be stimulated by people around him."

Few modern writers have proved more adaptable than Margaret Atwood, the Canadian poet and novelist who has bagged the Booker Prize, Giller Prize, and Governor General's Awards for both fiction and poetry. She has scribbled poems on bedside notepads in hotels around the world. "I've written quite a lot under those circumstances," she once said. "Perhaps it's being in a hotel room or a plane with no ringing phone and no supervision. Also, there is something about jet lag that breaks down the barriers."

Atwood has worked in a rented room in Toronto's Portuguese neighbourhood; a cottage in Norfolk, England; a walk-up flat in West Berlin, in which her typewriter had a German keyboard; a house in Tuscaloosa, Alabama, locally known as "the per capita murder capital of the U.S."; three successive houses in Lourmarin, Provence; a roomful of end tables arranged as a makeshift desk during another visit to France; and "a curious rented-by-Internet flat" in London. It was in Sydney, Australia, with the cries of kookaburras ringing in her ears, that she wrote the snowiest Canadian scenes in *Cat's Eye* (1991). Having barely recovered from scarlet fever and mourning the recent death of her father, in January 1993, she finished *The Robber Bride* aboard a train crossing Canada. In 2001, during a birdwatching trip in Queensland, Australia, she said, "I unaccountably found myself beginning another novel." It was *Oryx and Crake* (2003). She later wrote part of it on an island in Lake Erie, and several chapters aboard a ship beyond the Arctic Circle.

While living in Paris on a Guggenheim fellowship in the late 1940s, Saul Bellow began to write his breakthrough novel, *The Adventures of Augie March* (1953). "I wrote it in trains and cafés," he said. "I got used to writing on the roll. I hunted for the right café in Rome and, when I found it, I worked there all the time. . . . The great pleasure of the book was that it came easily. All I had to do was be there with buckets to catch it."

A single mother, unemployed, living on state benefits, J.K. Rowling sat in cafés in Edinburgh and, whenever her baby Jessica fell asleep in a stroller, wrote a few more sentences of *Harry Potter and the Philosopher's Stone* (1997). By 2004, that book, and the Harry Potter volumes that followed it, had sold more than 300 million copies and turned Rowling into the first person ever to earn a billion U.S. dollars by writing. She was richer than Queen Elizabeth, but she missed the cafés. "My ideal writing space is a large café with a small corner table near a window overlooking an interesting street," she said. "It would serve very strong coffee, and be non-smoking, and nobody would notice me at all. But I can't write in cafés any more because I would get recognized a lot."

Indeed, she would. Before she could apply ballpoint to exercise book, she'd be mobbed by autograph seekers.

THIRTEEN

Panoramas, Bare Walls, Strange Habits

B y the 1860s, when Emily Dickinson wrote most of her 1,775 poems, she almost never left her family home in Amherst, Massachusetts. She spoke to friends and relatives from around corners and through half-open doors, hid when strangers arrived, and used a rope and a basket to lower baked treats from her second-floor bedroom to neighbourhood children on the lawn below. They saw her hands and arms but never her face. Later in life she dressed entirely in white, and locals called her "the Myth." It was only after her death in 1886 that her poems found their way into print, and she was recognized as a great writer. From the big, bright bedroom where she wrote her poems in secret, she saw mountains in two directions.

The woman in white had a room with a view.

"I like a room with a view, preferably a long view," Norman Mailer said. "I prefer looking at the sea, or ships, or anything that has a vista to it." On the top floor of an elegant, five-storey John Nash house that dated back to 1820, Harold Pinter wrote his plays at a desk that overlooked a duck pond and a long wooded stretch of Regent's Park, London. Canadian novelist Jane Urquhart worked in both a cottage with a sweeping view of Lake Ontario and a dwelling in County Kerry, Ireland, where she gazed at mountains and heard winds gusting through valleys. "It's important to me to be in front of a window like this," she said. "I couldn't work on the thirty-second floor of a big chain hotel the way some writers do." At his home on Long Island, P.G. Wodehouse, still writing novels in his nineties, worked in a glass-enclosed study from which he could see nothing but greenery in the summertime.

When Victor Hugo was writing *Ninety-Three* – the last of his seven novels and, some say, the best – he lived in a mansion at the highest spot on Guernsey in the Channel Islands, and reported every dawn to a glass cage on his roof. There, he stood before a lectern and wrote, naked. On occasion, for variety, he dumped pails of cold water over his head and rubbed his torso with gloves made of horsehair. He liked the view up there; it "gave upon the sky, and on immensity."

Novelist and biographer Victoria Glendinning, on the other hand, lived in a house on the Thames in London, but chose to do her writing in a room in which she could not see the river. "No view," she said emphatically in 2002. "Otherwise, I'd just watch the boats go up and down."

No one has explained at more elaborate length the dangers to a writer that lurk in a busy and beautiful view than Henry James. In the preface to *The Portrait of a Lady* (1908), he said:

> I had rooms on Riva Schiavoni, at the top of a house near the passage leading off to San Zaccaria; the waterside life, the wondrous lagoon spread before me, and the ceaseless human chatter of Venice came in at my windows, to which I seem to myself to have been constantly driven, in the fruitless fidget of composition, as if to see whether, out in the blue channel, the ship of some right suggestion, of some better phrase, of the next happy twist of my subject, the next true touch for my canvas, mightn't come into sight. But I recall vividly enough that the response most elicited,

in general, to these restless appeals was the rather grim admonition that romantic and historic sites, such as the land of Italy abounds in, offer the artist a questionable aid to concentration when they themselves are not to be the subject of it. They are too rich in their own life and too charged with their own meanings merely to help him out with a lame phrase; they draw him away from his small question to their own greater ones; so that, after a little, he feels, while thus yearning toward them in his difficulty, as if he were asking an army of glorious veterans to help him to arrest a peddler who has given him the wrong change.

Blaise Cendrars, the Swiss-born Parisian who wrote poetry and novels and befriended the likes of Hemingway, Chagall, and Picasso, made the same point more succinctly: "A writer should never install himself before a panorama, however grandiose it may be. Like St. Jerome, a writer should work in his cell. Turn the back. Writing is a view of the spirit. . . . Today [1950], I even veil the mirrors."

Cendrars remembered that Guillaume Apollinaire, one of the foremost French poets of the early twentieth century, had a gigantic apartment with a belvedere and terrace on the roof, but chose to write in his kitchen, "at a little card table where he was very uncomfortable, having had to shrink this little table even smaller in order to succeed in sliding it under a bull's eye window in the mansard."

A ROOM WITH A VIEW? NO THANKS

Novelist and poet Annie Dillard, who at twenty-nine won a Pulitzer Prize for her non-fiction work *Pilgrim at Tinker Creek* (1974), insisted, "One wants a room with *no* view, so imagination can dance with memory in the dark." Another Pulitzer winner, Edna Ferber, said, "The ideal view for daily writing, hour on hour, is the blank brick wall of a cold-storage warehouse." William

Maxwell preferred small, messy rooms that overlooked nothing of the slightest interest. Fiction editor of *The New Yorker* for forty years and the author of six novels and two collections of short stories, Maxwell said, "I wrote the last two sections of *They Came Like Swallows* (1937) beside a window looking out on a tin roof. It was perfect. The roof was so boring it instantly drove me back to my typewriter." Canadian author Farley Mowat said with satisfaction that from the windows of his house on Cape Breton Island, "there's nothing to see but fog."

When Graham Greene was in his mid-forties, he began to write in the loft of a villa high in the mountains of Capri. The beauty of the island was spectacular but, up there, he saw none of it. His study had a skylight, a wooden trestle table, a rough wooden bed, and nothing on the whitewashed walls except one small cross. In that bare Mediterranean eyrie, he said, he got more writing done in three weeks than he did in three months back home in London, and it was there that he did most of his later work.

"Writing is the art of forgetfulness," said Canadian novelist Yann Martel, whose *Life of Pi* won the 2002 Booker Prize. "It's not about me. All I need is to get physically comfortable with some sort of padding on my chair because I'm a bony little fellow, and then I'm quite happy to work looking at a bare white wall."

EVERY LITTLE OBJECT HAD TO BE JUST SO

Some writers could not get down to work until they'd imposed a certain familiar order on their surroundings. The moment Dickens entered any rented room in which he intended to write, he pushed the tables and chairs into what he saw as precisely the right spots. At his home at Gad's Hill, Kent, he began his workdays by walking around the house and grounds to reassure himself that everything, even among the books and pictures, was exactly where it belonged. Only then could he start to write.

Perhaps the most beloved American essayist of the twentieth century, E.B. White, could not write until he'd set pictures straight and squared up rugs in rooms. In a typical twelve-hour period, he confessed, he made seven adjustments to rugs and pictures. "I believe this to be par for my private course," he once wrote. "Seven times three hundred and sixty-five is two thousand five hundred and fifty-five, which I think I can give as a fair estimate of my yearly penance."

When Dickens lived in Lausanne, Switzerland, his biographer Peter Ackroyd wrote, he could not work until "all the appurtenances of his desk [arrived]. These were not just his writing materials, his goose-quill pens and his blue ink, but also the bronze images of two toads dueling, of a dog fancier with puppies and dogs swarming all over him, a paper-knife, a gilt leaf with a rabbit upon it. He grouped all these images around him on his desk; as his son-in-law explained . . . these were the images 'for his eye to rest on in the intervals of actually writing,' and so great was his love of habit and order that he could not write without their silent presence in front of him."

Thomas Mann had a big desk, but he crowded its surface with so many comforting objects his working space was small. The desktop held a magnifying glass with an ivory handle, a leather-bound folder, Egyptian and Buddhist figurines, flowers in a vase, framed photographs, pen and pencil holders, and his late father's tortoiseshell tobacco box, inlaid with gold. One of his biographers, Ronald Hayman, wrote, "It was almost as if he wanted to feel cramped by the objects surrounding him as he committed himself to a draft he wouldn't feel free to change."

When interviewers from *The Paris Review* visited Robert Graves in Majorca, his desktop was crowded with pencils, marbles, jars of tobacco, tins of Dutch cigars, and porcelain heads of clowns. Perched on his fireplace mantel were Oriental, African, Roman, and Greek figurines. He told his visitors that everything in the

room, except the electric light fixtures, was handmade. In order
to think, you had to have "as little as possible around you that is
not made by hand."

Shortly after Freud's father died, he began to fill his Vienna
office with what he called "death deliria." In 2004, Canadian writer
Robert Fulford reported, "His consulting room had Egyptian
scarabs, Roman death masks, Etruscan funeral vases, bronze
coffins, mummy portraits, etc. In the study next door where he
wrote, he positioned some of his favourite figurines to face him on
his desk, a silent audience he confronted as he wrote his books."

Charles Wright, winner of both a National Book Award and a
Pulitzer Prize for his poetry, had a huge study in the attic of his
Victorian house in Charlottesville, Virginia, and kept it obsessively
neat. "Here is a poet for whom – as one looks around the room –
arrangements matter," fellow poet J.D. McClatchy wrote. "On one
wall of shelves his books are arranged by their size, not by author
or subject. In fact, there are fewer books than one might imagine,
but more images: stacks of postcards, a zebra rug, gadgets, bird
skulls, an heirloom sword – totems all." In a tin box near his desk,
Wright kept family documents, old land grant deeds, barely
legible letters by his nineteenth-century ancestors, and a lock of
Robert E. Lee's hair.

CURIOUSER AND CURIOUSER

In the basement of novelist Kent Haruf's house in Illinois, he converted a six-by-nine-foot coal room into an office in which he
hung, above his desk, the skull of a Hereford bull from Nebraska,
"complete with horns and dark gaping eye sockets." On one wall,
he had a plan of the Colorado county that he used as a prototype
for his fictional Holt County, "where all of my invented people
live and die and commit their acts of sudden kindness and unexpected cruelty." Also on display in the tiny room were pictures his

youngest daughter had drawn, four photos of western landscape paintings, and one of tumbleweeds smothering a barbed-wire fence. Those, however, were but a small part of Haruf's inspirational collection.

"On my desk," he wrote, "I keep a sapling chewed by a beaver . . . a bird's nest, a piece of black turf from Northern Ireland, a plastic bag of red sand from the stage at the new Globe Theatre . . . a piece of brick and some paddock dirt from Faulkner's home at Rowan Oak [Oxford, Mississippi], an old-fashioned hand warmer in a velvet sack, a blue bandana, a jackknife that once belonged to my maternal grandfather, Roy Shaver, who was a sheep rancher in South Dakota, and an obsidian arrowhead my father found in the North Dakota Badlands, where he was born almost one hundred years ago. . . . Every time I go down to work, I feel as if I'm descending into a sacred place."

While living outside Havana in 1958, Ernest Hemingway worked in a sunny ground-floor bedroom with white walls and a yellowish tile floor. Wearing loafers, he planted his feet on the skin of an African antelope and wrote while standing in a small space he'd cleared among the books, papers, pamphlets, and manuscripts on top of a bookcase that stood near his double bed. Atop other bookcases that lined the room, with books overflowing to the floor, lay piles of old newspapers and bullfight journals, and stacks of letters held together by rubber bands. Not every writer kept a gazelle's head, a leopard skin, and three water-buffalo horns in his bedroom, but Hemingway did. Remembering tense moments during the hunts that yielded the horns, he said, "It cheers me up to look at them."

Scattered about the room were not only a chaotic abundance of novels, non-fiction, and collections of poetry and drama, but also wooden carvings of African animals, a toy stuffed lion, a cast-iron turtle, a giraffe made of beads, a monkey with a pair of cymbals, a tin bear with a key in its back, and tiny models of a

Venetian gondola, locomotives, jeeps, and a U.S. Navy biplane. A burlap sack contained shotgun shells and carnivore teeth.

"The room, however, for all the disorder sensed at first sight," George Plimpton decided, "indicates on inspection an owner who is basically neat but cannot bear to throw anything away – especially if sentimental value is attached."

The British poet, short-story writer, and novelist A.S. Byatt, a Booker Prize winner (1990) who studied at both Cambridge and Oxford universities, has little in common with Haruf, much less Hemingway but, like them, she's a magpie. The attic in which she writes is like "a cabinet of curiosities." It includes glass paperweights; bits of lava from Iceland, phantom quartz from Norway, rose quartz from a Korean friend, chalk from a cliff in Yorkshire; a nineteenth-century book about ancient Norse and Icelandic tales, *Asgard and the Gods*; and "the Creature." Made of heavy, grey stone, it's a small, scaly monster with long hair, a big beak, and unforgiving yellow eyes with black eyeballs. Removing his head uncovers an inkwell. Like the book, Byatt says, the Creature "clearly belongs to the world of northern tales of trolls and goblins" that has fascinated her since childhood.

As playwright August Wilson grew older, he wrote less in restaurants and more in the basement of his house in St. Paul, Minnesota. "On some days it is a sanctuary," he said. "On others it's a battlefield and then at times it's a dungeon. It is a place surrounded by the familiar particulars of my life. Photographs, yellow tablets, pens, books, music. . . . I have quotes, no more than two or three, that I use to keep me focused and inspired. For my new play, *King Hedley II*, I had a quote by Frank Gehry on his plans for the Corcoran Gallery addition – 'I hope to take it to the moon.' And a quote attributed to Charlie Parker – 'Don't be afraid. Just play the music.' And from the *Bhagavagita* – 'You have the right to the work but not the reward.' Other than that, I'm on my own."

WILL DRIED SEAHORSES DO THE TRICK,
OR THIS WIND-UP DONKEY?

The writing room in downtown Toronto of novelist Austin Clark contained a photo of a school he attended in his native Barbados; a picture of an imaginary beast that his daughter drew in the early 1970s; the autograph of Margaret Trudeau, at one time the wife of Prime Minister Pierre Trudeau; the chair in which Malcolm X talked for five hours shortly before he was murdered; and a magazine cover about the assassination of Martin Luther King. Clark's novel *The Polished Hoe* (2002) won the Giller Prize, the Trillium Book Award, and the Commonwealth Writers Prize.

Vancouver Island novelist Gail Anderson-Dargatz worked in an orange and crimson office that overlooked the Pacific Ocean, and in the fall of 2002 kept on her desk a jar of rhinestone buttons she'd bought at thrift shops. "I love the look of them," she said. "When I'm working my way through an idea, I like dipping my hand in. It really seems to help." Her *Recipe for Bees* (1998) was a nominee for the Giller Prize and inspired one reviewer to write, "Margaret Laurence meets Gabriel García Márquez."

About the wooden carving of a grizzly bear and the piranha-jaw necklace in Andrew Pyper's writing cubbyhole in Toronto, he said, "Totems like these seem to collect of themselves. You don't say, 'Here's an office, let's design it.' You inhabit it first and then, like zebra mussels, these symbols just attach themselves. Your eye alights on these things and they give off a low thrumming of satisfaction." Pyper's first novel, *Lost Girls* (1999), was a thriller, ghost story, and murder mystery all rolled into one and emitted a thrumming that earned him six-figure advances from two international publishers.

More than any other modern book, *How I Write: The Secret Lives of Authors* (2007), reveals the ornaments and images that certain writers feel that, while working, they simply must have within sight or reach. In the entry about Booker Prize–winner (2004) Alan Hollinghurst, for example, he explains what his beloved engraving of ancient baths in Rome does for him: "As a slow, pen and ink, brick-by-brick kind of writer, I find it, when I look up, both sobering and reassuring." Jay McInerney, the first of whose nine novels, *Bright Lights, Big City* (1984), broke ground with its depiction of New York's cocaine culture, treasures a hand axe that's half a million years old. "I like to heft it and hold it between paragraphs," he explains. "It fits the palm beautifully."

British novelist Jill Dawson cherishes two dried seahorses. Heather Masonjones, the American biologist who gave them to her, said seahorses were lovable because "they often live in places with tremendous currents. They have an amazing ability to camouflage by changing colour. Their only defence mechanism is to blend into the background and hold on tight." Over the years, Dawson's seahorses have become as crispy as dry twigs, but their spines are intact and they still smell of the sea. To her, they represent chance, connectedness, and inspiration. "But mostly," she says, "they remind me to be patient and to trust my instincts."

The one essential desktop talisman for other writers ranges from a cypress cone plucked from Chekhov's garden to a picture of the gun-toting black cowboy, Nat Love; from a silver monkey to an inherited set of "unknown keys"; from a toy skeleton seated at a typewriter to the plaster head of a female saint with calm eyes; from a statuette of the Hindu Lord of Success, with his elephant head, to the cover art of the Frank Sinatra album, *Wee Small Hours*; from a forty-year-old wind-up donkey to a photograph of a rhinoceros that's dangling precariously in a belly sling. For various deeply personal reasons, the owners of these small treasures choose never to face the dreaded blank page without having them close by.

THE MUSE MAY LURK EVEN IN A
CREAKY CHAIR, OR A WORN RUG

Remembering when he wrote at a marble-topped table outside a café in Paris, Hemingway wrote, "For luck you carried a horse chestnut and a rabbit's foot in your right pocket. The fur had been worn off the rabbit's foot long ago and the bones and the sinews were polished by wear. The claws scratched in the lining of your pocket and you knew your luck was still there." He once told art historian Bernard Berenson he hated his new typewriter but refused to use his old one "because it has page 594 of the book in it . . . and it is unlucky to take the pages out."

If Hemingway had his rabbit's foot, Alan Sillitoe had his horseshoe. Sillitoe was once one of "the angry young men" on London's literary scene. In 2007, he was pushing eighty, the author of two dozen novels and several collections of short stories and poetry, and the owner of an "uneven" horseshoe that he used as a paperweight. His grandfather had made it to fit a lame horse, Sillitoe said, "and it's brought me a great deal of luck."

Erskine Caldwell's good-luck treasure was an old red rug. In his earliest days as a writer, he lived through a winter on the icy hardwood floor of an unheated room in Maine. Then, in South Carolina, he worked in a room with a linoleum floor so cracked that whenever he walked on it without shoes, splinters jabbed his feet. The moment he could afford to buy a good rug, he got a red one and, for the rest of his life, took it to wherever he was living. At seventy-nine, in his Spanish-style house near a desert mountain in Arizona, he told an interviewer, "We are sitting on it now, in fact. Why is it here? . . . It's part of my life."

The American fiction writer Jonathan Franzen scavenged an office chair off a street in Rockland County, New York, when he was twenty-three. Nineteen years later, his *The Corrections* (2001) earned both high sales and critical applause, but he did not let success go to his seat. By 2007, swaths of duct tape held together the chair's green leatherette cushion. "[The chair] squeaks horribly and irremediably," Franzen wrote, "but it's been many years since I've been able to hear the squeak, just as I can't hear myself talking when I write dialogue, even though when I leave the office, I can tell from my hoarseness that I've been talking loudly all day."

Never Underestimate the Power of a Superstition

When told certain numbers popped up repeatedly in his stories, Jorge Luis Borges said, "Oh, yes. I'm awfully superstitious. I'm ashamed of it. I tell myself that, after all, superstition is, I suppose, a slight form of madness, no?"

In Margaret Drabble's book *The Needle's Eye* (1972), one of the characters was a tragic eccentric named Rose. Drabble later admitted, "I was very keen that I shouldn't buy any new clothes until I had finished the book: that Rose wouldn't have done it. I was incredibly shabby by the end of the book." Carson McCullers wrote only while wearing her "lucky sweater." After donning slacks and a checked Abercrombie & Fitch shirt, Simenon would report to his desk at dawn and, writing thousands of words per hour, complete an eighty-page installment of a novel by 10:30 a.m. Every day until he finished the book, he had to wear that same shirt. Just as he refused to change it in mid-novel, whole teams of professional hockey players refuse to shave in mid-playoffs for the game's highest prize, the Stanley Cup. "If you were playing well, you didn't want to change anything," said Clark Gillis, a member of the Hockey Hall of Fame and former star of the New York Islanders. "I know this sounds gross but it was the same thing with underwear. Some guys would wear the same clothes for six weeks if they kept on winning. Our coach, Al Arbour, never said much about it, but our wives didn't like it." Simenon chose to prove his athletic prowess not on skates but in bed with women and, unlike the hockey players, at the end of each day of furiously hard work, he sent his sweat-stained shirt out for laundering.

When Rudyard Kipling, at twenty-four, returned from India to England in 1889, he so impressed critics, publishers, and editors that he feared he might become just another comet of the season. He therefore wrote "The Comet of the Season," a short story about a young writer who made a sensational debut, but then fizzled out. His biographer Harry Ricketts called the tale "an early example of how Kipling used his art as a form of natural magic to try to forestall Fate. . . . By imagining the possibility in fiction, he tried to prevent it happening in reality – a literary equivalent to knocking on wood. He would repeat variations of this superstitious gambit throughout his life."

Truman Capote, author of *In Cold Blood* (1966) and literary man about town, refused to fly on any aircraft whose passengers included two nuns; begin or end anything on a Friday; allow three cigarette butts in one ashtray; or be anywhere near yellow roses. He said he gained comfort "from obeying these primitive concepts."

To get rolling on their writing, some writers addicted themselves to strange habits. When the German poet, playwright, and novelist Goethe once sat by himself at the desk of his friend and fellow writer Schiller, he became aware of a nauseating stench. Opening a drawer, he found a hoard of rotten apples. "When he had recovered himself at the open window," John Middleton Murry wrote, "Frau Schiller came in and explained that her husband insisted that his drawer be kept full of rotten apples, 'because the smell did Schiller good, and he could not live or work without it.'" Research at Yale University in 1985 revealed that the smell of spiced apples relaxes people and increases their ability to focus and to receive new ideas. Whether putrid or pungent, perhaps an apple a day keeps the writer's block away.

No research, however, has explained what benefits the eccentric English poet Edith Sitwell derived from lying in an open coffin before beginning her day's writing; what good it did Henrik Ibsen to put off starting his morning's writing until he'd fed the scorpion inside a jar on his desk; why Thomas Hardy could not get down to work until he'd removed his boots or slippers; or why Colette preceded each day of writing by picking fleas from her cat. Samuel Johnson chose to write with not only gallons of tea nearby, but also scraps of orange peel and a cat, preferably purring. The celebrated orator and court preacher in seventeenth-century France, Jacques-Bénigne Bossuet, chose to do his writing in rooms so cold he wrapped his head in furs. Emile Zola, the French novelist of the late nineteenth century, found artificial light more stimulating than natural light, so he pulled down his blinds at midday.

William Carlos Williams said that Imagist poet Hilda Doolittle put herself in a creative mood by splashing ink from her pen all over her clothes. It's unlikely that any other important writer has ever tried this curious method of gaining inspiration, but Williams thought it gave Doolittle what she needed: "a feeling of freedom and indifference towards the mere means of writing." American novelist William Gass told author Diane Ackerman that he began most of his writing days by photographing "the rusty, derelict, overlooked, downtrodden parts of [St. Louis]. Filth and decay mainly."

Chilean-American writer Isabel Allende allowed each of her novels to grow within her for months, as though they were embryos, but did not sit down to begin writing any of them except on a January 8. Shortly after dawn on that day, she arrived at her office with fresh flowers, and then lit candles, burned incense, and meditated. "And I open myself completely to this experience that begins in that moment," she said. "I never know exactly what I'm going to write." It was on January 8, 1981, while she was in

Venezuela, that a phone call told her that her grandfather was dying. She immediately started to write to him. Her letter turned into her first novel, *The House of the Spirits* (1982), and January 8 became her "sacred day."

WOOING THE LUCK OF THE GAME

With their faith in rituals, symbols, and talismans, and their determination always to work in a certain way to keep luck on their side, big-league writers tended to be as superstitious as big-league ballplayers. Wade Boggs, one of the best third basemen and heaviest hitters in the history of the Boston Red Sox, made absolutely sure that, before every game he played, he ate chicken. During infield practice, he fielded no more and no fewer than 150 ground balls. Before night games, he entered the batting cage not a minute earlier or later than 5:17 p.m., and started to run wind sprints at exactly 7:17 p.m. He was not Jewish, but whenever he went up to bat, he wrote "chai," the Hebrew word for "life," in the dirt of the batter's box. Boggs had dozens of superstitions, but so did thousands of other players in a sport that's even more riddled with superstitions than hockey.

Lee Stevens, a first baseman whom the *Topeka Capital Journal* in 2002 called "the quintessential baseball veteran," might well have been describing certain novelists when he said, "Every guy in here [a baseball clubroom] is superstitious, and they're lying if they say they're not because that's part of your routine, and that's how you get mentally prepared to play this game. It's a crazy game. A real mental game, and everybody in here has a certain routine, whether it's your batting gloves, your clothes, what you eat for lunch, whatever. . . . Your routine *is* a superstition. When you break that routine, you kind of get out of whack." And as John Hersey warned, "Disturbing the rituals surrounding writing may be very confusing, very difficult."

While some of the world's finest ballplayers knew that if their pitcher seemed to be working on a no-hitter, they must not talk to him about it, some of the world's finest writers knew that if they were working on a novel, they must not talk to anyone about it. For the moment they did, surely they'd be sentencing it to death.

FOURTEEN

While Working on It,
Shut Up About It. Or Don't

W hile refusing *The Paris Review*'s request for a tape-recorded interview in 1966, John Updike said, "I really don't have a great deal to tell interviewers; the little I learned about life and the art of fiction I try to express in my work." In 1967, he agreed to the request, but insisted on seeing all the questions in advance. Then, during the interview, he blurted, "I'm interviewed too much. I fight them off, but even one is too many. However hard you try to be honest or full, they are intrinsically phony. There is something terribly wrong about committing myself to this machine and to your version of what you get out of the machine – you may be deaf for all I know, and the machine may be faulty. All the stuff comes out attached to my name, and it's not really me at all. . . . In any interview, you do say more or less than you mean. You leave the proper ground of your strength, and become one more gassy monologist."

"I don't have a schedule, but by preference I write in the morning," Pablo Neruda told an interviewer. "Which is to say, if you weren't here making me waste my time – and wasting your own – I would be writing." When a writer suggested to S.J. Perelman, "Perhaps you would talk about the incongruity that turns up so often in your use of language," the humorist shot back, "And perhaps I would not. Writers who pontificate about their own use of language drive me right up the wall. I've discovered that this is an occupational disease of those ladies with three-barreled names one meets at the Authors' League. . . . Vaporizing about one's own stylistic intricacies strikes me as being visceral, and, to be blunt, inexcusable."

An interviewer once reminded Edward Albee that he'd admitted he sometimes had no specific idea about the theme of a play he'd written and asked, "What about that?" Albee despised the very question. It was "a terrible invasion" of the kind of privacy writers must keep to themselves. "If you intellectualize and examine the creative process too carefully it can evaporate and vanish," he said. "It's not only terribly difficult to talk about, it's also dangerous. You know the old story about the very clever animal [a frog] – that saw a centipede he didn't like. He said, 'My god, it's amazing and marvelous how you walk with all those hundreds and hundreds of legs. How do you do it? How do you get them all moving that way?' The centipede stopped and thought, and said, 'Well, I take the left front leg and then I' – and he thought about it for a while, and he couldn't walk."

After Annette Grant interviewed John Cheever several times in 1976, she said he "talked freely about himself [but] he changed the subject when the conversation turned to his work. *Aren't you bored with all this talk? Would you like a drink? Perhaps lunch is ready. I'll just go downstairs and check. A walk in the woods, and maybe a swim afterwards? Or would you rather drive to town and see my office? Do you play backgammon? Do you watch television?*" After their last session together, "Cheever said, 'Go ahead and pack your gear, I'll be along in a minute to drive you to the station'. . . . He stepped out of his clothes and jumped with a loud splash into a pond, doubtless cleansing himself with his skinny dip from one more interview."

Plimpton's grilling of Hemingway proceeded amiably enough until, shortly after the twentieth question, Hemingway asked, "Doesn't this sort of talk bore you? This backyard literary gossip while washing out the dirty clothes of thirty-five years ago is disgusting to me." After Plimpton gamely produced another dozen questions and promptings, Hemingway snapped, "The fact that I'm interrupting serious work to answer these questions proves I am so stupid that I should be penalized severely." To be asked questions about his writing, Plimpton explained, "'spooks' him (to use one of his favourite expressions) to the point where he is almost inarticulate." His moments of testiness stemmed from "this strong feeling that writing is a private, lonely occupation with no need for witnesses until the final work is done." Hemingway had previously told Plimpton that any writer foolish enough to discuss a work-in-progress would "talk it out" and destroy it before finishing it.

One hundred and thirty-odd years earlier, Hazlitt said that if Coleridge "had not been the most impressive talker of his age, he would probably have been the finest writer; but he lays down his pen to make sure of an auditor, and mortgages the admiration of posterity for the stare of an idler."

Katherine Mansfield in 1921: "A bad spell has been upon me. I have begun two stories, but then I told them, and they felt betrayed. It's absolutely fatal to give way to this temptation."

Norman Mailer in 1964: "I just think it's bad to talk about one's present work, for it spoils something at the root of the creative act. It discharges the tension."

Don DeLillo in 2003: "When I work on a book, I don't talk to anybody about it until it's finished. And once it's finished I don't have much to say about it anymore."

Anne Tyler in 2006: "Any time I talk in public about writing, I end up not being able to *do* any writing. It's as if some capricious Writing Elf goes into a little sulk whenever I expose him."

And Then There Were the Garrulous Ones

Aldous Huxley was "surely the wittiest and most irreverent of serious novelists," and also "one of the most prodigiously learned writers not merely of this century but of all time." After interviewing him in 1960, that's how George Wickes and Roy Fraser saw him. They might have added that he was as amiable as he was learned. He happily told them all about the plot, setting, and philosophical thrust of his work-in-progress, the novel *Island*. "No, I don't mind talking about my writing at all," he said. "In fact, it might be a good practice; it might give me a clearer notion of what I was trying to do. . . . I don't think there's any risk that ideas or materials will evaporate."

Since Olga Carlisle was a granddaughter of Russian novelist Leonid Andreyev and the daughter of poet Vadim Andreyev, who had been imprisoned during the Bolshevik Revolution, Boris Pasternak greeted her warmly when she arrived at his door in Moscow in 1960. At seventy, she said, he was still "strikingly handsome; with his high cheek-bones and dark eyes and fur hat he looked like someone out of a Russian tale." He was also generous with his thoughts and memories.

During the last of several interviews he gave her, he said, "I think that on account of your background – so close to the events of the Russian nineteenth century – you will be interested in the outlines of my new work. I am working on a trilogy [of stage plays]. I have about a third of it written. I want to re-create a whole historical era, the nineteenth century in Russia with its main event, the liberation of the serfs." In great detail and with growing excitement, he then told the young woman about the plot, roles, scenes, and tone of each of the three plays. Hemingway would have dismissed all this as self-destructive babbling, but Pasternak seemed to feel he was granting a favour not only to his visitor but to himself.

Mary McCarthy was a formidable New York reviewer and literary figure who had been writing a novel off and on for a decade when in 1961, future publisher Elisabeth Sifton was so bold as to wonder, "Is it unfair to ask what it will be about?"

"No, it's very easy," McCarthy said. "It's called *The Group*, and it's about eight Vassar girls. It starts with the inauguration of Roosevelt, and – well, at first, it was going to carry them up to the present time, but then I decided to stop at the inauguration of Eisenhower. . . ." She went on to describe her book as "a kind of mock-chronicle novel," and "the history of the loss of faith in progress, in the idea of progress, in that twenty-year period." Her openness came nowhere near sabotaging *The Group*. After it appeared in 1963, Norman Mailer said that the reviews from all the most important book critics in America "came in on wings of gold, 'Brilliant' 'Sheer' 'Superlative' 'Highly' 'Generous' 'Wonderfully Worth' 'Great Joy.'"

Far from refusing to tell anyone about *Treasure Island* (1883) while working on it, Robert Louis Stevenson relied on his family to help him write it. They were living near Braemar in the Highlands of Scotland. While fooling around with his stepson's paints, Stevenson happened to draw a map of an imaginary island. Concocting a story to go along with the map seemed a natural thing to do. He wrote a chapter a day, which he read to his family each night. His father and stepson, in particular, got right into the spirit of the yarn and tossed out bits of detail that he liked enough to work into his manuscript. *Treasure Island* set Stevenson on the road to fame. Before he died, only eleven years after he finished it, it had appeared in editions of tens of thousands.

COUPLES

George Orwell regularly asked his wife, Eileen Maud O'Shaughnessy, to read his works-in-progress. She spoke to him frankly about them and may thereby have helped him develop his clean, muscular style. During the five years that Malcolm Lowry wrestled with the third and fourth drafts of *Under the Volcano*, his wife, Margerie Bonner, saw every word he wrote. In their tiny fisherman's shack near Vancouver, she was often beside him as he worked, and it was she who typed up his strange handwriting. But she contributed far more to *Under the Volcano* than stenographic services.

"It was only in 1939, when Lowry met Margerie, that the novel began assuming a coherent shape," D.T. Max wrote in 2007. "Margerie suggested characters and plot turns, added sentences, and cut back Lowry's wordiness. She was a good editor, and the only person who could manage her husband's reckless temperament." Lowry told his mentor, Conrad Aiken, "We work together on it day and night. . . . I'm more than glad I never got a chance to finish it without her." The odds are, he could not possibly have finished it without her. The book was a commercial and critical success, with reviewers hailing Lowry as the new James Joyce. He and Margerie, however, never again clicked as they did in the 1940s. By 1957, they had settled in Sussex and grown to hate each other so much that, after a drunken Lowry swallowed an overdose of barbiturates and choked to death on his vomit, some believed that Margerie had, literally, got away with murder.

When an interviewer asked Paul Bowles (*The Sheltering Sky*, 1949) if he and his wife Jane – who wrote short stories, plays, and a novel (*Two Serious Ladies*, 1943) – had influenced each other's work, he said, "Of course! We showed each other every page we wrote. I never thought of sending a story off without discussing it with her first. . . . I went over *Two Serious Ladies* with her again and again, until each detail was as we both thought it should be. Not that I put anything into it that she hadn't written. We simply analyzed sentences and rhetoric. It was this being present at the making of a novel that made me want to write my own fiction."

In the late 1960s, Kingsley Amis was writing *Ending Up* (1974) in the upstairs study at his house in London. Downstairs, his second wife, novelist Elizabeth Jane Howard, was writing *Something in Disguise* (1969), and a son from his first marriage, novelist Martin Amis, was writing *Dead Babies* (1975). On many evenings Kingsley and Jane met for cocktails and to read their day's work to each other. "We learned to criticize each other's work," she said. Indeed, that was "the most enjoyable and enduring part of our relationship." With his stupendous consumption of Scotch and other spirits, Kingsley so poisoned the relationship that Jane, after living with him for eighteen years, left him for good.

At Eagle Pond Farm in New Hampshire, where poet Donald Hall grew up "loving the landscape, loving the way people talked" and where his nineteenth-century forebears raised cattle, sheep, and pigs, he said, "Everything that my life has come to – coming back here, the church, my poems of the last fifteen years – derives from my marriage to Jane [Kenyon] in 1972. And I've watched her grow into a *poet*. Of course we work together; show each other what we're doing; occasionally getting a little huffy with each other, but helping each other all the same."

Jack Gilbert, whose poetry was nominated for two Pulitzer Prizes and inspired a reviewer in the *New York Times* to call him "inescapably gifted," recalled that when he lived with poet Linda Gregg, "we were intertwined. We read each other's poetry, appreciated each other's poetry, discarded each other's poetry. The presence of that spirit in my life – gentleness, beauty. . . . Pretty soon I'm going to start singing."

A Writer in Need Is a Friend Indeed

Remembering novelist and playwright W.O. Mitchell – for decades a frank, humorous, and boisterous character on Canada's literary scene – his long-time editor Douglas Gibson said, "He was always delighted to read pages of his work aloud on the phone to me – or in person to patient colleagues like Alistair MacLeod, who shared a corridor with him at the University of Windsor's English Department."

Few modern writers, however, have gabbed more incessantly to an editor about a work-in-progress than novelist and screen-writer Richard Price. While writing the first draft of *Clockers* (1992), he got editor John Sterling on the phone every day for a solid year and read to him everything he wrote. "It seems I needed to do that, to hear 'good dog,'" Price said. "His goal in humouring me like this was to get me to the end so he could have a manuscript to work with. For him, it must have been like talking to a head-job or a child, coaxing and comforting, and saying, Ooh, that's good. Wow. Oh, you're such a good writer. Very good. What page are we on? How many pages do you think we have left? What time is it? March?" The heroic Sterling finally got a manuscript from Price but it was more than a thousand pages long. "We wound up going back to page one three times," Price said, "and working our way through to page one thousand-plus – eighteen months of rewriting."

After Joseph Heller (*Catch-22*, 1961) said he did not think authors knew much about the effect of what they were doing, his inter-viewer asked if having such a tentative grip didn't bother him. "No," Heller replied. "It's one of the things that makes it inter-esting. I would only be nervous if I were told that what I'd done was no good and no one would want to read it. I protect myself from that by submitting the first chapter to my agent, and to my editor, and, after about a third of the book is done, to other friends. That can be tough on me."

When Wallace Stegner was struggling with his *Wolf Willow: A History, a Story, and a Memory of the Last Plains Frontier* (1962), his friend, the literary historian Malcolm Cowley, asked to see it. "He looked," Stegner recalled, "and he said, 'You know, I think if you just move this Dump Ground chapter from the beginning to the end' – or vice versa, I've forgotten which – 'the book will come together better.' And it did, like a puzzle when you find the key piece. I had a blind spot he did not have. So there is often a great usefulness in literary friends, but that isn't what you have them for. You don't have any friend *for* anything. You just have him. Or her."

Walker Percy and Shelby Foote, writers from deep in the American South, were the closest of friends for sixty years, and Percy so trusted his chum that he regularly showed him drafts of his novels, much to Foote's dismay. "I used to rage at him," Foote said. "He would send copies to Caroline Gordon [Southern fiction writer] and Allen Tate [Southern poet, and Gordon's husband], and ask them for criticisms and so forth, and I've always been opposed to that."

So was Vladimir Nabokov. When an interviewer asked to see some of his revisions, Nabokov gave him a supremely Nabokovian reply: "I'm afraid I must refuse. Only ambitious nonentities and hearty mediocrities exhibit their rough drafts. It is like passing around samples of one's sputum."

Next question, please.

FIFTEEN

They Wrote Lying Down, Standing Up, Stark Naked

In bed, behind locked doors, Thomas Hobbes not only sang loudly "to do the lungs good," but also wrote *Dialogue on Physics or on the Nature of Air* (1661). He used his bedsheets for paper and, when he'd completely covered them with words, scrawled on his thighs. "A possibly apocryphal story," Robert Hendrickson reported in his *World Literary Anecdotes* (1991), "has it that Voltaire did at least some of his writing in bed, using his naked mistress's back for a desk."

This invites questions like those John Steinbeck asked about Mark Twain's writing in bed. What exactly did Twain write while there, and what while sitting at his desk? And how often did he write in bed? Perhaps it was only twice, "and the story took hold. Such things happen." Whatever the answers, Steinbeck decided, "all of this has to do with comfort in writing. I should think that a comfortable body would let the mind go freely."

It was certainly more than once, however, that Twain wrote in bed, especially in his later years. Four days before his seventieth birthday, he told a reporter for the *New York Sunday Magazine*, "Often I lay in bed all day and wrote. It's a great luxury to arrange your desk in bed and write as long as you like. I've spent whole weeks that way." While enjoying the same luxury, Edith Wharton required skills similar to those that Thackeray employed while writing in stagecoaches. "She wrote, famously, in bed, tossing her handwritten pages onto the floor for her secretary to type," Updike wrote, "and balanced her writing desk on her knees with an inkpot in it and a pet Pekinese dog on the bed with her." It was in bed that Wharton not only wrote, her biographer Shari Benstock reported, but rewrote, "editing her work by the time-honoured method of scissors and paste; folding and cutting up pages, she created a layered manuscript whose seams hid earlier versions of her work."

A medallion that commemorates Robert Louis Stevenson shows him working in bed, with a pad on his lap, a pen in one hand, and a cigarette in the other. A childhood victim of Edinburgh's harsh climate all his life, he suffered from respiratory ailments. Bony, bug-eyed, sickly, susceptible to fevers, and racked by violent fits of coughing, he spent much of his life travelling in search of a climate good for his health. Before Stevenson died at forty-four, Henry James had this to say about his writing: "It adds immensely to the interest of volumes through which there draws so strong a current of life to know that they are not only the work of an invalid, but have largely been written in bed, in dreary 'health resorts,' in the intervals of sharp attacks."

One of the leading Italian writers of the twentieth century, Alberto Moravia, was only twenty-one when in 1929 he published his first novel, *Gli Indifferenti* (*Time of Indifference*), much of which he wrote in bed. It was about the moral corruption of a middle-class woman and her children in Rome, and indirectly condemned the Roman bourgeoisie under Mussolini's fascist regime. A quarter-century later, Moravia said the book he began to write as a prone teenager turned out to be the greatest success in "all modern Italian literature. . . . Certainly, no book in the last fifty years has been greeted with such enthusiasm and excitement."

Paul Bowles, the American writer and composer who spent more than half a century in Morocco, said, "Ninety-five percent of everything I've written has been done in bed." Jessamyn West, the Quaker whose best-known novel was *The Friendly Persuasion* (1945), said the advantage of writing in bed was that "you have on your nightgown or pajamas and can't go running to the door at the knock of a stranger. Also, once you're up and dressed you see ten thousand things that need doing." When Orson Welles died of a heart attack, at seventy, he was found in bed with a typewriter still perched on his ample belly. He had been writing a video version of *Julius Caesar*, in which he intended to play every character.

"I still lay down on the bed with a yellow pad and write," Woody Allen said in 2006. He had once composed on a typewriter, and wished he still did. "If you write on your typewriter, you act out the scene, and you type it down, and you sort of know how it works," he explained. When you lie back and handwrite on a pad, however, "you're hearing it in your head, and you don't know that it works when it becomes audible, but it goes so much faster that I've gotten into the bad habit, and I've been doing it for years."

"I can't think unless I'm lying down, either in bed or stretched on a couch and with a cigarette and coffee handy," Truman Capote said. Lying down, he wrote his first draft in longhand and did a complete revision, also in longhand. While still in bed and balancing a typewriter on his knees, he banged out a third draft on "a very special kind of yellow paper." He then typed a fourth and final version on white paper. Capote called himself "a completely horizontal author."

STANDING UP TO WRITE RIGHT

Some authors, however, were completely vertical. A website that advertises the J. Peterman Stand-Up Desk asks, "Notice how you get some of your best ideas when you're standing there shaving or taking a shower? How your thighs and toes squirm when you sit at a desk, then 'it comes to you' when you stand up and walk around? The fact is, *you think with your legs. . . .* If you want to increase the vigour and abundance of your thought, I recommend this time-tested Stand-Up Desk." Sitting at a desk put heavy pressure on "those shock absorbing discs between your vertebrae," but standing instantly relieved it and thus eliminated the risk of back pain.

Thomas Jefferson and Benjamin Franklin chose to express their vigorous and abundant thoughts by writing at stand-up desks, and that's how Lewis Carroll wrote *Alice's Adventures in Wonderland* (1865) and *Through the Looking Glass* (1872). "Standing at the upright desk he always used while writing," his biographer Morton N. Cohen said, "he managed to breathe life and laughter onto the dry leaves of paper that lay before him." Novelist (*The Scarlet Letter*, 1850) and short-story writer (*Tanglewood Tales*, 1853) Nathaniel Hawthorne had a stand-up writing desk in the study in his attic at Concord, Massachusetts, and, in the top level of a tower he added to the house, another one. It faced bookshelves rather than the south-facing window, which offered a beautiful and therefore distracting view.

While serving on the Supreme Court of the United States from 1902 to 1935, Oliver Wendell Holmes, "the Great Dissenter," stood at a high desk to write the pithy and lucid opinions that made him the most quoted of all American judges. "If I sit down, I write a long opinion and don't come to the point as quickly as I could," he explained. "If I stand up I write as long as my knees hold out. When they don't, I know it's time to stop."

Quentin Bell, a nephew of Virginia Woolf, said, "She had a desk standing about three feet six inches high with a sloping top; it was so high that she had to stand to do her work." Her "principal motive" was that her older sister Vanessa, a professional painter whom she both adored and saw as a rival, stood before an easel as she worked. Virginia feared her writing would appear less worthy than Vanessa's painting "unless she set matters on a footing of equality," and that was why "for many years she stood at this strange desk, and, in a quite unnecessary way, tired herself."

Winston Churchill composed his prose while standing and walking. "He wrote forty-two books, five thousand speeches and articles – in all roughly thirty-million words," said Richard M. Langworth, founder of the Churchill Centre in Washington, DC. "When he went to work, usually late at night, he shut himself up in his study, banned loud noises, hired teams of stenographers, and arranged his papers at a stand-up desk. And there, padding up and down in his slippers, he reeled off prose in the small hours. . . . 'Nearly 3,000 words in the last two days!' he told his wife in 1928. 'I do not conceal from you that it is a task. But it is not more than I can do.'"

E.B. White, having been invited to experience silence and solitude as a writer-in-residence at Yaddo, the artists' community in upstate New York, told its executive director, Elizabeth Ames, "If I ever arrive at the point where I sit down to do some writing, I shall remember your invitation, but I'm still writing standing up. . . . Even at home in Maine, where I have a 'study' of my own, I seldom use it for writing, but instead work in the middle of the living room where the household tides run strongest."

Playwright August Wilson "wrote standing up, at a high, cluttered accounting desk," said John Lahr, drama critic of *The New Yorker*. "For years, an Everlast punching bag was suspended from the ceiling about two steps behind. When Wilson was in full flow and the dialogue was popping, he'd stop, pivot, throw a barrage of punches, then turn back to work."

Wilson said his stand-up desk allowed him to pace around, but perhaps no American writer has done more pacing than Philip Roth. At seventy-one, he'd written more than twenty novels and won a dozen awards for fiction and, despite agonizing back pains, had not slowed down. "He works standing up . . . and has said he walks half a mile for every page he writes," Al Alvarez reported in *The Guardian* in 2004. "Even now, when his joints are beginning to creak and fail, energy still comes off him like a haze."

Nabokov, who never learned to type, wrote standing up, sitting, and lying down. "I generally start the day at a lovely, old-fashioned lectern I have in my study," he said in 1964, six years after the U.S. publication of *Lolita*. "Later on, when I feel gravity nibbling at my calves, I settle down in a comfortable armchair alongside an ordinary writing desk; and finally, when gravity begins climbing up my spine, I lie down on a couch in a corner of my small study. It is a pleasant solar routine. But when I was young, in my twenties and early thirties, I would often stay all day in bed, smoking and writing."

Water Nourished the Muse

To encourage their creativity to blossom, Nabokov and Saul Bellow liked to soak themselves in bathtubs. While lying in one at his house in Vermont, Bellow gazed through skylights at twinkling constellations. Benjamin Franklin wrote not only standing up but, at times, stretched out in America's first bathtub. French dramatist Edmund Rostand (*Cyrano de Bergerac*, 1897) found the uninvited visits of his friends so maddeningly distracting that he ended up writing his plays in his bathtub.

Since the American poet and non-fiction writer Diane Ackerman wrote the best-selling *A Natural History of the Senses* (1990), perhaps it is not surprising that she worked under sensuous conditions: "I have a pine plank that I lay across the sides of the tub so that I can stay in a bubble bath for hours and write. In the bath, water displaces much of your weight and you feel light. When the water temperature and the body temperature converge, my mind lifts free and travels by itself." Lolling in baths one summer, she wrote an entire verse play about a woman poet in seventeenth-century Mexico; her lover, an Italian courtier; and various characters in her tumultuous life. "I wanted to slide off the centuries as if from a hill of shale," Ackerman said. "Baths were perfect."

By the time American novelist Jane Smiley reached her late fifties, she knew she could melt the hardest writer's block with a hot bath or shower. The when, where, and why this Pulitzer winner (1992) wrote, and the equipment she used, the pictures on her walls and ornaments on her desks had all varied over the years, but not that simple unclogger of her mind. "I disrobe," she writes. "I step in. It's hot, almost hotter than I can stand for almost ten seconds. Within moments, I know what to write next." Washing her hair, rinsing it, conditioning it, rinsing it again, she stays right where she is, feeling the delicious flow of heat, "cultivating my little thought," often until she runs clean out of hot water. She gets out, gets dry, and gets to work. Throwing on a pink terry-cloth robe, she rushes back to her writing chair. "It could be worse," Smiley says, "and a lot more trouble – drinking, driving, fighting, shopping, something like that, but after all these years, it's only hot water."

WANT TO WORK IN YOUR UNDERWEAR?
WRITING AWAITS YOU.

In 1819, at twenty-three, Keats wrote, "I rouse myself, wash, and put on a clean shirt, brush my hair and clothes, tie my shoestrings neatly, and in fact adonize [dandify] as if I were going out – then all clean and comfortable I sit down to write. This I find the greatest relief." August Wilson, when asked if he observed any rituals "to get [him] going," said, "I always approach my work with clean hands. I will do a symbolic cleansing with my morning coffee, if nothing else is available." It was only after shaving and pulling on slacks and a gaudy sports shirt that Canadian novelist Hugh

Garner sat down at his typewriter in the morning. Pulitzer Prize–winning Amy Lowell, a leader of the Imagist school of American poetry early in the twentieth century, wrote while wearing men's shirts and severely tailored suits.

As assistant editor of *Bus and Truck Transport* magazine in Toronto in the 1950s, young Arthur Hailey dressed in a white shirt, subdued tie, conservatively cut business suit, and polished shoes, and that's how he continued to dress after he became a screenwriter and novelist. In an office with plywood walls in the basement of his home, he worked from nine to five, Monday to Friday. His second wife, Sheila, called him "fanatically clean" and "maniacally tidy." The sales of his novels, which included *Hotel* (1965), *Airport* (1968), and *Wheels* (1971), surpassed 170 million in forty languages.

Long before John Cheever, "the Chekhov of suburbia," won both a U.S. National Book Award and a Pulitzer Prize, he lived with his wife, Mary, and their two children in an apartment in Manhattan and, every morning, his daughter Susan remembered, "my father would put on his one good suit and his gray felt hat and ride down in the elevator with the other men on their way to the office. From the lobby he would walk down to the basement, to the windowless storage room that came with our apartment. That was where he worked. There, he hung up the suit and hat and wrote all morning in his boxer shorts, typing away at his portable Underwood set up on the folding table. At lunchtime he would put the suit back on and ride up in the elevator."

Shortly after Tom Wolfe wrote *Bonfire of the Vanities* (1987), Joseph Epstein said, "Tom Wolfe may be the only writer since Mark Twain to dress for the job. Two white-suited southerners, Twain and Wolfe resemble nothing so much as characters who have somehow wandered off the stage of a production of Jerome Kern's *Show Boat*. . . . Plainspoken and decorous in his personal utterances, Wolfe has written as he has dressed, which is gaudily."

For writing, and simply to enjoy being a noticeable dandy, Wolfe had more outfits than his white suits. Mort Sheinman of *Women's Wear Daily* interviewed him in 1983 and remembered, "He was wearing a navy blue blazer of unfinished worsted with gray buttons that matched his gray trousers and a big-lapeled, covered-button, double-breasted gray vest; a white silk tie with a small knot hiding under a high stiff collar ('my latest pretension, my Herbert Hoover look'); patterned hose of blue and white, and single-buckle blue suede shoes."

While nearing the end of *The Right Stuff* (1979), about astronauts and others involved in America's first manned space program, Wolfe ran into trouble. His publisher kept demanding the manuscript, but he couldn't quite close it out. In desperation, he took off his fancy duds and pulled on "a pair of khakis" and a turtleneck sweater. "Dressing that way forced me to work," he told Sheinman. "I knew I could just *never* leave the house looking like that, so I had to finish the book."

For many writers, however, the freedom to earn a living while wearing whatever sloppy old clothes they chose was precious compensation for the misery their lonely calling imposed on them. Ex-journalist Wendy Holden, the English author of seven humorous novels, said that what made her keep on writing was "the lurking horror of having to go back and get a proper job. . . . I'm a complete hermit, so it suits me perfectly. It also means that I don't have to dress up or wear make-up. After years of doing just that, I find it so relaxing not having to." The best thing about being a writer, said Canadian novelist and humorist Will Ferguson, was this: "You get to work in your underwear and scratch yourself whenever you want. Try doing that in your standard office work environment."

William Maxwell of *The New Yorker* rolled out of bed in the morning and, wearing bathrobe and pyjamas, wrote until early afternoon. He refused the office that the magazine offered him because "I would have to put my trousers on and ride the subway downtown to my typewriter. No good."

Harry Hoff worked in the nude. Under the name William Cooper, he wrote *Scenes from a Provincial Life* (1950) and other novels that earned him a reputation in England as a trailblazer for Kingsley Amis and others among the Angry Young Men. Hoff was a civil servant, and in the mid-1970s, his mentor, the scientist and novelist C.P. Snow, introduced him to Leslie Millin, a Canadian civil servant and writer of non-fiction who'd been posted to London. Hoff and Millin became good friends and, a few years after the novelist died at ninety-two in 2002, Millin, who'd settled in Vancouver, remembered that he wrote with a fountain pen, on school exercise books, while standing before a lectern, as naked as the day he was born and, whenever possible, in bright sunshine.

"I write nude, seated on a thick towel, and perhaps with a second towel around me," said the British-born American poet and novelist Paul West. "Something atavistic prevails and helps me relax." His wife was that writer-in-a-bubble-bath, Diane Ackerman.

SIXTEEN

Horror Rolls in,
"Like Some Poisonous Fogbank"

Why does a writer, at work, choose a pen rather than a computer, yellow paper rather than white, to stand rather than sit, to face a blank wall rather than a busy river, and to keep company with a little statue, wind-up toy, pale-olithic find, stuffed animal, faded photo, or dried seahorses?

To unleash creativity.

Unlike a Waterman, IBM Selectric, or desktop Buddha, however, the source of the creativity is neither visible nor tangible. It lies among the deep entanglements of the mind. Some writers have calm, balanced, and relatively untroubled minds, but so many others suffer from severe depressions, other mood disorders, and even suicidal urges that surely there's a connection between emotional turmoil and getting the right words down on paper – between mental illness and literary genius. That, too, is part of the wond'rous mystic art.

BEWARE OF VISITS BY "THE BLACK DOG"

Knowing what you want to write about, you sit down before your computer. "Then your mental illnesses arrive at the desk like your sickest, most secretive relatives," San Francisco novelist and non-fiction writer Ann Lamott wrote in 1994. "And they pull up chairs in a semicircle, and they try to be quiet but you know they are there with their weird coppery breath, leering at you behind your back."

Insomnia tortured Virginia Woolf in 1913, and she wrote, "After such nights there were days of headaches, drilling the occiput [back of the head] as though it were a rotten tooth and then come worse nights of anxiety and depression." Twenty-eight years later, at fifty-nine, she wrote to her husband, Leonard, that she was "going mad again," and "I feel we can't go through another of those terrible times. And I shan't recover this time. I begin to hear voices, and I can't concentrate. So I am doing what seems the best thing to do. You have given me the greatest possible happiness. . . . I don't think two people could have been happier till this terrible disease came. I can't fight any longer. . . ." With that, she left their home in Sussex, walked across familiar fields to the River Ouse, filled her coat pockets with stones, and strode into the water. Three weeks later, children found her corpse.

Shortly after Hemingway's sixty-first birthday in July 1960, he suffered a deep depression. "His symptoms were fear, loneliness, ennui, suspicion of the motives of others, insomnia, guilt, remorse, and failure of his memory," psychiatry professor Russell R. Monroe wrote in *Creative Brainstorms: The Relationship Between Madness and Genius* (1992). "He had a number of physical complaints and nightmares and expressed the fear that he was having a complete physical and nervous crackup." In the following November and April, Hemingway was hospitalized for extreme depression with suicidal impulses and underwent electroconvulsive therapy. On July 2, 1961, at his home in Ketchum, Idaho, he loaded a double-barrelled shotgun, put the muzzle to his forehead, and pulled both triggers.

Emily Dickinson, whom Monroe called "an inhibited recluse with massive neurotic symptoms," began one of the grimmest of her many grim poems with "I felt a Cleaving in my Mind – As if my Brain had split," and another with "I felt a funeral in my brain." She also wrote, "And then a plank in reason, broke, / And I dropped down and down – / And hit a world at every plunge."

But it was Gerard Manley Hopkins, a Victorian poet, Catholic priest, and manic depressive, who wrote perhaps the darkest poem in the English language about plummeting into deep depression. He called it "No Worst, There Is None":

No worst, there is none. Pitched past pitch of grief,
More pangs will, schooled at forepangs, wilder wring.
Comforter, where, where is your comforting?
Mary, mother of us, where is your relief?
My cries heave, herds-long; huddle in a main, a chief-
woe, world-sorrow; on an age-old anvil wince and sing –
Then lull then leave off. Fury had shrieked "no ling-
ering! Let me be fell: force I must be brief ".
O the mind, mind has mountains; cliffs of fall
frightful, sheer, no-man-fathomed. Hold them cheap
May who ne'er hung there. Nor does long our small
Durance deal with that steep or deep. Here! Creep,
Wretch, under a comfort serves in a whirlwind: all
Life death does end and each day dies with sleep.

Like other artists, writers have always been vulnerable to dreadful crashes of spirit. Even in Plato's time, people linked mood disorders to creativity, and the notion of the "mad genius" has survived for centuries. Shakespeare well knew depression. "I have of late – but wherefore I know not – lost all my mirth, forgone all custom of exercises," Hamlet says. "And indeed it goes so heavily with my disposition that this goodly frame the earth seems to me a sterile promontory. This most excellent canopy, the air, look you, this brave o'erhanging firmament, this majestical roof fretted with golden fire – why, it appeareth nothing to me but a foul and pestilent congregation of vapours."

Samuel Johnson, Walter Scott, and Winston Churchill each called his bouts of depression visits by "the black dog." This creature, Scott said, was "that vile palpitation of the heart . . . that hysterical passion which forces unbidden tears and falls upon a contented life like a drop of ink on white paper which is not the less a stain because it conveys no meaning."

Byron's lover, Lady Caroline Lamb, famously called him "mad, bad and dangerous to know" but, according to clinical psychologist Kay Redfield Jamison, herself a victim of bipolar disorder, he was also "virulently melancholic, and in lifelong fear of going insane." He "represented the fine edge of the fine madness – the often imperceptible line between poetic temperament and psychiatric illness."

Poe was still in his mid-twenties when he wrote to a friend, "I am suffering under a depression of spirits such as I have never felt before. I have struggled in vain against the influence of this melancholy. . . . I am wretched, and know not why. Console me – for you can. But let it be quickly – or it will be too late. Write me immediately. Convince me that it is worth one's while – that it is at all necessary to live. . . ."

Dostoevsky was also a young man when he wrote, "With the first approach of twilight, I gradually begin to succumb to that state of soul which now comes to me so frequently at night, in my sickness, and which I call *mystical terror*. It is a most oppressive, tormenting fear of something I myself cannot define, of something that is not understood and that does not exist in the natural order of things, but that without fail, perhaps this very minute, will happen, as though in mockery of all the arguments of reason, and will come to me and stand before me as an undeniable fact – horrible, unseemly, and implacable."

One night in 1875, when Tolstoy was forty-seven and his wife

Sonya thirty-one, his screams of terror awakened his whole family, but what worried her more was the depression that seemed to be draining the very life out of him: "It hurts me to see him the way he is now; despondent, sunken, he sits without working, without effort, without energy, without joyful purpose for days and weeks as though he condoned this condition. . . . I don't want this for him and he himself cannot live like this for long."

A bout of depression grew so monstrous in the mind of William Styron in 1985 that, if he hadn't allowed his wife, Rose, to check him into a hospital, he'd have killed himself. He later wrote, "The pain of severe depression is quite unimaginable to those who have not suffered it, and it kills in many instances because its anguish can no longer be borne." Depression was "a true wimp of a word for such a major illness. . . . Nonetheless, for over seventy-five years the word has slithered innocuously through the language like a slug, leaving little trace of its intrinsic malevolence and preventing, by its very insipidity, a general awareness of the horrible intensity of the disease when out of control."

He endured "dreadful, pounding seizures of anxiety." His mind was "an organ in convulsion," and his "psychic energy throttled back close to zero." Every afternoon, he wrote, "I'd feel the horror, like some poisonous fogbank, roll in upon my mind, forcing me into bed." Death became "a daily presence, blowing over me in cold gusts," and a "gray drizzle of horror" took on the "the quality of physical pain."

You Don't Have to Be a Mad Genius . . .

Not every writer, however, suffers an emotional disturbance that comes anywhere near being suicidal, or believes it's essential to sweat out a severe depression to create art. Margaret Atwood was only twenty-nine when, in reply to a friend who asked if artists must suffer to be creative, she wrote, "Everyone has neuroses, granted, but the artist has a way of working them out (his art) not available to those who ain't; the latter have to work them out in their lives. Therefore the artist is likely to be better adjusted (to his own neuroses) than someone with an equivalent intensity of neurosis who isn't an artist. That's probably a lot of crap too, but I find it more viable than the suffering one. At least you don't feel guilty if you enjoy yr. life or happen to have a good relationship with someone."

A decade later, Atwood told Joyce Carol Oates, "I certainly don't feel that all art is a consequence of neurosis. I tend to see it as the opposite. Not that some artists aren't neurotic . . . but that art, the making or creating, is made in spite of the neurosis, is a triumph over it."

Atwood biographer Nathalie Cooke links her to American poet Denise Levertov who, after the suicide of poet Anne Sexton, urged a redirection of attention from the destructive fascination with suffering among artists to "the 'romantic' aspects of artists' 'tenacity' and 'devotion' to their art. . . ." Cooke explained, "By recasting art as a gesture of defiance rather than an articulation of surrender, both Levertov and Atwood consciously invert the equation of art and suffering."

. . . BUT QUITE A FEW WRITERS WERE

In *Touched with Fire: Depressive Illness and the Artistic Temperament* (1993), Kay Redfield Jamison acknowledges that many writers are psychiatrically normal, but nevertheless makes a strong case for "a compelling association, not to say, an overlap, between two temperaments – the artistic and the manic depressive – and their relationship to the rhythms and cycles, or temperament of the natural world." She insists "that a much-higher-than-expected rate of manic-depressive illness, depression and suicide exists in exceptionally creative writers and artists."

Jamison lists eighty-three poets and forty-two writers of fiction, non-fiction, and plays "with probable cyclothymia [marked swings of mood from cheerfulness to misery], major depression, or manic-depressive illness." The poets, thirty-three of whom committed or attempted suicide, include Baudelaire, Burns, Coleridge, Eliot, Goldsmith, Lowell, Pound, Shelley, Tennyson, Whitman, and, as we've seen, Byron, Dickinson, and Hopkins. The prose writers, eleven of whom either killed themselves or tried to, include not only Hemingway, Fitzgerald, and Tolstoy, but Balzac, Conrad, Dickens, Faulkner, Gibbon, Gogol, Gorky, Hugo, Greene, Ibsen, James, Melville, Ruskin, Strindberg, Turgenev, and Zola.

The bouts of deep depression that tortured these and other creative writers may well have been inextricable from their talent and indispensable to their work. Their mental agonies taught them things that the emotionally stable could not fully understand. "And he who has never felt, momentarily, what madness is," Melville claimed, "has but a mouthful of brains." He elaborated on this shortly after the publication of *Moby Dick* in 1851: "The intensest light of reason and revelation combined can not shed such blazonings upon the deeper truths in man, as will sometimes proceed from his own profoundest gloom. Utter darkness is then his light, and cat-like he distinctly sees all objects through a medium which is mere blindness to common vision."

"Most wretched men are cradled into poetry by wrong," Shelley wrote. "They learn in suffering what they teach in song."

Manic-depressive illness, Jamison says, not only adds "depth, fire and understanding to artistic imagination" but also "forces a view on reality, usually neither sought nor welcome, that looks out onto the fleeting nature of life, its decaying core, the finality of death, and the finite role played by man in the history of the universe." Was that not the view on reality that Tolstoy needed in order to write *War and Peace*, Dickens to write *Bleak House*, and Dylan Thomas to write "Do Not Go Gentle into That Good Night"?

Woolf knew her creativity sprang directly from her illness. "As an experience madness is terrific . . . and in its lava I still find most of the things I write about," she told a friend in 1930. "It shoots out of one everything shaped, final, not in mere driblets as sanity does." Columbia University psychologist Katherine Dalsimer wrote, "After a period when [Woolf] was paralyzed by depression, withdrawn from human contact, when the horror and terror of her experience made her long for death, she reflected, 'But it is always a question whether I wish to avoid these glooms. . . . These 9 weeks give one a plunge into deep waters. . . . One goes down into the well & nothing protects one from the assault of truth.'"

ALL THINGS MUST PASS, EVEN CLINICAL DEPRESSION

She was a twenty-nine-year-old survivor of a short, miserable marriage to a Portuguese journalist, a single mother of a baby girl, a receiver of welfare cheques, and the hard-up occupant of a cramped Edinburgh flat for which a friend paid the rent. She plunged into a horrible depression. Four years had passed since her mother had died of multiple sclerosis, but she still mourned her deeply. Her father had terrified her since her childhood, and now, she recalled, "I was definitely clinically depressed." She felt "a numbness, a coldness, an inability to believe [I would ever] feel happy again." During her most nightmarish moments, something dreadful hovered over her baby, Jessica. "I kept expecting her to die," she said. "It was a bad bad time."

In danger of killing herself, she reported to her doctor, who lined up cognitive behavioural therapy for her. If this saved her life, however, so did absorbing herself in finishing a manuscript with which she'd started to mess when her mother was alive. It was *Harry Potter and the Philosopher's Stone* (1997). She was J.K. Rowling, and that volume launched the series of Harry Potter books that made her fabulously rich and happier than she had ever been before.

The grief Rowling suffered after her mother's death enabled her to write movingly about how young Harry felt about losing those he loved. Moreover, Rowling milked her depression to enrich her story. "The most obvious depressive element is her representation of 'Dementors,' frightening shrouded monsters that glide around spreading horror in their wake," British science-fiction writer Kit Whitfield explained on her blog. "In the presence of one, you flash back to all the most painful experiences of your life and become convinced you'll never be happy again; in the worst circumstances, it'll suck out your soul and leave you hollow for the rest of your life. That's a pretty good description of depression."

LET THE LAVA ERUPT

"If I lose my demons," said German poet Rainer Maria Rilke, "I will lose my angels as well." The New York theatrical producer and director Joseph Papp went so far as to warn writers that therapy for their mental disorders would destroy their ability to write. Lauren Slater's experience suggests that, for some, he was right. A psychologist and author of six books, she had always thought of herself as a writer, "all tortured and intense," but in the entire year after she began to down Prozac pills, she failed to compose even one short story or poem. "I can just manage this journal," she wrote. "So maybe I'm not a writer anymore. Maybe Prozac has made me into a nun, or a nurse, or worse, a Calgon Lady. Why can't I write a simple story? Why is my voice – all my voices – so lost to me?"

"I have a great fear of happiness making me stupid," said Italian novelist Italo Svevo (1861–1928). John Fowles said all creative writers were "victims of some form of manic depression" and "that is the price of being what we are. I would never choose – even if I could! – to be a more 'normal' human being. I would never choose something without that emotional cost, severe though it can become."

Perhaps no poet ever made a more extreme pronouncement about the link between suffering and creativity than the Pulitzer-winning John Berryman: "The artist is extremely lucky who is presented with the worst possible ordeal which will not actually kill him. At that point, he's in business. Beethoven's deafness, Goya's deafness, Milton's blindness, that kind of thing. . . . I hope to be nearly crucified."

Unfortunately, he was soon presented with an ordeal that did actually kill him. From a bridge in Minneapolis, he hurled himself into the Mississippi River. Although writing did not save his life, however, it may well have prolonged it. In 1974, another winner of a Pulitzer for poetry, Anne Sexton, killed herself by sitting in her car with the engine running in a closed garage. Five years before, however, she had written, "Poetry led me by the hand out of madness."

"The only way I keep afloat is by working," Virginia Woolf wrote. "Directly I stop working I feel that I am sinking down, down."

Graham Greene, a manic depressive with suicidal urges, said, "Writing is a form of therapy. Sometimes I wonder how all those who do not write, compose or paint can manage to escape the madness, the melancholia, the panic fear which is inherent in the human situation."

Poetry, Byron said, was "the lava of the imagination whose eruption prevents an earthquake – they say poets never or rarely go *mad* . . . but are generally so near it – that I cannot help thinking rhyme is so far useful in anticipating & preventing the disorder." Or, as Neil Simon put it, writing a play is "like analysis without going to the analyst. The play becomes your analysis."

"Writing is tough, but it's a lot less tough than depression," Erica Jong wrote. "Which basically leads to suicide. Unless you make a joke. Writing is the first antidepressant. It came before Prozac or Effexor. And it was cheaper. All you needed was a blank piece of paper and a pencil. . . . If you were lucky, you might even make some dough. But even if you didn't, you were doing something godlike – emblazing words of fire on a tablet of stone and handing them to Moses, any Moses."

Leon Edel, who spent twenty years on his five-volume biography of Henry James, said that a part of what James called the madness of art "resides in the artist's search for some exit from the labyrinth of the imprisoned and despairing self – the verbal structure, the philter, the anodyne, that will somehow provide escape and surcease."

The escape and surcease that Gao Xingjian spent much of his life seeking was from the oppression of his native China. A compulsive scribbler from childhood on, he was still writing or painting for sixteen hours a day in 2000 when, at sixty, he became the first Chinese-language author ever to win the Nobel Prize for Literature. But during the Cultural Revolution, which began in 1966 when he was in his mid-twenties, he was forced to burn "kilos and kilos" of his novels, plays, and articles. His wife publicly denounced him, and he endured six years of hard labour at "a re-education camp." In secret, however, he kept right on writing. That was his only way to find freedom. "Writing eases my suffering," he explained decades later. "When you use words, you're able to keep your mind alive. Writing is my way of reaffirming my own existence."

The exclusive focus that writers bring to their work, their total absorption in the task at hand, may float them free of mental anguish, or deaden it. Tennyson wrote:

> But, for the unquiet heart and brain
> A use in measured language lies;
> The sad mechanic exercise
> Like dull narcotics, numbing pain.

While a degree of depression is both therapeutic for some writers and essential to their creativity, the horrors of the kind that Styron barely survived lead to the emergence of a writer's block. "All your juices dry up – your creative juices, your procreative juices – everything is withered," he wrote. "There's nothing there. That's one of the characteristics of depression. All the life, the vital biological processors are dust." And the writer's block is impenetrable, impassable, insurmountable.

SEVENTEEN

Blocked!

One of America's finest novelists and short-story writers, Carson McCullers, an alcoholic, suffered an incurable writer's block in her forties and died at fifty. "It was a murderous thing, a deathblow, that block," said novelist William Goyen, a friend with whom she sometimes stayed in her last years. "She said she just didn't have anything to write. And really, it was as though she had never written. This happens to writers when there are dead spells. We die sometimes. And it's as though we're in a tomb. It's a death. That's what we all fear, and that's why so many of us become alcoholics or suicides or insane – or just no good philanderers."

"Block is the supreme torture for a writer," essayist Joseph Epstein says. "When a writer is blocked, he cannot write; his craft and talent and energy suddenly flee him. The condition can last a week, a month, a year, a lifetime. And like inspiration, writer's block can show up utterly without warning. It is a condition that seems inexplicable, and is painful in the extreme."

If you don't feel pain while not writing, you haven't got writer's block. You're just a writer who doesn't happen to be writing. But it's in response to that pain – to the terror of being blocked – that writers cling to their favourite equipment and, while alone at their desks, obey private rituals and put their faith in good-luck charms and graven images.

The most determined writers learn to exploit their own terror. In *The Courage to Write* (1975), Ralph Keyes revealed that, after publishing eight books, he finally realized that "a rising tide of anxiety isn't necessarily bad. Nervousness keeps me alert. Fears force me to focus and to work longer hours. Restless nights mean I'm gaining momentum. The end is in sight. Getting there isn't always pleasant."

Nor, for some, possible.

No Writer Wants "Page Fright"

Coleridge, in 1802, happened to be writing letters, journalism, and metaphysical speculation but, he complained, every time he tried to write poetry, which mattered most to him, he "beat up Game of other kind – instead of a covey of poetic Partridges with whirring wings of music . . . up came a Metaphysical bustard, urging its slow, heavy, laborious, earth-skimming flight over dreary and level wastes." He wrote his finest poems in his mid-twenties but, as early as his thirties, his attempting to write at that level filled him with "an indefinite indescribable Terror."

Coleridge was a blazing comet of the Romantic Movement, which introduced writers to new notions about the source of their inspiration. They previously thought their work was deliberate and rational, and that *they* controlled it. To the early Romantics, however, poetry came into being only at the whim of a mysterious, external force that might or might not bestow it on them. "A man cannot say, 'I will compose poetry,'" Shelley explained. No, sir. It came only from "some invisible influence, like an inconstant wind." Thus, there was no point in the writer's picking up his quill pen until the breeze deigned to favour him. This belief fertilized writers' blocks so formidable that only hurricanes could blow them away.

What was also new among the Romantics, Alice W. Flaherty wrote, was "their emphasis on the sublime, the experience of transcendence in the presence of a phenomenon – frequently a natural object – with grandeur too great to be expressed. If the sublime is that which cannot be expressed, painful inarticulateness and writer's block seem inevitable."

A block often arises from the victim's realizing that writing lasting literature is so fiendishly hard to do there's no longer any point in trying. It may loom up when he begins to feel he just hasn't got what it takes to write what he promised himself to write or, when halfway through a novel, she decides that everything she's written is hogwash, and she hasn't the heart to start all over again. Some would-be writers never get around to writing because they can't bear to give any editor a chance to reject their work. Others tremble at the possibility that, if their work does get into print, it will be ridiculed for as long as they live, or longer. "Page fright" can be worse than stage fright.

Freud's explanation of writer's block was, well, Freudian. He believed that "as soon as writing, which entails making a liquid flow out of a tube onto a piece of white paper, assumes the significance of copulation," the writing stopped because it represented "the performance of a forbidden sex act." Hmmm. If a writer suffers a block while writing not with a pen but with a keyboard, one wonders what kind of forbidden sex act the performance represents.

Another Vienna-trained psychoanalyst, Dr. Ludwig Eidelberg, wrote in 1968, "Various unconscious factors may be responsible for [writer's block]. The writer's analysis usually discloses that the creative activity has become connected with infantile repressed wishes (e.g., identification with the preoedipal mother, the wish to have a baby). In addition to oral material, anal and phallic, sexual and aggressive, exhibitionistic and scopophilic [voyeuristic] wishes are responsible for this inhibition." Eidelberg endorsed the theory of his colleague, Otto Fenichel, that "all types of inhibitions may form the basis of a block. In our present day society, working may lead to success and to the consequent fear of reawakening the oedipal fears and threats of having to compete with the father for the love of the mother."

As if that weren't alarming enough, Eidelberg cited the case of a certain "Donald," whose monumental block was caused by the fact that his writing had become an outlet for his unconscious wish to rape: "By writing, he gratified his desire to force his readers to submit to what he wanted to have them read and his pen unconsciously became the penis of the brute who ravishes an unwilling woman." Eidelberg, however, offered no insight into why a woman might suffer writer's block. By writing, did a woman, like Donald, gratify her desire to force her readers to submit to what she wanted them to read and, if so, what was it that her pen unconsciously became?

It got worse. Poor Donald had an unconscious wish not only to rape, but to *be* raped: "Writing symbolized being raped by the publishers who, by paying him, were able to force him to write what they wanted. . . . But eventually what put a stop to his writing was the frustrated wish to rape and be raped. . . . Once a normal function of the body is used for the discharge of infantile wishes, it becomes blocked either by fear or by other paralyzing emotions. These are the punishments inflicted by our conscience, which is not fooled by the ostensibly innocuous conscious meaning of what we are doing."

While explaining writer's block, Eidelberg sounded like Balzac's card player: "As cocksure as if he had a fistful of aces." Was the good doctor a quack? Apparently not. He was editor-in-chief of *Encyclopedia of Psychoanalysis* (1968). To the lay mind, however, his theories about writers have not weathered well.

You're Not Blocked, Just "Re-energizing"

By the 1950s, many Americans dismissed highly prolific writers, to whom writing came easily, as hacks, and expected every good novelist to endure a block or two. A surge in the popularity of psychoanalysis coincided with much self-imposed pressure on writers to achieve the virtually impossible – the Great American Novel – and to write as well as such emerging stars as Mailer, Salinger, Bellow, Capote, Ralph Ellison, and Tennessee Williams. The result? Blocks. Blocks all over the place. Canny psychoanalysts let it be known they were specialists in the arcane (and expensive) practice of writer's-block-removal.

Working before breakfast, the machine-like Anthony Trollope churned out nearly seventy books in the late nineteenth century, and in 1991 the American poet and novelist Jay Parini called Trollope's calmly professional attitude "a kind of unspoken ideal for contemporary British writers like Graham Greene, Anthony Burgess, Iris Murdoch, and A.N. Wilson – all of whom regard productivity as a virtue." According to Parini, however, American writers such as Bellow, Styron, Mailer, Mary McCarthy, and Thomas Pynchon "often harbour long silences, publishing in gigantic, well-publicized spasms. A few of our best writers – J.D. Salinger, Ralph Ellison, Grace Paley and Harold Brodkey – have fashioned whole careers out of the sound of one hand clapping."

British writer Anthony Burgess could not understand the American writer's block, "unless it means that the blocked man isn't forced economically to write (as the English writer, lacking campuses and grants, usually is) and hence can afford the luxury of fearing the critics' pounce on a new work not as good as the last (or first)." In England apparently, the prime motive for authors was still much as it had been when Virginia Woolf's father, man-of-letters Sir Leslie Stephen (1832–1904), said that "the great secret of the literary profession" was that "a clever man can write when he has to write, or starve."

Introducing the American literary and cultural commentator Harold Bloom, *The Paris Review* said that no critic in the English language since Samuel Johnson had been more prolific but, in the interview that followed, Bloom himself confided that, owing to "despair and exhaustion," there were times when he could not write at all. "Long, long periods, sometimes lasting many years," he said. "Sometimes one just has to lie fallow." American poet and essayist Julia Spicher Kasdorf argues, "Quiet periods when the creative juices are re-energizing are just as important as periods of production. . . . Just because there aren't any leaves on the trees doesn't mean the trees are dead or broken."

"There's a time to go to the typewriter," Thurber said. "It's like a dog – the way a dog before it craps wanders around in circles – a piece of earth, an area of grass, circles it for a long time before it squats. It's like that – figuratively circling the typewriter."

No Pity for the Blocked Plumber

If some believe that writer's block is not an affliction but a driver of creativity, others think it's merely an excuse for laziness. "It's so noble to suffer," says science-fiction writer Bruce Holland Rogers. "When you suffer in a very public way, you get some of the glamour of art without all the risk. So some writers dress in black, hang out at the café with their blocked friends, supporting one another's writing identity without writing word one."

Allan Gurganus, a North Carolinian whose fiction has won comparisons with that of Faulkner and Welty, says, "You don't get [writer's block] if you don't believe in it. I've never heard of anyone getting plumber's block, or traffic cop's block." Mark Helprin, another accomplished American novelist, uses a similar analogy: "If an electrician said, 'I have electrician's block. I just can't bend conduit. I can't! I can't! I can't run wires. Help me, please!' he would be committed. . . . I would call writer's block laziness, lack of imagination, inflated expectations, or having-spent-your-entire-advance-in-Rio-de-Janeiro-and-taking-taxis-and-going-to-restaurants-you-can't-afford-before-you-have-written-a-single-word-of-the-book-you-pitched-to-a-cretin-with-an-out-of-control-cash-flow."

Not surprisingly, the writers with the least respect for writer's block tend to be those who've produced the most books. About that happy master of science fiction, Isaac Asimov, a colleague said he "had writer's block once. It was the worst ten minutes of his life." Elmore Leonard, whose published novels numbered forty-four in 2007, said, "I don't believe in writer's block. I don't know what that is. There are just certain little areas that I know I'm going to get through."

"With a play I go straight on until I'm finished," Noel Coward said. "I do it straight on the typewriter. It was five days for *Blithe Spirit*. No, no changes. It was all complete. Maybe a few typographical errors. The quicker I write my plays, the better they are. . . . What I adore is this supreme professionalism. I hate more bitterly than anything an unprofessional job in a profession.

"I'm bored by writers who can only write when it is raining."

Very Bad, Worse Than Bad. It's All Over

Despite such critics, however, blocks have tormented and silenced countless writers, including some of the immortals. While writing *The Adventures of Huckleberry Finn* in 1876, Mark Twain had no trouble until he launched Huck and the runaway slave, Jim, on the Ohio River. He planned to float them northward to freedom for Jim. He could not do it, and *Huckleberry Finn* stayed where it was for eight years. Then, in 1884, he decided to send Huck and Jim down not the Ohio, but the Mississippi. The Ohio meant nothing to Twain, but he'd once been a steamboat pilot on the Mississippi and loved it. The block vanished. Writing four thousand words during some sittings, he finished the book in three months.

Joseph Conrad was a great writer who overcame great blocks. While constantly moaning in letters to friends about his futile staring at blank sheets of paper, he published nineteen novels and scores of novellas and short stories. Even a Mark Helprin would have to concede that Conrad was not lazy.

Yet in 1894, he complained: "I am completely stuck. I have not written a single word in a fortnight. It's all over, I think. I feel like burning what there is. It is very bad! It is worse than bad!"

In 1898: "I sit down for eight hours every day – and the sitting down is all. In the course of that working day of eight hours I write three sentences which I erase before leaving the table in despair. Sometimes it takes all my resolution and power of self-control to refrain from butting my head against the wall. I want to howl and foam at the mouth but I daren't do it for fear of waking the baby and alarming my wife."

In 1911: "Full 3 weeks – no two consecutive ideas, no six consecutive words to be found anywhere in the world. I would prefer a red hot gridiron to that cold blankness."

"I long and long to write, and the words just won't come," Katherine Mansfield confided to her diary. "It's a queer business."

Thurber told a friend, "I have not been able to write a God damn thing for eight months. Which, combined with a cold and gloomy view of man, makes me feel like an empty raspberry basket – frail, stained, and likely to be torn to pieces by a child."

But compared to the block of his colleague, Joseph Mitchell, Thurber's was a passing distraction. Mitchell joined *The New Yorker* in 1938 and for twenty-six years gave its readers a steady stream of beautifully written profiles of New York's most quirky and colourful characters. His prose was so spare and clean that Calvin Trillin, another staff writer at the magazine, called him "The *New Yorker* reporter who set the standard." Starting in 1964, however, Mitchell reported to his office nearly every day until his death thirty-two years later, without submitting a single word for publication.

"Each morning, he stepped out of the elevator with a preoccupied air, nodded wordlessly if you were just coming down the hall, and closed himself in his office," wrote Roger Angell, another *New Yorker* writer, in 1996. "He emerged at lunchtime, always wearing his natty brown fedora (in summer, a straw one) and a tan raincoat; an hour and a half later, he reversed the process, again closing the door. Not much typing was heard from within, and people who called on Joe reported that his desktop was empty of everything but paper and pencils. When the end of the day came, he went home. Sometimes, in the evening elevator, I heard him emit a small sigh, but he never complained, never explained."

No one will ever know what caused Mitchell's block, the most notorious in the history of magazine writing, but Trillin recalled hearing "that he was writing away at a normal pace until some professor called him the greatest living master of the English declarative sentence and stopped him cold."

In a survey in 2003, British readers chose the gloomy Philip Larkin as the best-loved poet of the previous half-century, and in 2008 *The Times* named him number one on its list of Britain's "50 greatest postwar writers," but during the last decade of his life he could bring himself to write scarcely a line of verse. To Kingsley Amis, he wrote, "So we face 1982, sixteen stone six, gargantuantly paunched, helplessly addicted to alcohol, tired of livin' and scared of dyin', world-famous-unable-to-write poet." He died the following year, at sixty-three.

What slams a block into place in the heads of some writers is their merciless self-criticism, their self-contempt for not achieving the perfection they're aiming for. Thus, Kafka bewailed having "to see the pages being covered endlessly with things one hates, that fill one with loathing, or at any rate with dull indifference." He failed to finish any of his three novels.

THE SIXTY-YEAR BLOCK. SURELY, A WORLD'S RECORD

A divorce, a betrayal, a death in the family, or some other emotionally traumatic event can also cause writer's block. In 1935, Isaac Bashevis Singer, at thirty-three, left Poland, where he was a promising writer of novels in Yiddish, to settle in America and sailed not only into New York Harbour but into a writer's block. He eventually published more than thirty novels and collections of short stories and became perhaps the greatest Jewish writer of the twentieth century but during his first seven years in Manhattan he wrote virtually nothing.

"Coming from one country to another, immigrating, is a kind of crisis," he said in 1968. "I had a feeling that my language was lost. My images were not anymore. Things – I saw thousands of objects for which I had no name in Yiddish in Poland. Take such a thing as the subway – we didn't have a subway in Poland. And we didn't have a name for it in Yiddish. Suddenly I had to do with a subway and with a shuttle train and a local, and my feeling was that I lost my language and also my feeling about the things which surrounded me. Then, of course, there was the trouble of making a living and adjusting myself to the new surroundings. All of this worked for a number of years so that I couldn't write."

He wrote in the Yiddish of Poland, but his readers in New York had betrayed him by speaking what David Roskies, an expert on Yiddish literature, has called "a *patois*, a pidgin Yiddish, beneath contempt." Roskies continued, "No self-respecting writer could write the language that is spoken in the streets of New York and Miami Beach. So what is a writer to do? In his own brilliant dialectical way, [Singer] decides that the answer . . . is to renounce the

American present, renounce his readers, renounce the degraded state of Jewish culture in America, and go back to some re-imagined past. To me, that's the root of his greatness from beginning to end."

If arriving in Manhattan silenced Singer, several traumatic memories and experiences ganged up on novelist Henry Roth, also a Jewish immigrant, to cause a gap between the publication of his first and second novels that lasted no fewer than sixty years. His *Call It Sleep* appeared in 1934. He was twenty-eight. His second novel, the four-volume *Mercy of a Rude Stream*, began to appear in 1994. He was eighty-eight. He had spent much of his life as a duck farmer, ditch digger, tool grinder, hospital attendant, substitute high school teacher, and aimless and miserable man. *Call It Sleep* gained critical acclaim in the Dirty Thirties, but few sales. In 1964, however, Roth unexpectedly received a fabulous bonanza. A paperback reprint of the book caused a sensation. Here was a Depression-era masterpiece of Jewish-American literature that had been neglected for three decades. It quickly sold a million copies. The good news, however, did not inspire Roth to rush to his typewriter.

"The reasons for Roth's monumental block, which include but are not limited to Communism, Jewish self-loathing, incest and depression," Jonathan Rosen wrote in 2005, "are ultimately as mysterious as the reasons for his art and are in some ways inseparable from them."

At fifteen Roth began a sexual affair with his twelve-year-old sister, Rose, and at sixteen he was having regular intercourse with her. Rosen met Roth in 1993 and decided that the guilt the elderly novelist still felt about having sex with Rose in the early 1920s "hung over him like a kind of Biblical curse." No incestuous episodes occur in *Call It Sleep*, and one had to wonder about "the agony Roth felt in writing an autobiographical novel that concealed the most traumatic fact of his own autobiography."

It took Roth almost a lifetime of blockage to get around to describing in print what he'd done to his sister. In *A Diving Rock on the Hudson* (1995), the autobiographical second volume of his second novel, the computer of the sinner, now an old man, tells him that "the unspoken and unspeakable must become spoken and speakable, and the taboo broken and ignored." The novel therefore includes the protagonist's beginning an affair with his sister when he's fifteen and she's twelve. The sex scenes leave nothing to the imagination. If this gave Roth the relief of confession, it dumped on Rose – who'd typed out the manuscript of *Call It Sleep* for him sixty-one years earlier and was now eighty-six – a truckload of embarrassment. After *A Diving Rock* came out, she publicly denied the incest had ever occurred in real life, and told *The Jewish Weekly*, "This is not pleasant for me. I'm a very old woman."

THE CURSE OF THE SECOND NOVEL

Novelist and essayist Arthur Koestler, who had lived and worked in half a dozen European countries before he was forty, happened to be in New York in 1951 and complained, "In America the social climate has made the creation of art into an essentially competitive business."

Koestler was almost certainly talking about Norman Mailer when, to prove his point, he added, "I know of a young American writer who once headed the best-seller list, but is now paralyzed and on the verge of a nervous breakdown because of the fear that if he doesn't repeat his success he will be regarded as a passé novelist. And this very excellent young writer is still under thirty. Can you fathom the whole horror of what this implies?"

Mailer was still only twenty-eight. In 1948, the smashing success of his war novel, *The Naked and the Dead*, had turned him into an instant celebrity, but he'd published nothing since. For three years he'd been futilely wrestling with his second novel, *Barbary Shore*. After writing fifty pages, he remembered, "it stopped, just ground down. . . . My novelistic tanks ran out of gas. I dropped it completely." He started to write an entirely different novel, but soon abandoned it. "In desperation (I was full of second-novel panic), I picked up [*Barbary Shore*]," he continued. "And found something there I could go on with. . . . [But] I never knew where the book was going, I had no idea where it was going to move from day to day. I'd wake up and push the typewriter in great dread, in literal terror, wondering when this curious and doubtful inspiration was going to stop. It never quite did. It ground along at the rate of three pages, three difficult pages, a day."

Critics were not kind to *Barbary Shore*. *Time* said *The Naked and the Dead* had "the juice of life," but the only juice in *Barbary Shore* was "embalming fluid." *The New Yorker* sneered at the "monolithic, flawless badness" of Mailer's second book. "If first novels are the golden children," Australian novelist Malcolm Knox said in 2006, "second novels are the little monsters." Mailer, however, kept plugging away until his confidence returned, and, when he died at eighty-four in 2007, he had written more than thirty books of fiction and creative non-fiction.

Another American who fought his way through the "second-novel syndrome" was Jeffrey Eugenides. Critics welcomed his *The Virgin Suicides* (1993) as a "piercing first novel" and a "tour de force." The *Independent* in London called it "wonderfully original" and, uttering precisely the sort of expectation that triggers the second-novel syndrome, added, "It could prove to be the start of an important writing career." Explaining why it took him nine years to write his second novel, the Pulitzer-winning *Middlesex* (2002), Eugenides said, "No one is waiting for you to write your first book. No one cares if you finish it. But after your first, if it goes well, everyone seems to be waiting. You're suddenly considered to be a professional writer, a fiction machine, but you know very well that you're just getting going. You go from having nothing to lose to having everything to lose, and that's what creates the panic."

Eugenides therefore took all the time he needed to learn everything he had to know in order to write his second novel. To regain his "blessed anonymity" and concentrate fully on his work, he settled in Berlin for five years.

Some victims of the second-novel syndrome are not so resilient. It silences them forever. In 1960, the Pulitzer Prize–winning *To Kill a Mockingbird*, by Harper Lee, was an enormous critical and commercial success. The plot spins around a white lawyer's defending a black man against a charge of having raped a white woman in an Alabama village, and the narrator is the lawyer's six-year-old daughter. In 1999, participants in a poll by the American *Library Journal* voted *Mockingbird* "Best Novel of the Century." In 2006, it topped a poll that asked British librarians, "Which book should every adult read before they die?" The Bible finished second.

Having sold thirty million copies in forty languages, *Mockingbird* remained a best-seller. In 2007, President George W. Bush presented to Lee, now eighty-one, America's highest civilian award, the Presidential Medal of Freedom, but since her first novel had gone on sale forty-seven years earlier, she had published nothing. Back in 1964, in the last interview she ever gave, she said that while writing *Mockingbird*, she expected it would meet only "a quick and merciful death at the hands of reviewers," but hoped someone would like it enough to give her a little public encouragement. Trouble was, she said, "I got rather a whole lot, and in some ways this was just about as frightening as the quick, merciful death I'd expected." The final sentence in that interview was "All I want to be is the Jane Austen of south Alabama."

Black novelist Ralph Ellison also won the Presidential Medal of Freedom. President Lyndon B. Johnson gave it to him in 1969. Seventeen years had passed since the publication of Ellison's *The Invisible Man* (1952), which beat out Hemingway's *The Old Man and the Sea* for the National Book Award, and the countless fans of that terrific first novel were wondering where his second one was. Ellison called that *Juneteenth*, and in 1994, forty-two years after critics praised *The Invisible Man* to the skies, he died at eighty with it still unfinished.

Critic Irving Howe in 1952 hailed *The Invisible Man* as "a soaring and exalted record of a Negro's journey through contemporary America in search of success, companionship and, finally, himself. . . . For Ellison has an abundance of that primary talent without which neither craft nor intelligence can save a novelist; he is richly, wildly inventive; his scenes rise and dip with tension, his people bleed, his language stings." Bellow called *The Invisible Man* "a superb book," "a brilliant individual victory," and "an immensely moving novel." *Time* praised it as "a remarkable first novel that gives 38-year-old Ralph Ellison a claim to being the best of U.S. Negro writers. It makes him, for that matter, an unusual writer by any standard."

The Invisible Man shot a powerful spotlight on Ellison, and he strove to keep it there for the rest of his life. He wrote essays, sat on boards and panels, accepted chairs at universities, gave lectures on American culture, harvested a fine crop of honorary degrees, and served as a consultant on such matters as "the role of Negroes in American society." He became what more than one critic called "a grand old man of letters" and found this career not only pleasing and lucrative, but perhaps both easier and less risky to his self-esteem than finishing *Juneteenth*.

While reviewing Arnold Rampersand's biography of Ellison, Hilton Als wrote, "The pain that Ellison must have experienced during his long fallow period should not be underestimated, but one comes away from Rampersand's book feeling that even that anguish was a little engineered: the longer Ellison took to write his second novel, the more serious an author he would appear to be, the less vulnerable to criticism. One feels oppressed by the emotional and intellectual knots in which Ellison bound himself at the end of his life; had he been able to conquer his own caginess and social ambition, he might have produced the work that he and the world were waiting for."

"Whom the Gods wish to destroy," English journalist Cyril Connolly wrote, "they first call promising."

EIGHTEEN

"I'm a Drinker with a Writing Problem"

Countless authors have used tea or coffee to kick-start their creativity or to keep their focus sharp while writing, but Samuel Johnson, who sometimes drank twenty-five cups of tea at one sitting, and Balzac, who downed up to fifty cups of sludgy coffee per night of writing, are literature's all-time champion guzzlers of these beverages. Moreover, no caffeine-hooked writer has ever described the benefits of coffee with more passion and eloquence than Balzac.

"It brutalizes these beautiful stomach linings as a wagon master abuses ponies; the plexus becomes inflamed; sparks shoot all the way up to the brain," he wrote. "From that moment on, everything becomes agitated. Ideas quick-march into motion like battalions of a grand army to its legendary fighting ground, and the battle rages. Memories charge in, bright flags on high; the cavalry of metaphor deploys with a magnificent gallop; the artillery of logic rushes up with clattering wagons and cartridges; on imagination's orders, sharpshooters sight and fire; forms and shapes and characters rear up; the paper is spread with ink – for the nightly labour begins and ends with torrents of this black water, as a battle opens and concludes with black powder."

If Balzac was the only great writer who drank himself to death with coffee, quite a few, some of them also great, seemed bent on drinking themselves to death with hard liquor.

COULD AN ALCOHOLIC WIN THE NOBEL IN LITERATURE? SURE. FIVE DID

Poet, novelist, soldier, raconteur, beekeeper, world traveller, pioneer filmmaker, and, at one time, drinking companion of the most famous writers and artists in Paris, Blaise Cendrars was in Rome in late 1930 when he heard from Sinclair Lewis. The author of *Main Street* (1920), *Babbitt* (1922), *Arrowsmith* (1925), and *Dodsworth* (1929) was bound for Stockholm to pick up the Nobel Prize for Literature, but he'd stopped off in Italy and, Cendrars said, was now "trailing about with a squadron of jolly New York girls who were causing a scandal."

Cendrars knew Hemingway and Henry Miller and, since Lewis urgently wanted to meet him, went to his hotel suite. There, he found the jolly girls. They were drunk and, while making a gigantic cocktail in a soup tureen full of whipped cream, squabbled over how many litres of vermouth to add. After one girl offered Cendrars scissors and dared him to cut her hair, he went looking for Lewis. Water flowed out of the half-open door of the bathroom.

"I went in," Cendrars remembered in 1966. "The bathtub was overflowing and the faucets were wide open. Two feet, dressed in polished dancing pumps, hung out of the tub, and at the bottom a man in a tuxedo was drowning. It was my Sinclair Lewis. I pulled him out of his unfortunate position, and that was how I saved his life so he could take the train the next morning for Stockholm and his prize."

Far-fetched? Perhaps, but when the teetotaller and muckraking novelist Upton Sinclair listed writers he'd known who were alcoholics – they included O. Henry, Stephen Crane, F. Scott Fitzgerald, Sherwood Anderson, and Hart Crane – he said, "Never had anybody gotten so blind drunk as Sinclair Lewis." Of the seven native-born Americans who won Nobel Prizes for literature, Lewis, Faulkner, Hemingway, and Eugene O'Neill were alcoholics, and if Steinbeck was not, he drank so heavily that some thought he was. Only Bellow and Pearl Buck had no drinking problem. (Irish playwright Brendan Behan, a notorious lush, once said, "I'm a drinker with a writing problem.")

Alcoholism landed Faulkner in hospital over and over again. In the mid-thirties, Fitzgerald was hospitalized eight times for alcoholism and was repeatedly jailed on drunkenness charges. Gin hastened his death at forty-four. Hemingway drank as his characters did, and in *The Sun Also Rises* (1926), Jake Barnes and Brett Ashley downed three martinis each before lunch, and five or six bottles of wine with it. "In 1939, Hemingway was ordered to cut down on his drinking," author Ann Waldron wrote. "He tried to hold himself to three Scotches before dinner but he couldn't do it and, in 1940, he began breakfasting on tea and gin and swigging absinthe, whiskey, vodka and wine at various times during the day. He even let his boys drink hard liquor when one of them was only ten."

Hemingway and Fitzgerald "pickled their brains," John Irving said, thereby destroying their talent. Both were twenty-seven when they wrote *The Sun Also Rises* (1926) and *The Great Gatsby* (1925) respectively and, he says, "They should have gotten better; *I've* gotten better. We're not professional athletes; it's reasonable to assume that we'll get better as we mature. . . . Hemingway and Fitzgerald really lived to write; their bodies and their brains betrayed them." Drinking sabotaged the "interrelatedness" that gave good novels their narrative momentum. "Drunks ramble; so do books by drunks."

Recalling the hugely talented young poet Hart Crane at drinking parties in the twenties, Malcolm Cowley wrote, "Gradually he would fall silent, and a little later he disappeared. In lulls that began to interrupt the laughter, now Hart was gone, we would hear a new hubbub through the walls of his room – the phonograph playing a Cuban rumba, the typewriter clacking simultaneously; then the phonograph would run down and the typewriter stop while Hart changed the record, perhaps to a torch song, perhaps to Ravel's 'Bolero.' . . . An hour later . . . he would appear in the kitchen or on the croquet court, his face brick-red, his eyes burning, his already iron-gray hair bristling straight up from his skull. He would be chewing a five-cent cigar which he had forgotten to light. In his hands would be two or three sheets of typewritten manuscript, with words crossed out and new lines scrawled in. 'R - read that,' he would say. 'Isn't that the grreatest poem ever written?'"

At thirty-two, while bound for New York, Crane killed himself by jumping off the ss *Orizaba* into the Gulf of Mexico.

Modern Literature's Biggest Boozers: A Distinguished Roster

Edgar Allan Poe and Herman Melville were alcoholics, and Sinclair Lewis once asked, "Can you name five writers since Poe who did not die of alcoholism?" It was in the twentieth century, however, that the disease became an epidemic among American creative writers. "Recent medico-literary studies now at the bookstore suggest that American writing rests very heavily on alcohol abuse," humorist Russell Baker wrote in 1989. "These books have left little doubt that we owe much of the glory of American literature to a bunch of drunks."

In the public mind, the hard-drinking writer was somehow more romantic and authentic than the non-drinking writer, and the calling and the addiction became so interconnected that novelist James Jones, himself no slouch at downing liquor, said he wanted to make it clear that "boozing does not *have* to go hand in hand with being a writer, as seems to be the concept in America. I therefore solemnly declare to all young men trying to become writers that they do not have to become drunkards first." He was right. Among the American writers who've had no trouble staying away from the bottle are Robert Frost, Henry James, Edith Wharton, Willa Cather, Flannery O'Connor, James Michener, Lillian Hellman, Arthur Miller, Mary McCarthy, Kurt Vonnegut, Joyce Carol Oates, Philip Roth, John Updike, and Tom Wolfe. Among the Canadians are Margaret Atwood, Robertson Davies, Mavis Gallant, Alice Munro, and Michael Ondaatje.

On the other hand, not only the aforementioned Nobel laureates, but Pulitzer Prize–winners James Agee, John Cheever, James Gould Cozzens, William Styron, William Inge, and Tennessee Williams were all alcoholics, and so were Jack London, Ring Lardner, Thomas Wolfe, Dorothy Parker, John O'Hara, Carson McCullers, Truman Capote, and Raymond Carver. Prominent on the long list of alcoholic American poets are the one-time poet laureate of the Library of Congress, Allen Tate (whose wife, novelist Caroline Gordon, was also an alcoholic), Pulitzer Prize–winners Edna St. Vincent Millay, Theodore Roethke, Conrad Aiken, John Berryman, and Robert Lowell, and National Book Award–winner James Dickey.

"American writers drink a lot when they're 'blocked," Anthony Burgess said, "and drunkenness – being a kind of substitute for art – makes the block worse." Among the best British writers, alcoholism did not seem to cut the swath that it did among the Americans, but Philip Larkin, Kingsley Amis, and Paul Scott were alcoholics. Scott wrote the four-volume, novel sequence *The Raj Quartet* (1966–74), upon which the televisions series *The Jewel in the Crown* was based. Malcolm Lowry, Dylan Thomas, and Brendan Behan were spectacular drunkards. In the entire twentieth century, no famous writer on either side of the Atlantic Ocean regularly lashed his family, friends, admirers, and strangers alike with more vicious words than that supremely peevish alcoholic, Evelyn Waugh.

He was infamous for getting outrageously besotted and then using his wicked tongue to enrage or humiliate just about everyone within earshot. One example: when Cecil Beaton, England's most celebrated portrait and fashion photographer, amiably approached him at a cocktail party, Waugh shouted, "Here's someone who can tell us all about buggery!" Drinking heavily every day, Waugh verbally abused his children so cruelly that his son Auberon said his death "lifted a great brooding awareness not only from the house but from the whole of existence." An unusual eulogy, to say the least.

DANGER LURKED IN "THIS SOOTHING, OFTEN SUBLIME AGENT"

Some writers turn to drink because they experience neither the camaraderie nor workday rules of a factory or business office, but fearfully face that daunting blank page all by themselves. And they set their own hours. Unlike a postman, hairdresser, or banker, they can drink liquor or take drugs whenever they want. Or perhaps the reasons for their addictions lie deeper in their psyches. Among people with the kind of mood disorders so many writers endure, alcohol and drugs are particularly tempting. Writers may turn to these substances to escape what Kay Redfield Jamison calls "painful depressions and agitated manic states" and "to provoke or recapture freer, less inhibited states of mind and emotion." American short-story-writer Donald Barthelme "was dependent on alcohol and dependent on work," literary historian Louis Menand wrote in 2008, and, "The combination of melancholia, compulsive typing, and too much alcohol might describe a lot of writers."

Writing does not cause drinking, and drinking does not cause writing, New York journalist and critic Christopher Lehmann-Haupt said in 1988, but "the two activities have a cause in common, be it genetic endowment or whatever connects creativity with insanity."

"We know now that what made Poe write was what made him drink," one of his biographers explained. "Alcohol and literature were the two safety valves of a mind that eventually tore itself apart."

Joseph Tartakovsky, associate editor of the *Claremont Review of Books* in California, has suggested that getting drunk may actually help writers write. "Intoxication, if not the source of literary creation, creates a cerebral aura congenial to it," he writes. "It recasts the glare of life in a softer hue. It soothes anxiety and other stultifiers of reflection. It warms the mind and thaws thoughts frozen in timidity. The fruit of the vine does not give us insight but aids our discovery of it; it can allow you to eavesdrop on yourself."

Early in the careers of many young writers, according to Malcolm Cowley, they discover that getting drunk is part of the creative process, "that it opens up visions. It's a terrible sort of creative device, because three out of four who involve themselves in it become alcoholics. But it does open doors in the beginning."

For much of Styron's life, he drank so late into the night and slept so late into the day that he could write only in the afternoon. Like most alcoholic writers, including Hemingway, he never tried to work and drink at the same time, but he called alcohol "this soothing, often sublime agent, which had contributed greatly to my writing." It had enabled him to "conceive visions that the unaltered, sober brain has no access to" and served as "an invaluable senior partner of my intellect."

It must have been invaluable to James Gould Cozzens, as well. A heavy drinker and prolific novelist, he quit drinking on doctor's orders at sixty-five. During his last decade, he drank nothing alcoholic – and wrote nothing for publication. For him, the link between alcohol and creativity was no myth.

"I've gone on the wagon but my body doesn't believe it," Irwin Shaw said in 1979. "It's waiting for that whiskey to get in there. To get me going. I never drink while I'm working, but after a few glasses I get ideas that would never have occurred to me dead sober. And some of the ideas turn out to be valuable the next day."

Barry Hannah, a novelist and short-story writer from the American South, was sixty-one when asked if drinking had stimulated his creativity. "Gosh, I hate to publish this, because young [would-be writers] will do anything it takes," he replied. "But at first, yes. Teaching . . . was very hard work. I'd come home, put down the babies – and I was trying to be a good father and I think I was – but then that freedom, it was astonishing. My god! Every man or woman who comes home and takes a couple of hits of bourbon on the rocks knows what I mean. Just this total loosening and release from the white noise of the day." Instead of going to bed at night, the totally loosened Hannah banged away on his typewriter, sometimes until four in the morning. His habit became a sickness, however, and the sickness became a nightmare. He kept waking up in hospitals and jails. "So yeah, I learned things that way," he concluded, "but on the other hand I'd have learned things had I been sober."

Kingsley Amis said that approaching his typewriter to do a day's work made him so nervous that one drink of Scotch could be "very useful as a sort of artistic icebreaker." It provided an "artificial infusion of a little bit of confidence, which is necessary in order to begin at all." Thus he made himself sound like E.B. White, a model of temperance, who said, "Before I start to write, I always treat myself to a nice dry martini. Just one, to give me the courage to get started." In truth, however, Amis was anything but temperate. He once confessed to "having the reputation of being one of the great drinkers, if not one of the great drunks, of our time." His son Martin said the only thing Kingsley loved more than a drinking party was adultery and called him "the laureate of the hangover."

While at lunch and dinner, the senior Amis often passed out from drink; a friend recalled, "We used to take more or less a drinks cabinet with us [to movie theatres]. We used to go and sit in the front row . . . and then Kingsley would say, 'What's yours, a gin and tonic?' And out of pockets would come bottles and glasses and then a thermos with some ice in it and somebody would cut up a lemon."

American novelist Robert Stone, whose voice an interviewer described as "branded by Scotch and smoke," used drink not to ease his way into writing but – after he'd done a good day's work and a kind of manic exhilaration flooded his mind – to calm himself. In the basement of a college library at night, after the rest of the building was closed, he finished a section of *Dog Soldiers* (1974), which later won a National Book Award: "I staggered out in tears, talking to myself, and ran into a security guard. It's hard to come down from a high in your work. It's one of the reasons writers drink. The exhilaration of your work turns into the daily depression of the aftermath. But if you heal that with a lot of Scotch you're not fit for duty the next day."

Novelist Stephen King, a recovered alcoholic, has argued that male alcoholic writers employ the Hemingway defence: "As a writer, I am a very sensitive fellow, but I am also a man, and real men don't give in to their sensitivities. Only *sissy*-men do that. Therefore I drink. How else can I face the existential horror of it all and continue to work? Besides, come on, I can handle it. A real man always can."

SOMEHOW, SOME WRITERS DRANK AND WROTE ALL DAY

"It is more or less impossible to write when drunk, which is just as well, given how much and how many writers drink," British novelist John Lanchester wrote in 2003. "Imagine the amount of booze they would put away if it actually helped."

A few have proved, however, that it is more or less possible to write, if not exactly drunk, while continually drinking. Robert Stone said, "Paul Scott, who wrote *The Raj Quartet*, according to his biographer, used to drink all day. . . . He seems to somehow have been able to sit there and drink and write. I can't do it. I just can't."

Faulkner could. "I usually write at night," he said. "I always keep my whiskey within reach." He was probably sober when he did his extensive revisions, but it was while drinking that he wrote his finest novels. By the time the sickly Carson McCullers was twenty-three, she had already published *The Heart Is a Lonely Hunter* (1940) and, while working, drank what she called her "sonny boy" mixture. This was sherry and hot tea, with which she refilled her Thermos several times a day. In the evening she switched to cocktails. Between 1941 and 1951, she nevertheless completed *Reflections in a Golden Eye, The Member of the Wedding, The Ballad of the Sad Café*, and stories for *The New Yorker, Mademoiselle*, and *Harper's Bazaar*.

A biographer of F. Scott Fitzgerald wrote, "He often composed in the evenings, clouded by the smoke of Chesterfields and propelled (according to whether or not he was drinking) by astonishing quantities of gin or Coca-Cola." Fitzgerald's daughter Scottie remembered him "sitting at his desk in his bathrobe and slippers, writing, or rereading Keats or Shelley – although there was often a faint aroma of gin in the air to dispel too romantic a picture." Tennessee Williams based the last play he wrote, *Clothes for a Summer Hotel* (1980), on the lives of F. Scott and Zelda Fitzgerald and, although it bombed on Broadway, he kept right on writing and drinking. In 1981, at seventy, he told an interviewer he habitually rose before dawn in Key West and reported to his studio, where "I usually have some wine. And then I carefully go over what I wrote the day before. You see, baby, after a glass of wine or two I'm inclined to extravagance. I'm inclined to excesses because I drink while I'm writing, so I'll blue-pencil a lot the next day."

Williams never again wrote anything publishable, but in 1966, another playwright, the English jack-of-all-theatrical-trades Harold Pinter, drank beer and Scotch throughout his working day; for four decades to come, he wrote successful dramas and screenplays.

When a man from *The Paris Review* told Hunter S. Thompson, inventor of the wildly personal gonzo style of journalism and champion of psychedelics, that "almost without exception writers we've interviewed over the years admit they cannot write under the influence of booze or drugs," Thompson snapped, "They lie. Or maybe you've been interviewing a very narrow spectrum of writers. It's like saying, 'Almost without exception women we've interviewed over the years swear that they never indulge in sodomy' – without saying that you did all your interviews in a nunnery. Did you interview Coleridge? Did you interview Poe? Or Scott Fitzgerald? . . . Did Faulkner tell you that what he was drinking all the time was really iced tea, not whiskey? Please. Who the fuck do you think wrote the Book of Revelations? A bunch of stone-sober clerics?"

NINETEEN

The Wrong Stuff

John Cheever said his short stories were about "a long-lost world when the city of New York was still filled with a river light, when you heard Benny Goodman quartets from a radio in the corner stationery store, and when almost everybody wore a hat. Here is the last of that generation of chain-smokers who woke the world in the morning with their coughing. . . ." Among the writers of his day, the chain-smokers must have outnumbered even the boozers. A cigarette seemed to belong in every novelist's mouth as surely as it belonged in Humphrey Bogart's.

"After I get up, it takes me an hour and a half of fiddling around before I can get up the courage and nerve to go to work," James Jones said. "I smoke half a pack of cigarettes, drink six or seven cups of coffee, read over what I wrote the day before. Finally, there's no further excuse. I go to the typewriter." He called this routine "pretty normal," as though half the writers in the world could not start working until they'd smoked a dozen cigarettes, and he may well have been right.

Smoking was so widely seen as an attractive habit that, in the 1942 movie *Now Voyager*, Paul Henreid and Bette Davis gaze adoringly into each other's eyes as he places two cigarettes between his lips, lights both, and hands one to her. Non-smokers were squares, dullards, and Sunday-school teachers. But if tens of millions of cigarette lovers saw their addiction as fashionable and alluring to members of the opposite sex, writers had further reasons for sucking tobacco smoke into their lungs.

Nicotine rewards the brain's pleasure system with a flood of dopamine, a hormone and neurotransmitter that not only makes the smoker say to himself, "Aaaahh, hit me again," but also starts an adrenalin rush, relieves anxiety and depression, weakens inhibitions, sharpens focus, and strengthens creative drive. In *Cigarettes Are Sublime* (1994), Richard Klein calls the cigarette the "wand of dreams" and insists that "each puff is like total immersion: it baptizes the celebrant with the little flash of renewed sensation, an instantaneous, fleeting body image of the unified *Moi*." What more could a block-wary writer ask for?

Long after the wands lost their fashionableness and began to smell less glamorous than cancerous, they remained so addictive that some writers still could not work without inhaling them night and day. Among the more shameless was Anthony Bourdain, a former New York chef, sometimes novelist, and writer of the outrageous, and outrageously entertaining, exposé of the least appetizing practices of the most pricey restaurants, *Kitchen Confidential* (2001). Against the toughest odds, Bourdain conquered his heroin and cocaine habits but, he said in 2007, "other than a writing implement and paper, the single item essential to my writing career – and indispensable to the very task of setting words to paper – is a pack of cigarettes. No smokes? No writing. However unhealthy or unlovely that equation – there it is. I can't do without them."

DOSTOEVSKY, CONRAD, ORWELL, SIMENON –
CHAIN-SMOKERS, ALL

Stephen Spender remembered Walter De la Mare saying, "If there's a leak of attention when you are trying to concentrate, the leak can be stifled by smoking a cigarette." Jack London must have been prone to such leaks. He smoked sixty Russian cigarettes per day and smelled like burning tarpaper. Erskine Caldwell was a cigarette addict almost his entire life, but conquered his habit in his early seventies. After a doctor at the Mayo Clinic told him he had to quit if he wanted to go on living, he remembered, "I crossed the street to a bar and ordered a drink. I had two cigarettes left in a pack, and I put both in my mouth and smoked them at the same time. I haven't had one since." He lived until he was eighty-four.

In 2005, Kurt Vonnegut, Jr., said he'd been chain-smoking Pall Malls ever since he was twelve and threatened to sue their manufacturers "for a billion bucks" because their advertising was false. He felt it was past time he was dead, "and for many years now, right on the package, [they] have promised to kill me. But I am now eighty-two. Thanks a lot, you dirty rats. The last thing I ever wanted was to be alive when the three most powerful people on the whole planet would be named Bush, Dick and Colon." Vonnegut died two years later.

George Sand wore men's suits and smoked cigars, and the mannish, 200-pound Imagist poet Amy Lowell alarmed her eminent Massachusetts family by chain-smoking stogies while she wrote. She claimed that, since they lasted longer than cigarettes, they were not as distracting. Fearing World War I would cut off her supply, she ordered ten thousand of her favourite brand from the Philippines. Simenon owned three hundred pipes, most of them Dunhills, and on the night before he began a novel he selected several and lined them up on his desk beside a supply of his special Coupe Maigret tobacco. At dawn, he started to write and smoke at the same feverish pace.

Dostoevsky suffered from epilepsy, asthma, and emphysema and, according to literary scholar Gary Adelman, what finished him off was "chain-smoking hand-rolled, thickly packed, Russian cigarettes." Lung diseases tormented Orwell all his life but, like Dostoevsky, he enjoyed rolling his own cigarettes and smoking them incessantly. Tuberculosis killed him at forty-six. Conrad smoked so much his fingers were brown and, after he spent twenty-one consecutive hours penning the ending of Lord Jim, he told John Galsworthy that his cigarette butts had grown into "a mound similar to a cairn over a dead hero."

"Any smoker will sympathize when I say that after your first cup of coffee you have a sobbing, pleading feeling in the lungs as they cry out for the first cigarette of the day," Martin Amis said, "and my desire to write is rather like that. It's rather physical." He suspected that if he ever quit smoking, he'd start to write sentences like "It was bitterly cold" and "It was bakingly hot."

Despite vowing to quit thousands of times, Italian novelist Italo Svevo smoked cigarettes throughout his adult life and, in his last years, puffed away on thirty or forty a day. On his deathbed, he saw his nephew, also his doctor, light up a cigarette. He asked for one, but the doctor refused him. Svevo is said to have sighed, "That really would have been the last cigarette."

EVERYBODY'S FAVOURITE CURE-ALL: OPIUM JUICE

In 1797, Samuel Coleridge, at twenty-five, wrote "Kubla Khan." He never finished it but with its not-of-this-world imagery – dancing rocks, a lifeless ocean, caverns measureless to man, the milk of Paradise, a sunny pleasure dome with caves of ice – it was one of the strangest and finest poems he ever wrote. He said he composed it during an opium-induced sleep, and that the moment he awoke, he grabbed a quill to write it out. "A person" from the nearby village of Porlock interrupted him, however, and by the time he returned to his desk, he'd forgotten the rest of the poem.

Laudanum was a mixture of spices, alcohol, and opium and, from the late 1700s onward, a wildly popular medicine. It was a soporific and painkiller. Doctors prescribed it for everything from head colds to meningitis, from flu to cardiac disease, and from backache to yellow fever, but variations of this "tincture of opium" were also available over the counter. Like everyone else, writers drank laudanum when they were sick, but also because it gave them magical visions.

In an obituary in 2006 of Alethea Hayter, a British authority on the link between narcotics and literary creation, the *Telegraph* said laudanum was "particularly attractive to writers such as Coleridge, Keats and De Quincey because it seemed to provide a means whereby the dreamer could control his dreams, switching them on and off and having access to the marvellous at will." While Keats, Byron, Shelley, Dickens, Longfellow, Lewis Carroll, and Elizabeth Barrett Browning all sought access to the marvellous with laudanum, none became a hopeless addict like Coleridge or Thomas De Quincey.

In *Confessions of an English Opium Eater* (1822), De Quincey, somewhat gloatingly, offered readers a catalogue of the horrors that descended on him after taking laudanum:

I was stared at, hooted at, grinned at, chattered at, by monkeys, by paroquets, by cockatoos. I ran into pagodas: and was fixed for centuries, at the summit, or in secret rooms; I was the idol; I was the priest, I was worshiped; I was sacrificed. I fled from the wrath of Brama through all the forests of Asia: Vishnu hated me; Seeva laid wait for me. I came suddenly upon Isis and Osiris: I had done a deed, they said, which the ibis and the crocodile trembled at. I was buried, for a thousand years. In stone coffins, with mummies and sphinxes, in narrow chambers at the heart of eternal pyramids. I was kissed, with cancerous kisses, by crocodiles; and laid, confounded with all unutterable slimy things, amongst reeds and Nilotic mud. . . . The cursed crocodile became to me the object of more horror than almost all the rest. I was compelled to live with him; and (as was always the case, almost, in my dreams) for centuries. I escaped sometimes and found myself in Chinese houses with cane tables, etc. All the feet of the tables, sofas, etc. soon became instinct with life: the abominable head of the crocodile, and his leering eyes, looked out at me, multiplied into a thousand repetitions; and I stood loathing and fascinated.

"Wow! Yuck! Or at least that's how we're supposed to react," British novelist John Lanchester wrote in 2003. "Like a freak-show barker, De Quincey stresses that we are sure to be appalled by the sights we are about to witness. The *Confessions* dwells on the horrors of opium in a way that seems close to boasting. Its author has gone places, seen things we wouldn't dare to; so the book pretends to be a warning, while also acting as something of an Advertisement for Myself."

Since Sir Walter Scott was too ill in 1819 to write *The Bride of Lammermoor* with pen and paper, he dictated it to amanuenses from his bed and, at the same time, fended off his agonizing stomach cramps with hefty doses of laudanum. When he read the finished novel, he could not recollect any of its scenes, characters, conversations, or incidents. Alethea Hayter called this "one of the best attested examples of an opium interlude in the work of a non-addicted writer." While Wilkie Collins was composing *The Moonstone* (1868), he treated his attacks of gout with laudanum. Screaming with pain from time to time, he dictated much of his novel. Like Scott, he did not recognize the finished work as his own. Unlike Scott, he became an addict who suffered terrifying hallucinations. In one, phantoms followed him upstairs to his bed where a green woman with tusks awaited him. Over the years, he built up such tolerance to laudanum that, when he died, an obituary said he'd been drinking more of it per day "than would have sufficed to kill a ship's crew or company of soldiers."

Robert Louis Stevenson took hashish and opium. Scholars long believed he was on cocaine when he wrote *The Strange Case of Dr. Jekyll and Mr. Hyde* (1886), but in 2005 evidence surfaced that he was under the influence of a hallucinogenic drug similar to LSD. In the novella, the kindly scientist Dr. Jekyll invents a potion that separates the good and evil within him. It purifies him, but also transforms him into the unspeakably evil Hyde. At first, Jekyll can turn himself back into a decent fellow without much trouble, but the monstrous Hyde grows ever more dominant in him and clubs an old man to death. Before the police can arrest him, Jekyll-Hyde commits suicide.

Stevenson, who suffered from tuberculosis, wrote his 26,059-word story at furious speed in six days. Around that time, a doctor was trying to stop the bleeding in his lungs by injecting him with a derivative of the hallucinogenic fungus ergot. In a letter to a friend, Stevenson's wife, Fanny, mentioned "Louis's mad behaviour." He was enduring spasms and hallucinations and, she continued, "I think it must be the ergotine that affects his brain at such time."

"*Dr. Jekyll and Mr. Hyde* is about drug-taking and the power of drugs, which overtake his body completely, and drive Dr. Jekyll in a way that is really completely alien to him," said British medical scientist Robert Winston. "Maybe that's what Stevenson is feeling with the use of the drugs he's taking, particularly ergotine. Perhaps he becomes a Mr. Hyde himself."

POT, SPEED, HEROIN, COCAINE, LSD, AND ALL THAT

While writing an essay on the imagination in 1935, Jean-Paul Sartre decided he did not know enough about hallucinations and dreams.

He therefore arranged for a hospital in Paris to inject him with mescaline. Made from peyote cactus, mescaline radically alters the consciousness of its users and rewards some with visions that are pleasant, illuminating, or even ecstatic. Sartre was not so lucky. As he lay under observation in a dark room at the hospital, the hallucinations that flooded his mind were grotesque. His umbrella turned into a vulture, and a clock into an owl. Crabs and slimy polyps swarmed about in the corners of his eyes. For weeks after that, nothing seemed to interest him, and he struck his friends as half-dead. "Finally, he admitted that he was fighting off serious depression," biographer Hazel Rowley wrote. "He still had freakish visions. Houses had leering faces. Lobsters trotted along behind him."

All through the twentieth century, writers who wanted to mess with their brains had their choice of not only hallucinogens and such traditional substances as cocaine (a stimulant), hashish and heroin (narcotics), and good, old opium (soother, painkiller, narcotic), but a vastly wider range of mind-altering powders, pills, potions, and injections than ever before.

If amphetamines feel to writers like a long and stimulating adrenalin rush that allows them to work the way marathoners run, barbiturates bring them back down, calm them, and make them sleepy. Cannabis intoxicates them and gives them hallucinations. Lysergic acid (LSD), like mescaline, is hallucinogenic, but its natural source is not a cactus but ergot. The amphetamine-based ecstasy, which came into vogue in the 1970s, is a powerful stimulant that can make its users both euphoric and hallucinated. In addition to these and other illegal drugs, doctors around the world every day prescribe a Niagara of antidepressants and tranquillizers like Prozac and Valium.

"There is no question that the modern era has been a heroic period for the invention and ingestion of pharmaceuticals," John Lanchester wrote. "And writers have taken all these drugs, often in heroic quantities. So where are the literary results? . . . Where are the bodies of work that have come to us as a result of this explosive expansion of the pharmacopeia, this unprecedented transformation of possibilities for tinkering with the mind's chemistry?"

Most writers who take drugs do so not to improve their work, but simply to unwind or feel euphoric during their spare time, and that's one reason that their habit has given us few books of even the slightest literary merit. Another is that, as a rule, they can no more write well on drugs than they can on booze.

While Sartre was writing his 750-page *The Critique of Dialectical Reason* (1960) he was gobbling amphetamines and, to conquer the sleeplessness they caused, also taking barbiturates. Much of *The Critique*, like other works that he wrote as a speed freak, was a jungle of ludicrous incomprehensibility that not even his fellow philosophers could penetrate. In 1963–1964, Philip K. Dick, dosing heavily on amphetamines, wrote no fewer than eleven science-fiction novels but, although his fans regard him as a genius, others see little literary value in his work. *The Power and the Glory* (1940), however, which Graham Greene wrote while downing Benzedrine, struck Lanchester as "that superb novel," whose "paranoid and menacing atmosphere" surely owed something "to Greene's pill-chugging."

W.H. Auden may have been the only great writer who systematically used speed to energize himself for work. Every morning during the twenty years in which he wrote his best poems, he took Benzedrine, and then, when he wanted to sleep, the barbiturate Seconal. He believed that Benzedrine, like alcohol, coffee, and tobacco, was one of "a few labour-saving devices" that, over centuries, had "been introduced into the mental kitchen." He warned, however, that "these are very crude, constantly breaking down, and liable to injure the cook."

One of the many cooks whom drugs injured was William S. Burroughs, the famous junky whose best-known novel was *Naked*

Lunch (1959). Just as he indulged in almost every kind of sexual practice imaginable (with men, women, and children), he took virtually every kind of drug he could get his shaky hands on. None, however, enslaved him more than heroin, and it was to heroin that *Naked Lunch*'s protagonist was addicted. *Midwest Book Review* pronounced the novel "a classic of modern literature . . . the unnerving tale of a narcotic addict's monumental descent into hell." *Newsweek* called it "a masterpiece . . . a brutal, terrifying and savagely funny book that swings between uncontrolled hallucination and fierce, exact satire." Dame Edith Sitwell spoke for many, however, when she dismissed it as "psychopathological filth."

Burroughs spent from 1954 to 1958 mostly in Tangier, where drugs and male prostitutes were as easy to buy as cigarettes. It was here that he also wrote the fragments that Allen Ginsberg and Jack Kerouac helped turn into *Naked Lunch*. To intensify his inspiration, he took both marijuana and a German-made derivative of codeine called Eukodol. "Trust the Germans," he wrote, "to concoct some really evil shit." Eukodol was six times stronger than codeine, and the euphoria it delivered "hits like speedball."

In the semi-autobiographical *Naked Lunch*, Burroughs wrote, "Shooting Eukodol every two hours. I have a place where I can slip my needle right into a vein, it stays open like a red festering mouth, swollen and obscene, gathers a slow drop of blood and pus after the shot." Burroughs had De Quincey's flair for nightmarish imagery. In his novel *Junky* (1953), the narrator says, "Doolie, sick, was an unnerving sight. The envelope of personality was gone, dissolved by his junk-hungry cells. Viscera and cells, galvanized into a loathsome insect-like activity, seemed on the point of breaking through the surfaces. His face was blurred, unrecognizable, at the same time shrunken and tumescent."

De Quincey said he wrote *Confessions* after he'd kicked his habit for good but, when he died at seventy-four, he was still hooked on laudanum. More than once, Burroughs, too, claimed he'd conquered his addiction. "Now," he said in 1965, "heroin is no temptation for me." Amazingly he did not die until he was eighty-three but, when he did, he was taking methadone as treatment for his heroin addiction. As he himself had said during a lucid moment, "Once a junky, always a junky."

CALLING DR. FEELGOOD

"By the late 1930s, German refugee Max Jacobson, M.D., had established a general practice on the Upper East Side catering to writers, musicians and entertainers who nicknamed him 'Miracle Max' or 'Dr. Feelgood' for the 'vitamin injection' treatment that made them happy and gave them seemingly limitless energy," William Bryk told readers of the *New York Sun* in 2005. "Jacobson's panacea was 30 to 50 milligrams of amphetamines – the mood-elevating neural energizers also known as speed – mixed with multivitamins, steroids, enzymes, hormones, and solubilized placenta, bone marrow and animal organ cells."

Before President Kennedy's debates with Nixon, his major state addresses, and his summit conference with Khrushchev, Dr. Feelgood obligingly shot him up. By May 1962, Jacobson had "treated" his most famous patient no fewer than thirty-four times, but, when Robert Kennedy urged his brother to stop taking the injections, the president said, "I don't care if it's horse piss. It works." Truman Capote agreed. Jacobson, he said, gave him "instant euphoria. You feel like Superman. You're flying. Ideas come at the speed of light. You go seventy-two hours straight without so much as a coffee break."

Deeply depressed, Tennessee Williams turned to Jacobson, and in the late sixties, the doctor mailed him disposable needles and vials full of his concoction. Williams found it "marvelously stimulating to me as a writer," but nothing he created then has passed the test of time. After three years, he suffered what he called "my collapse," and blamed it not on the shots but on his continuing to drink while taking them.

Williams had "a bad heart," but during visits to Jacobson's clinic, the doctor "never listened to my heart. Never took my pulse. Never took my blood pressure. He would just look at me. He was really sort of an alchemist. He would look at me for a long time. He had all these little vials in front of him. He'd take a drop from one, and a drop from another, and then look at me again, and take another drop or two. . . . And after I had a shot, I'd get into a taxi and my heart would begin to pound, and I'd immediately have to have a drink or I wouldn't be able to get home. I'd have died in the cab otherwise."

Looking back, one wonders why it took until 1975 for New York State to revoke the licence of Miracle Max, and why so many rich and talented people lined up to pay him to endanger their lives. Top fashion and magazine photographer Mark Shaw was a Jacobson patient and, after he expired at forty-seven, New York's medical examiner said he died of "acute and chronic intravenous amphetamine poisoning."

TUNE IN, TURN ON, AND PLUMMET OUT

In 1955, Aldous Huxley took LSD for the first time and, he said, it gave him "the direct, total awareness, from the inside, so to say, of Love as the primary and fundamental cosmic fact." When Auden tried LSD, the insight he gained was less divine. "Nothing much happened," he said, "but I did get the distinct impression that some birds were trying to communicate with me." Perhaps this only confirmed his opinion that "there's an enormous variation in the way people respond to lysergic acid."

Huxley was English literature's pre-eminent pioneer in the self-directed use of psychedelic drugs, but he did not take them to help him write novels. "The lysergic-acid experience is a revelation of something outside of time and the social order," he explained. "To write fiction, one needs a whole series of inspirations about people in an actual environment, and then a whole lot of hard work on the basis of those inspirations."

As early as 1960, however, Huxley told an interviewer that any poet who took LSD "would certainly get an extraordinary view of life, which he wouldn't have had in any other way, and this might help him a great deal." Not while taking LSD, but *after* taking it, "people would see the universe around them in a very different way and would be inspired, possibly, to write something about it." For some, the experience was liberating. "It shows that the world one habitually lives in is merely the creation of this conventional, closely conditioned being which one is, and that there are quite other kinds of worlds outside. It's a very salutary thing to realize that the rather dull universe in which most of us spend most of our time is not the only universe there is. I think it's healthy that people should have this experience."

While Huxley was being interviewed, Timothy Leary was preparing to visit Mexico to eat "magic mushrooms." He loved them. Later that year, with the approval of David McClelland, director of the Center for Personality Research at Harvard, Leary set up the Harvard Psychedelic Project. He was not yet notorious as the champion of LSD and coiner of "Turn on, tune in, and drop out" but, having admired *The Doors of Perception* (1954), in which Huxley described how mescaline had affected him, he was delighted to meet the novelist. Over lunch at the Harvard Club in late 1960 they discussed what psychedelic drugs might do for society. Huxley believed that if a way could be found to "turn on" world leaders, the result would be peace everlasting.

"The vision was appealing to Leary," Louis Menand wrote. "It was, after all, simply psychiatric work on a global scale, and administered not to convicts and juvenile delinquents but to the political, social, and artistic elites – much more fun."

Huxley did not live long enough to help Leary have fun. On the morning of December 22, 1963, the day President Kennedy was assassinated, he was dying. Unable to speak, he asked his wife in a note to inject him with enough LSD to finish him off. She did. He died peacefully at 5:20 p.m. "The person Leary eventually teamed up with in the business of spreading acid illumination . . . was Ginsberg," Menand said, "a man who took pride in knowing the address and phone number of everyone who mattered in the cultural world."

Leary descended into a life in which he betrayed some of those closest to him and some of them betrayed him, a life of law-breaking, jail terms, a jail break, a witness-protection program, and short-lived friendships of convenience with the likes of Eldridge Cleaver of the Black Panthers. Ginsberg, however, who took bar-biturates, marijuana, and several hallucinogens, became the prophet of "flower power" and America's most celebrated poet.

"Drugs were obviously a technique for experimenting with consciousness, to get different areas and different levels and dif-ferent similarities and different reverberations of the same vision," Ginsberg said in 1965. "Marijuana has some of it in it. That awe, that cosmic awe that you sometimes get on pot." A year later, he wrote that marijuana enabled him to see "anew many of nature's panoramas & landscapes that I'd stared at blindly without even noticing before; thru the use of marijuana, awe and detail were made conscious."

Ginsberg took lysergic acid; peyote and mescaline; psilocybin (derived from mushrooms); and ayahuasca (from a vine in the Amazon rain forest). By 1965, however, hallucinogens were giving him such hideous visions he swore off all of them. He'd been seeing "great scaly dragons in outer space. They're winding slowly and eating their own tails. Sometimes my skin and all the room seem sparkling with scales, and it's all made out of serpent stuff. And as if the whole illusion of life were made of reptile dream. . . .

I was getting in a real terrible situation. It finally would get so if I'd take the drugs I'd start vomiting."

A year later, however, he took small doses of LSD in "a secluded tree and ocean cliff haven at Big Sur" and had a fine time. "No monster vibration, no snake universe hallucinations. Many tiny jeweled, violet flowers along the path of a living brook that looked like Blake's illustration for a canal in grassy Eden: huge Pacific watery shore, Orlovsky dancing naked like Shiva long-haired before giant green waves, titanic cliffs that Wordsworth mentioned in his own Sublime, great yellow sun veiled with mist hanging over the planet's oceanic horizon."

Ginsberg, whose *The Fall of America: Poems of These States, 1965–1971* won a National Book Award in 1974, took a strong interest in yogic practices and Buddhism as he grew older and gave up drugs for good.

COCAINE-INSPIRED WRITING EQUALS "BURBLY BULLSHIT"

Asked if taking acid had influenced him as a novelist, Canadian writer Matt Cohen, whose *Elizabeth and After* won the Governor General's Award for fiction in 1999, said, "It's undoubtedly true that I have been. I think drugs definitely influence my view of reality." He wrote his early novels and short stories while taking drugs, but did not think the doses gave him any ideas he would not have had otherwise. "It's just that the hesitation between thinking something and writing it down disappeared."

Drugs also unblocked American poet Robert Creeley. For almost a year, his marriage had been rocky, and "a stale sense of effort" and "confusions of feeling older" had tormented him. A logjam clogged his mind. And how did he think hallucinatory drugs affected the creative process? "Terrific!" he replied. "LSD just wiped that out – and fears and tentativeness and senses of getting lost or of being endlessly separated from the world, all that just went. . . . The thing is, it's *information* – extraordinary and deeply *relieving* information. Just as if one were to hear that the war was over, that some imminent peril and/or bitter waste of time had been *stopped*. . . . It's a vision of life, *all* life."

Poet Charles Wright drank whiskey, smoked pot, and tried peyote because writing was work, and it was fun he wanted. He "tooted some cocaine after supper one night" in Laguna, California, reported to the writing shack in his back yard, and wrote a perfect poem in ten or fifteen minutes. "I was amazed," he said. "Total concentration, total focus and magnification. I was even more stunned the next day when I realized I didn't have to change a thing. I published it just the way I wrote it that night. It scared the hell out of me and I never tried it again. Ever. I realized that if I did it a second time – or so I thought at the time – I'd have to use coke every time I tried to write."

Cocaine, however, bestowed no such favour on most of the writers who took it. The trouble is, said novelist and Hollywood screenwriter Richard Price, cocaine merely makes you think you're being creative. Looking at what you wrote yesterday, you realize it's "burbly bullshit," and "you start to panic because now you're *really* behind your deadline . . . and you better get cracking, but you're too depleted, physically and mentally, and therefore what you realize is, in order to jump-start yourself, maybe just a wee hair of the dog would be in order, so you go out and score again."

American poet Conrad Aiken, friend of T.S. Eliot and mentor to Malcolm Lowry, recalled his experiments with hashish and peyote as "fascinating, yes, but no good." Like alcohol, such drugs were "an *escape* from reality, a cheat, a momentary substitution, and in the end a destruction of it. With luck, someone might have a frag-mentary 'Kubla Khan' vision. But with no meaning. And with the steady destruction of the observing and remembering mind."

During a time in which Burroughs thought he'd kicked his habit forever, he described hallucinogens like LSD as extremely dangerous. "They can produce overwhelming anxiety states," he said. "I've seen people trying to throw themselves out of windows; whereas the heroin addict is mainly interested in staring at his big toe." He also denounced "the whole range of sedative drugs," including alcohol, barbiturates, tranquillizers, and morphine and all its derivatives. They were simply pain-killers. They decreased "awareness of inner processes, thoughts and feelings" and were therefore "absolutely contraindicated for creative work."

Perhaps no one better understood the price a writer paid for taking too many drugs. "There is a sadness in reading [Burroughs]," Mailer wrote, "for one gets intimations of a mind which might have come within distance of Joyce, except that a catastrophe has been visited on it, a blow by a sledgehammer, a junkie's needle which left the crystalline brilliance crashed into bits."

TWENTY

Walking the Walk,
and Other Steps to Creation

D uring the 1770s, a short, pompous bachelor, whom Samuel Johnson's biographer James Boswell called "an ugly, affected, disgusting fellow," spent much time walking alone in the garden at his house on Bentinck Street in London. Roughly 160 years later, Virginia Woolf described this same solitary walker as "ridiculous – prodigiously fat, enormously top-heavy, precariously balanced upon little feet upon which he spun round with astonishing alacrity." He was Edward Gibbon and, as he spun around among his flowers and shrubs, he wrote *The History of the Decline and Fall of the Roman Empire*, which would run to six volumes.

"Gibbon composed his work in his head, as he took turns about his large and peaceful garden," Frank Conway, a bibliographer at the University of Chicago, wrote in 2007. "When he had worked and reworked a paragraph to his satisfaction, perfecting every phrase, he would come in to his desk and transcribe it."

Thus it was while walking that Gibbon not only organized in his brain the stupendous hoard of information that he'd gathered from ancient documents, but arranged it in one and a half million words of prose that still strikes readers as beautiful and magisterial.

"In accuracy, thoroughness, lucidity and comprehensive grasp of a vast subject, the 'History' is unsurpassable," Oxford's *Dictionary of National Biography* said in 1921. "It is the one English history which may be regarded as definitive. . . . The book is artistically imposing as well as historically unimpeachable as a vast panorama of a great period."

However Gibbon's appearance struck Woolf, she saw nothing ridiculous in his *Decline and Fall*. Reading it, she wrote in 1937, was like being "mounted on a celestial rocking-horse." The toy becomes a "winged steed," and then "we are sweeping in wide circles through the air and below us Europe unfolds; the ages pass; a miracle has taken place."

While Wordsworth Walked, "Consummate Happiness" Was His

When Gibbon died in 1794, William Wordsworth, at twenty-four, was a published poet. He would become the most celebrated walking poet in the history of English literature. Wordsworth, however, did not walk in circles within an urban garden, or out to some little shop around the corner. Walking mostly in the Lake District of northwestern England, he tramped among wild forests, hulking peaks, lonely valleys, rattling brooks, grassy hills, sheep farms, and mirror-calm lakes. He hiked in sunshine and shadow, on ice, mud, gravel, and wildflowers, and through downpours, blizzards, and blossom-fragrant breezes. He could walk thirty miles on a good day. In December 1799, he wrote, he and his sister Dorothy hiked ten miles – on mountain roads and in "driving snow showers" – in two hours and fifteen minutes. That's faster than power walkers moved on flat, comfortable city streets in 2009. Wordsworth lived to be eighty, having walked a distance that Thomas De Quincey figured was 180,000 miles (290,000 kilometres), the equivalent of more than seven times around the world.

With respect to how he felt while walking, Wordsworth was a
spiritual descendant of the father of Romanticism, Jean-Jacques
Rousseau. In his *Confessions* (1882), Rousseau wrote, "Never did I
exist so completely, never live so thoroughly, never was so much
myself . . . as in those journeys made on foot. Walking animates
and enlivens my spirits; I can hardly think when in a state of inac-
tivity; my body must be exercised to make my judgment active."
Walking freed his soul, emboldened his thoughts, and threw him
into "the immensity of beings." He felt "an indescribable ecstacy
and delirium in melting, as it were, into the system of beings, in
identifying myself with the whole of nature."

Until the arrival of Romanticism in English literature, walking
in Britain was just walking. It was how those who could not afford
horses got from one place to another on land. Nobody took walks
just to view scenery. For Wordsworth, however, long walks in the
country put him in the mood to write poems, aroused memories
that stimulated his muse, and offered him a stream of images:
withered briars, tremulous cliffs, a dark sycamore, a sounding
cataract, a whole field of golden daffodils. He, too, identified
himself with all of nature. In "Lines Composed a Few Miles Above
Tintern Abbey," he called himself "a lover of the meadows and the
woods, and mountains." He wrote all 159 lines of "Tintern Abbey"
in his head, on a single day in 1798, while walking with Dorothy
from Wales to Bristol. He claimed, "Not a line of it was altered and
not any part of it written down till I reached Bristol." For
Wordsworth then, walking was both a way to collect material and
a way to turn it into poetry. His shoes were almost as important
to his art as his quill pens. Walking made him feel good, too:

Those walks did now, like a returning spring,
Come back on me again. When first I made
Once more the Circuit of our little Lake
If ever happiness hath lodg'd with man,

That day consummate happiness was mine,
Wide-spreading, steady, calm, contemplative.

In 1797, Samuel Coleridge walked forty miles from Somerset to the Wordsworth house in Dorset for a visit that *New York Times* critic Richard Edel described as "three weeks of tramping the countryside, nightlong talk about a new world and the poetry that was to shape it, and long sessions of feverish writing at a common table. Lines and images were swapped back and forth, often literally, as one poet used the other's notes or supplied a missing stanza." The two poets had begun "the most remarkable literary friendship and collaboration we know."

They both composed poetry while walking, but chose different paths. William Hazlitt wrote, "Coleridge has told me that he himself liked to compose in walking over uneven ground, or breaking through the straggling branches of a copse-wood; whereas Wordsworth always wrote (if he could) walking up and down a straight gravel walk, or in some spot where the continuity of his verse met with no collateral interruption."

Coleridge so entranced William and Dorothy that they moved to Alfoxden, a mansion near his place in Somerset and, as literary historian Molly Lefebure wrote, "The 'Alfoxden Circle' passed the wonderful summer of 1797 with almost ceaseless laughter and high spirits, constant visits, talk and sociability, love and warm happiness, excitement and buoyancy."

In 1798, Wordsworth and Coleridge jointly published their *Lyrical Ballads*. The collection rejected what Wordsworth saw as the "gaudiness and inane phraseology of many modern writers" in favour of "fitting to metrical arrangement a selection of the real language of men in a state of vivid sensation." Poetry, he wrote in the preface to *Lyrical Ballads*, was "the spontaneous overflow of powerful feelings" and sprang not from rhetorical tricks and affected language but from "emotion recollected in tranquility."

Many of the twenty-four poems in *Lyrical Ballads* expressed a Rousseau-like respect for country folk and a Rousseau-like reverence for nature. Strong feelings, everyday words, creative pantheism. With this slender book, Wordsworth and Coleridge ushered in the whole Romantic Movement in English literature. As Hazlitt wrote, the arrival of *Lyrical Ballads* was "like the turning up of fresh soil." Neither poet had reached thirty.

By 1808, Wordsworth's poetry had begun to decline, he found Coleridge's addiction to opium unforgivable, and word reached Coleridge that Wordsworth had called him "a rotten drunkard." Their celebrated friendship ended in bitterness and mutual antagonism. Wordsworth's relationship to his younger sister Dorothy, however, lasted all his life. From 1795 until his death fifty-five years later, and even after he married Dorothy's friend Mary Hutchinson in 1802, brother and sister shared the same dwellings. One of those was Dove Cottage at Grasmere in the Lake District, where in 1799 his most creative period began.

Dorothy was an exceptional spinster and chronic romantic.

"While other women were fainting with exhaustion after a journey down the garden path," her biographer Frances Wilson wrote, "Dorothy was braving mountain glaciers in her homemade shoes, lying under the stars on Grasmere Vale, watching the shifting shapes of the night sky, and writing out hundreds and thousands of William's sublime words."

She did far more, however, than merely transcribe his work.

"The two walked together, observing and sometimes composing while walking," wrote Anne Wallace of the University of Southern Mississippi. "William composed to Dorothy's ear or passed his written work on to her for comment; Dorothy wrote in journals open to William's eye, at times specifically for his use; William reworked Dorothy's journals in his poetry; Dorothy reworked William's poetry in her own; and Dorothy copied and reworked William's work, and her own, in innumerable manuscript versions."

No one walked further with William than Dorothy. They were an odd couple. "Wordsworth was of a good height, and not a slender man," De Quincey wrote. "On the contrary, by the side of [Robert] Southey, his limbs looked thick, almost in a disproportionate degree." Hazlitt saw "something of a roll, a lounge in his gait." Tripping along beside or behind him came his short, skinny, fast-talking, quick-moving, brown-faced, and wild-eyed sister and soul mate. "William and Dorothy failed to see how comic they seemed to the villagers," Wilson wrote. "'Mr. Wordsworth went bumming and booing about,' recalled one local of Wordsworth's compositional walks, 'and she, Miss Dorothy, kept close behint him, and she picked up the bits as he let 'em fall, and tak 'em down, and put 'em on paper for him.'"

Robert Southey said that "of all human beings whom I have ever known," this brother and sister were "the most intensely selfish," but they were far from selfish to each other. Without Dorothy, William might never have become the poet he did. Without her, he might never have become any kind of poet at all. He thanked her in his verse for awakening him to all the beauties of the countrysides that they trekked through together, and said, "She gave me eyes, she gave me ears."

FOR DICKENS, THE CHOICE WAS SIMPLE: WALK FAST OR EXPLODE

Throughout most of Jane Austen's life, she walked six miles a day. She believed walkers were morally superior to horseback riders, and Charles Dickens described his daily walks as a "moral obligation." At twenty-seven, he had already given to Britain *The Pickwick Papers*, *Oliver Twist*, and *Nicholas Nickleby*, and he now knew that he had to spend as much time walking – and walking *fast* – as he did writing. All his life, his restlessness drove him as spurs drove horses. Like Nicholas, "he felt so nervous and excited that he could not sit still. He seemed to be losing time unless he was moving." Nicholas said, "I must move rapidly, or I could not draw my breath," and Dickens himself, in a letter to a friend in 1854, said, "If I couldn't walk fast and far, I should just explode and perish."

As Dickens fretted over beginning a new novel, he walked at night "into the strangest places . . . seeking rest, and finding none." That last phrase, his biographer Peter Ackroyd wrote, "is strikingly reminiscent of the fate of the unclean spirit in the Bible, as Dickens stalks the streets of London, both by day and night, the amorphous shape of the narrative within him like some burden from which he needs to be relieved."

In March 1851, Dickens treated his insomnia by walking throughout several nights on the deserted streets of London, going to bed exhausted only at sun-up. Years later, remembering the Thames as he'd seen it from Waterloo Bridge, he wrote, "But the river had an awful look, the buildings on the banks were muffled in black shrouds, and the reflected lights seemed to originate deep in the water, as if the spectres of suicides were holding them to show where they went down. The wild moon and clouds were as restless as an evil conscience in a tumbled bed, and the very shadow of the immensity of London seemed to lie oppressively on the river."

Dickens usually reported to his neat study at nine in the morning and, taking only a short break for a light lunch, which he ate mechanically, sat at his desk to write, think, or worry until two in the afternoon. He then charged out on a three-hour walk. "I go at once," he said, "hardly waiting to complete a sentence." As he strode, however, his story strode with him. One of his sons described "his eyes looking straight before him, his lips slightly working, as they generally did when he sat writing and thinking." In his own words, Dickens was "searching for some pictures I wanted to build upon."

Walking at four and a half to five miles per hour, Dickens covered roughly fourteen miles every afternoon, but the older he grew, the more his restlessness tormented him, and the further he went. By his mid-forties, he was taking what Ackroyd called "his customary twenty-mile walks." Sometimes his demons drove him to more dangerous exercise. He once described himself, at Dover, as "swarming up the face of a gigantic and precipitous cliff in a lonely spot overhanging the wild sea-beach."

Nigel Tranter Wrote in the Rain

"It isn't surprising that Walt Whitman should have tramped impressive distances, for you can feel the pulse beat of the walker in his slightly breathless, incantatory poems," Joyce Carol Oates wrote. "But it may be surprising to learn that Henry James, whose prose style more resembles the fussy intricacies of crocheting than the fluidity of movement, also loved to walk for miles in London."

From 1933 to 1939, when Thomas Mann lived high above Zurich, he wrote only in the morning and, every afternoon, organized his thinking while walking downhill, past a fast-flowing stream, and through forests of pine, cherry, and sycamore trees. Throughout Simenon's writing life he took daily strolls and, when he was seventy-six, he revealed, "All my books have come to me while I was walking." Thornton Wilder said that, to start himself off on each day's writing, "my springboard has always been long walks." In his late sixties, Isaac Bashevis Singer, who lived to be eighty-eight, looked frail and feeble, yet every day he walked fifty to sixty Manhattan blocks. Author D.T. Max called him "an Upper West Side cynosure, a besuited elf in a hat, feeding the Broadway pigeons."

For three hours every day, Scottish novelist and historian Nigel Tranter walked along the south coast of the Firth of Forth, eighteen miles east of Edinburgh, while writing in longhand. He wrote 137 books, the most popular of which were novels based on Scottish history. Michael Russell, now Scotland's Minister for

Culture, called Tranter "a storyteller of rare power, whose genius was his ability to excite new audiences with imaginative and detailed tales of Scotland's past. He brought Scottish history to life and made it accessible to all."

At ten each morning, Tranter left Quarry House, the seventeenth-century dwelling he lived in for half a century, to walk beside the sand dunes, dark cliffs, and echoing surf of Aberlady Bay. Not even wind-driven rain – not even *Scottish* rain – could halt his writing; he used a waterproof pen on waterproof paper. As he started out, he crossed a footbridge. Thus the book he wrote about his beloved stretch of coastline was entitled *Footbridge to Enchantment* (1992).

His friend and ardent fan Cameron Cunningham said that as Tranter walked the same route, day after day, decade after decade, he was "conceiving, imagining, visualizing and recreating in his own mind the 'enchantment' of Scottish history. It is as if, when he steps off that bridge, he enters a timewarp that transports him deep into Scotland's past, bringing it back to life, virtually becoming the character about whom he is writing. This he shares with his readers. This is enchantment."

Tranter arrived back home for lunch at 1 p.m. and then, on an ancient manual typewriter, typed out up to twelve hundred words exactly as he'd scrawled them outdoors. He held together the pages of his finished manuscript with, appropriately, a shoelace. His walks not only got his muse working for him, but kept him healthy. When he died of flu in 2000, he was ninety.

FOR NOVELISTS AND POETS ALIKE, A GOOD WALK WORKED

"I always go for a walk by the river at the end of the day," said British novelist J.G. Ballard in 2000, "to clear my mind." At seventy, Canadian novelist Richard Wright, winner of both a Governor General's Award and the Giller Prize, still took long afternoon walks in old St. Catharines and said, "If I'm writing, that walk sometimes helps to sort out problems."

"There are certain ways of becoming attentive," Margaret Drabble said in 1978. "Like walking. I can think better because I don't have to worry about what I'm doing. But sometimes you can walk for three hours and it's only just as you're putting the supper in the oven that you realize exactly what the answer is." Twenty-nine years later, she was still walking to find answers, and still dealing with ovens: "My absolute favourite walk is from the back of my house in the country. It goes along the edge of Exmoor National Park up to a little church called Cullborne. To go there and back is about the time it takes to roast a chicken."

When Carlos Fuentes was at Princeton University, he composed his fiction in his head while walking, just as Gibbon had composed his non-fiction and Wordsworth his poetry. Late in the afternoon, he said, "I take my walk for the next day's writing. I must write the book out in my head now, before I sit down. I always follow a triangular pattern on my walks here. I go to Einstein's house on Mercer Street, then down to Thomas Mann's house on Stockton Street, then over to Herman Broch's house on Evelyn Place. After visiting those three places, I return home, and by that time I have mentally written tomorrow's six or seven pages." From eight-thirty the next morning until twelve-thirty, he laid out in longhand what he'd "written" in his head.

While walking two miles from his house in Hartford, Connecticut, to his job as an insurance-company executive, Wallace Stevens, a big, taciturn man who never learned to drive, wrote some of America's finest poetry. Literary critic Harold Bloom once named Chaucer, Shakespeare, Milton, Wordsworth, Whitman, Dickinson – and Stevens – as the "exemplars" that any would-be poet must keep in mind.

Poet and non-fiction author Diane Ackerman might well have been thinking of Stevens when she wrote, "Many nonpedestrian writers have got their inspiration from walking. Especially poets – there's a sonneteer in our chests; we walk around to the beat of iambs." Stevens told a reporter he liked to match the words in his head to the rhythm of his strides. Locals claimed they'd seen him lumber along, stop, walk backwards, stop again, and repeat his forward steps as he reworked a line in his head. "From all accounts, the insurance company indulged Stevens in his second vocation," Christine Palm of the *Hartford Courier* wrote. "After his leisurely walk to the office, he would take notes and scraps of paper out of his pockets and transcribe – or have his secretary transcribe – his morning musings into a poem. His colleagues left him alone when he was in a reverie and knew not to ask too much about his creative life."

At home in the Berkshire Mountains of Massachusetts, poet Richard Wilbur led "a fairly physical life," which included "a lot of long walks." He said, "I do things that are non-verbal so that I can return to language with excitement, and move towards language from kinds of strong awareness for which I haven't instantly found facile words. It is good for a writer to move into words out of the silence."

As the Writer Runs, "the Mind Flies with the Body"

As far back as 1982, literary critic and memoirist Malcolm Cowley said, "I wonder if the decline of walking will lead to a decline of the creative process." Twenty-two years later, Joan Acocella wrote that, since American writers now drank much less liquor than their predecessors, she had asked a psychoanalyst what they did instead to conquer their inhibitions and calm their anxieties. His answer? "Exercise."

Not content with walking, many writers were now running. "I work in the morning at a manual typewriter," Don DeLillo said. "I do about four hours and then go running. This helps me shake off one world and enter another. Trees, birds, drizzle – it's a nice kind of interlude. Then I work again, later in the afternoon, for two or three hours." By 2006 Joyce Carol Oates had published more than one hundred books of fiction, non-fiction, and poetry but, at sixty-eight, she still found the strength and time to run nine miles a day. Five years earlier, she had explained the huge importance to her work of running.

"If there's any activity happier, more exhilarating, more nourishing to the imagination, I can't think what it might be," she said. "In running the mind flies with the body; the mysterious efflorescence of language seems to pulse in the brain, in rhythm with our feet and the swinging of our arms. Ideally, the runner who's a writer is running through land- and cityscapes of her fiction, like a ghost in a real setting. . . . In running, 'spirit' seems to pervade the body; as musicians experience the uncanny phenomenon of tissue memory in their fingertips, so the runner seems to experience in feet, lungs, quickened heartbeat, an extension of the imagining self. The structural problems I set for myself in writing, in a long, snarled, frustrating and sometimes despairing morning of work, I can usually unsnarl by running in the afternoon."

"To be a good writer," Gabriel García Márquez said, "you have to be absolutely lucid at every moment of writing – and in good health. . . . I think you have to be in a very good emotional and physical state."

"Sometimes I go for a swim at lunchtime," said British novelist Wendy Holden. "I would seize up otherwise. I do rather think that writing is an Olympic sport – you have to be fit to do it."

At forty-four, John Irving, who'd been a wrestler in college, kept fit by jumping rope, lifting weights, riding a stationary bike, and jogging in Central Park.

At forty-nine, J.P. Donleavy said, "An author must be very self-disciplined and have a driving, desperate control of his resources. My physical regimen and workouts are part of this discipline. The body is not made to sit for long stretches of hours. Your heart has to be stimulated and you must get the blood through the system just to clean the sides of the blood vessels. At four o'clock in the afternoon my ears will turn red from work. . . . I sometimes have to make myself get up from the desk and do thirty sit-ups and thirty back exercises just to shift the blood around. If I go past four o'clock I begin to notice that my guts start to get all pressed down, and it's time to get up and move around. And at times when I can't indulge the luxury of stopping, by late afternoon I'm kneeling at my desk."

At fifty-two, poet James Dickey, "the bare-chested bard," believed in "a great deal of exercise, to keep the body moving, because when the body moves the mind is inclined to move with it." A skilled archer and canoeist, Dickey, the author of *Deliverance* (1970), also lifted weights.

At seventy-three, Philip Roth regularly interrupted his gruelling night-and-day schedule of writing to work out with exercise gear.

At ninety-one, P.G. Wodehouse rose at seven-thirty every morning and did not sit down to breakfast until he'd completed his "daily dozen exercises."

Music Hath Charms to Dissolve the Savage Block

As plants need fertilizer, many writers have needed music. Peter C. Newman, chronicler of the doings and misdoings of rich and powerful Canadians, wore earphones while he worked and listened to the driving rhythms of Stan Kenton. The American novelist May Sarton, who wrote more than forty books, preferred Bach, Mozart, Tomaso Albinoni, and Haydn. "I feel the tremendous masculine joy of Haydn," she said. "That gets me going." Did it *keep* her going? "Yes. It's probably a terrible thing to do to the music but it does a lot for me."

Joseph Heller relied on music to overcome "those noises that might distract me – a leaking faucet, my daughter's rock music in the other part of the apartment, or someone else's radio across the courtyard. I mostly listen to Bach, his choral music. Beethoven is OK; he's great, but Bach, for me, is best."

"I write daily on a Smith Corona SL 580 from midnight to two, mostly to the sounds of classical music," poet and novelist Paul West said, "no doubt a throwback to my mother's constant pianoforte, cocooning me from the first, even in the womb."

The novelist, biographer, cultural critic, and chronicler of gay life in the United States Edmund White said, "I've never willingly written a word without listening to music of some sort." He was born in 1940 and grew up in a house "flooded after dark with music." At night, he'd listen to his father's seventy-eight RPM records of music by Beethoven, Brahms, Mahler, and Debussy, of Kathleen Ferrier singing Bach, and Fritz Kreisler playing violin.

White went so far as to vary the composers he played while writing to "program my moods." In the morning, to conquer laziness or banish gloom, he might listen to a tenor sing Bach's "Christ unser Herr zum Jordan kam." In the afternoon, to steel himself during a long session at his desk, he might choose Wagner's five-and-a-half-hour opera *Parsifal*. A Strauss waltz sometimes brought a smile to White's lips. He played Stravinsky's ballet *Agon* to gain rigour for his tasks and Chopin's *Nocturnes* "to make me more introspective after a jarring conversation."

If music had not been a force in William Styron's life, he said, he'd never have been able to write a word. As with West and White, it lodged itself in his soul during his boyhood. His mother had studied voice in Vienna, and he grew up hearing her sing, often accompanying herself on piano. She played classical, baroque, and romantic music on a primitive phonograph. "I remember how appalled my mother and father were when they found out that I was in love with hillbilly music," he said. "But for me music has an eclectic appeal – classical, country, jazz, the swing music of the

Forties, some of the rousing Protestant hymns. At their best all of these modes can transport me."

Styron loved Mozart's *Sinfonia Concertante* for violin and viola. "It runs the gamut of human emotion," he said. "It's like opening up windows onto all the magic of the world. . . . But there are dozens of compositions – not all of them classical – that come close to affecting me with the same power. In the proper mood I have been as deeply moved by a ballad sung by Emmylou Harris as by the *Missa Solemnis.*" Music was "the ultimate inspiration – the wellspring for my creativity."

Diane Ackerman invited not only music to get her creativity flowing, but quite a range of other bodily pleasures.

"The truth is," she wrote, "that, besides opening and closing mental drawers (which I actually picture in my mind), writing in the bath, beginning each summer day by choosing and arranging flowers for a Zenlike hour or so, listening to music (Alessandro Marcello's oboe concerto in D minor, its adagio, is what's nourishing my senses right now), I go speed walking for an hour every single day. Half of the oxygen in the state of New York has passed through my lungs at one time or another. I don't know whether this helps or not. My muse is male, has the radiant silvery complexion of the moon and never speaks to me directly. I suspect he's too busy catching his breath."

TWENTY-ONE

Burning Kisses, Animal Magnetism

Colette seduced her sixteen-year-old stepson, kissed a female lover onstage while performing in a risqué pantomime, flaunted her naughty liaisons with women and men, and used her exotic and feverish sexual entanglements to enrich passages of her fiction. She may, however, have been the spectacular exception to a rule. No matter how important to most women writers their love affairs may be in some respects, these relationships influence their work far less than the love affairs and sexual adventures of men writers influence theirs. Either that, or the men are simply less able or willing to hide the importance of their lovers to their literary creation.

Consider Ernest Hemingway and Katherine Anne Porter.

Hemingway had four wives, dedicated a novel to each of them, and said, "The *best* writing is certainly when you're in love." Porter, who had four husbands, said, "I don't know whether you write better [when in love], but you feel so good you *think* you're writing better!" Being in love so lifted her spirits that it made "everything you do seem easier and happier," but it was not something a writer could ever count on for help. Her mind mattered while she wrote, not her heart, and no bond she ever had with "any human being" was as strong as "this thing between me and my writing."

Graham Greene, by contrast, felt he could not do his best work if he did not have this thing between him and his woman. Film director Otto Preminger, for whom Greene created the screenplay of *Saint Joan* in 1957, once wrote that although the writer "gives a first impression of being controlled, correct and British he is actually mad about women. Sex is on his mind all the time." For no other woman, however, was Greene ever more mad than Catherine Walston. By 1949, he still had a wife and an emotional commitment to his mistress of the previous ten years, but he was, in his own words, "wildly, crazily, hopelessly" in love with the famously beautiful and inconveniently married Walston. She "dominated his thoughts for over a decade," his biographer Norman Sherry wrote, and was his lover during "the most productive and the most emotionally wrenching period of his life." Without her, he could never have finished *The Heart of the Matter* (1948) or started *The End of the Affair* (1951). With her by his side, and this was crucially important to both his mental health and his creativity, he was never bored. He was "productive, volatile, sexually potent." He was "elevated and expansive" and worked "with great concentration and fluency of thought."

Love, Literature, the French Connection

At twenty-nine, George Sand (born Aurore Dupin) began a tempestuous affair with the dashing twenty-three-year-old poet, dramatist, and novelist Alfred de Musset. Sand was already notorious in Paris not only for taking a man's name, but for wearing men's suits and boots, and smoking cigars in public. Her mannishness, however, did not prevent Musset from falling desperately in love with her. She had long, curly, black hair and dark, expressive eyes. "She was a thinking bosom," V.S. Pritchett wrote, "and one who overpowered her young lovers."

Musset was a heavy drinker and an opium-eater, and the romance was stormy. At one point, Sand cut off her hair and mailed it to him. Another time, he threatened both her and himself with a knife. When they decided they could live neither apart nor together, they vowed to kill themselves in a forest outside Paris. Fortunately for Sand's fans, they changed their minds. She eventually wrote eighty novels. Her writing schedule was rigid, and to avoid Musset's passionate but badly timed advances, she sometimes worked behind closed doors. It angered him that, the moment they finished their lovemaking, she leapt out of bed, raced to her desk, and began to write. After two years, she ended the relationship by retreating to her beloved estate in the village of Nohant in central France. The breakup devastated Musset. He remained sombre and dissipated for the rest of his life, but it was his romance with Sand that inspired him to write his finest poems.

If that affair lasted only two years at best, Victor Hugo's with Juliette Drouet lasted half a century. After a falling-out with his wife, Adèle, the mother of their five children, he fell deeply in love with Juliette, an actress in one of his plays. She was an impulsive, humorous, hot-tempered spendthrift, and perhaps the most gorgeous courtesan in Paris. Hugo decided to save her, and she was more than willing to obey him. He installed her in a tiny apartment near the Hugo house in Place des Vosges, the oldest square in Paris, and paid her a less-than-generous monthly allowance, for which she kept detailed accounts.

"It was now that there began the most astonishing life of penitence and confinement ever willingly entered upon by any woman outside a conventual order," André Maurois wrote in his biography of Hugo. "Victor Hugo had promised to forgive the past, but he had laid down conditions and they were hard. Juliette, who only yesterday had been one of the most widely admired women in Paris, adorned with lace and jewels, had now to live for nobody but him, go out only with him, abandon all coquetry, all ways of luxury – in short lead the life of a penitent."

She strove never to displease him and served not only as his lover and confidante but as his copyist and travelling companion. "You are not only the solar spectrum with the seven luminous colours, but the sun himself, that illumines, warms and revivifies!" she told him in a letter in 1835. "This is what you are, and I am the lowly woman who adores you." He gave her a notebook, bound in black and encrusted with gold and, before leaving her every evening, left a loving thought in it: "Your kisses make me in love with the earth; your eyes make me understand Heaven. . . . Society could have done no more than make you a queen; nature has made you a goddess."

Nature, however, had made him a chronic seducer. Hugo loved good food, good wine, hard work, and beautiful women. Early in his affair with Juliette, she had often climbed a secret staircase to meet him in his studio at the house in Place des Vosges, and later, during his forties, actresses who wanted parts, women who wanted to be novelists, and female students who wanted to see the great man in the flesh, as it were, all made their way up those same steps and into his arms. He was a womanizer and in 1845, when he turned forty-three, still a highly romantic one.

To Léonie Biard, a young married woman with whom he enjoyed an intensely sexual affair that year, he wrote, "To dream of you is sweet, but sweeter still to have the feel of you, to talk with you, to take you on my knee, to put my arms about you. To cover you with burning kisses, to see you redden and go pale, to feel you trembling in my arms. That is life – life full, entire and real. That is the light of the sun; that is the glow of paradise."

His romanticism, however, gave way to sexual greed. "Surrounded by debutantes and adventuresses, by chambermaids and courtesans," André Marois wrote, "he seemed, in these years from 1847 to 1850, as though he had become prey to a sort of gloomy craving for fresh meat. The romantic lover now gave himself the airs of a roué. . . ."

At sixty-nine, Hugo bedded an eighteen-year-old girl. At seventy-six, he suffered a mild stroke during a liaison with his ever-willing maid, Blanche Lavin. Even in his last days he wooed women. In a diary he started on New Year's Day, 1885, he recorded eight sexual performances, the last of which was on April 5. He was eighty-three. A few weeks later, more than two million people joined his funeral procession.

Despite Hugo's philandering, his understanding wife Adèle chose to live with him until she died in 1868, and Juliette, who showered him with more than twenty thousand passionate love letters, remained faithful to him until her death in 1883. "Nothing more redounds to the credit of Victor Hugo," wrote poet and dramatist Paul Claudel, "than the calm and tender devotion given to him by that wonderful creature, Juliette Drouet."

Back in the 1830s, when she still had what one admirer called "this delicious face" and "abundant black hair, with wonderful reflections in it," Hugo's love for her moved him to write some of his best and most romantic poetry. Indeed, Maurois believed that every one of Hugo's love affairs – throughout a long and amazingly prolific career as a poet, playwright, and novelist – stimulated his creative powers.

DREISER: A STRANGE, DRIVEN, LONELY SEDUCER

Malcolm Lowry expected the women who loved him "to mother him, to nurture him verbally, spiritually, and physically," wrote Sherrill E. Grace, an authority on him and his work. A psychologist, she added, "might explain Lowry's constant demand for mothering as the need to feel at ease with language, the mother tongue, in order to be able to write. A more traditional literary explanation would be that Lowry made his women into muses, and then turned on them when the inspiration failed."

Theodore Dreiser also craved a certain amount of mothering, but demanded from his lovers a whole lot more. He was neither handsome nor rich, neither charming nor loyal, yet H.L. Mencken said he enjoyed the sex life of a chimpanzee. At twenty-seven in 1898, Dreiser married a Missouri schoolteacher, but soon left her for a nomadic and phenomenally promiscuous life. At thirty-eight, his goatish pursuit of the seventeen-year-old daughter of a fellow employee cost him a well-paid job at a publishing house. At forty-five, he juggled simultaneous sexual affairs with at least three women. At forty-eight, he took as his lover a young actress, Helen Richardson, and despite his serial seductions of other women, she was with him when he died twenty-six years later. At fifty-eight, he launched an affair with sixteen-year-old Yvette Szekely. "Their relationship began," Dreiser scholar Thomas P. Riggio wrote, "as a strange, even clumsy, seduction." At sixty-two, Dreiser ardently wooed a first-year student at Bryn Mawr College for women.

Well over six feet tall and weighing nearly two hundred pounds, he was physically and socially awkward. He had buck teeth, an undershot chin, and a wandering eyeball, yet he managed to carry on several love affairs at the same time. He was egotistical, bigoted, suspicious, prone to fits of jealous rage, and, while trying to keep his lovers from knowing about one another, a traitor to all of them. Half a century after actress Kirah Markham loved him, however, she remembered him as a strong-willed "emotional steam-roller" who had "animal magnetism" and "an utter sense of loneliness."

He demanded absolute fidelity from her. But one reason he fled New York on a steamship bound for Savannah in 1916 was his fear that she'd learn about his outrageous cheating on her. As he said farewell to her at the North River pier on the evening of January 26, he was enormously relieved that none of his other lovers showed up. But two days after reaching Savannah, according to his biographer W.A. Swanberg, "he was actually ill because he had not received letters from *any* of his women, sleepless, frantic. He needed a woman – a mother – to pet and pamper him." He suffered a headache, and a sick stomach, and claimed he could not read, write, or eat. Then, a loving telegram from Miss Markham instantly cured him. The next day, he told his diary he hated "life without a woman."

"Dreiser believed love to be a force so powerful that it could send waves through long spaces," Swanberg wrote, "but the waves emanating from New York seemed weak or unsatisfactory in Savannah. In his diary he mentioned interest in six women." They included Miss Markham. He urged her to join him in Savannah but when she did, he was cranky. She complained that he made "snide remarks about my interfering with his life."

Dreiser was not only unusually horny; horniness was the key to his art. In *An American Tragedy* (1925) – and other works in which his power and insight conquer his sloppy, overstuffed prose so convincingly that some critics still call him America's greatest novelist – the writing flows out of his belief that men and women, all their lives, endure emotional and erotic yearning, and that their most powerful appetite is sexual. As much as that appetite ruled his characters, it ruled him. About the sexual adventures of his big brother, Paul Dressler, a Tin Pan Alley songwriter ("My Gal Sal" and "On the Banks of the Wabash, Far Away"), he coyly wrote, "I have never known a man more interested in women from the sex point of view (unless it might perchance be myself)."

Perchance? "[Dreiser] used women as other men used cigars," essayist Joseph Epstein wrote, "and frequently had more than one a day. . . . He believed in the close connection between erotic and creative energy – and acted upon his belief. He was not a man you would want to leave alone in a room with your grandmother, and certainly not with your granddaughter."

Nor was the Pulitzer-winning novelist Bernard Malamud a man to trust with your granddaughter. He taught creative writing at three universities and, among his students, many were the grand-daughters he seduced. "But there is something disconcertingly poseurish about all these loveless affairs with all these young women," wrote Deborah Friedell, an editor at *London Review of Books*. "'I *deserve* you,' he wrote to one of them. He had decided that a writer – certainly a great one – should have affairs even if he didn't really want to." In *Dubin's Lives* (1979), perhaps the most autobiographical of Malamud's novels, the wife of a biographer tells him his infidelities mean nothing to her because "everything sooner or later goes back to your biographies. That's your grand passion – if you could fuck your books you'd have it made." Malamud had no qualms about inserting in his fiction some of the real utterances of his girlish conquests.

It was in the 1960s that he wrote some of his best fiction, includ-ing his Pulitzer Prize–winning *The Fixer* (1966) and, according to essayist Gerald Howard, that was when "a whole mystique of sexual potency gathered about the novelist, cultivated by writers from Henry Miller to Norman Mailer; penmanship and cock-manship clearly went hand in hand."

A Great Spanish Novelist's Unseemly Secret Addiction

Emile Zola married Alexandrine-Gabrielle Meley in 1870, and in 1875 fellow novelist Edmond de Goncourt wrote in his diary, "Two or three years ago . . . he wouldn't sit at his desk after a night of conjugal effusion, knowing beforehand he couldn't construct a sentence, write a line. Now it's the opposite. After eight or ten days of mediocre work, coitus induces a slight fever that unblocks him."

If Zola was happy to reveal the most intimate details of his sex life during a *tête-à-tête* with a diarist, his Spanish contemporary Benito Pérez Galdós was not. An unmarried writer of Balzacian genius who published eighty novels, he managed to hide from his adoring readers that he enjoyed sex with prostitutes virtually every afternoon of his entire adult life. His novels revealed an intimate knowledge about the gritty lives of the derelicts, bums, thieves, street peddlers, and whores of Madrid's most teeming slum, and readers long wondered how this gently reared man could possibly have gained this insight.

"The answer is simple," C.P. Snow wrote. "Galdós had an indefatigable appetite for women. He appears to have had a special addiction to women of the lowest classes – prostitutes, semi-prostitutes, women of the slums who heard gossip about this nice, kind, rich and generous man. He didn't much want anything in the way of a sustained relationship. He did have several upper-class mistresses, but seems to have extricated himself with some dexterity. He had affection for most things about women, but above all he wanted women's flesh, as quickly and as easily as it came."

Galdós kept two or three rented rooms in Madrid's sordid *barrios bajos* neighbourhood, but he met his illiterate partners in sex not only in these quarters but in their own dwellings. While journeying to and from his trysts, he got to know the streets, lanes, ramshackle storefronts, and rickety stairways of the district better than any other middle-class Spaniard, and he befriended men and women who were fated to spend their lives there. While the clothes of many were little better than rags, he walked among them in a black business suit. His gait was distinctive, and he had an air of wisdom. During his last seven years, Galdós was blind, and a trustworthy manservant escorted him on his daily visits to the neighbourhood.

"They became a familiar sight in the streets of the *barrios bajos*," Snow continued, "the tall old man on the arm of his attendant. Galdós was greeted with the love that he had always found among the derelict. The servant had to ask the way to some of Galdós's rendezvous. He was answered with respect and without inquisitive questioning. . . . They venerated the old man, and they behaved as though to preserve his dignity."

Guy de Maupassant's addiction to prostitutes was every bit as strong as Galdós's but, Snow explained, the Frenchman was uncontrolled in everything he did, while the Spaniard, except perhaps for his afternoon habit, was a paragon of self-control. Every morning, with the efficiency of Trollope, he wrote for hours on end. Maupassant, a syphilitic, died at forty-two, and Galdós at seventy-seven.

At Last, Simenon Found His One True Love

Unlike Galdós, Simenon talked freely about his addiction to sex with "all women – tall, short, fat, thin." He claimed to have had sexual intercourse with ten thousand women, eight thousand of them prostitutes. As an old man, he allowed, "I never sought records or anything like that. A journalist came up with that figure [ten thousand] by multiplication, figuring on the basis of two or three women a week, and I suppose it's about right. I am insatiable for contact with women." Whatever the exact number, he wished it were higher. He told a reporter for *People*, "I literally suffered from knowing there were millions of women in the world that I would never know."

When he was eighty, in 1984, he told American journalist Leslie Garis, "Since the age of thirteen, when a girl made me a man, I have been hungry for all women. I consider that if I can't have a woman, I lose something. Because you know a woman only when you have slept with her." His voice, Garis wrote, "trembled with emotion."

While she interviewed him in the living room of his pink eighteenth-century farmhouse in Lausanne, Teresa was with them. A petite, dark-eyed Venetian with shoulder-length black hair, she was in her mid-sixties and, while he'd continued to churn out novels in his seventies, she'd been his secretary, nurse, confidante, and lover.

Garis marvelled over the number of women to whom the old man had made love, and "Teresa, who is taking a keen interest in the turn of our conversation, holds up her hand and counts her fingers. 'Three, four . . . sometimes five a day!' She smiles proudly."

In reply to the interviewer's astonishment, Simenon laughed and modestly explained that, since his partners were five *different* women, and mostly prostitutes, "it's not so much."

Did he feel any passion for them?

"'No, it was a question of contact,' Simenon says, his voice high and youthful. 'Carnal contact. You know, to have the skin of a woman in my hands, to caress her. . . . I never made love cynically or cold-bloodedly. Even when I did the same things five time a day with five different women, it was always . . . *la chair* . . . flesh. It's a feeling that exists in your hands, in your body, in everything.'"

Gazing tenderly at Teresa, Simenon said, "I had to wait fifty-eight years for love. It was a long time."

Was he still hungry for women?

"Yes, still. But not for other females, because now I've found my female. And for twenty years I haven't needed others."

"Before he felt empty," Teresa explained. "He lacked a feeling of wholeness."

"Yes, that's true," he said. "But I still make love, like when I was young. At eighty!"

That same year, he wrote, "In the end, what I have searched for all my life, so curious about all women, getting married twice, disappointed twice, always running after something I didn't know, I finally learned. The goal of my tireless quest was not a woman but '*the* woman,' the true. And I found her!"

Teresa was still with him when, five years later, he died in his sleep.

TWENTY-TWO

The Daily and Nightly Grind

At 5:30 every morning, Anthony Trollope placed his watch on his desk, spent thirty minutes reading what he'd written the day before, and then, for two and a half hours, wrote 250 words every fifteen minutes. If he finished a novel before his three hours were up, he started another on a fresh sheet of paper. At 8:30, he headed off to put in a full day at the Post Office, for which he worked for thirty-three years in Ireland and England. Somehow, in addition to inventing Britain's red pillar letter-box, he found time, at least twice a week, to indulge his passion for riding to hounds. Yet he wrote not only forty-seven novels, including *Barchester Towers* (1857) and the Palliser yarns, but short stories, travel books, biographies, and his autobiography.

"A small daily task, if it be really daily, will beat the labours of a spasmodic Hercules," he averred. "It is the tortoise which always catches the hare. The hare has no chance. He loses more time in glorifying himself for a quick spurt than suffices for the tortoise to make half his journey." About the notion that no novelist should dip his pen until a flash of inspiration had struck him, Trollope wrote, "I have hardly been able to repress my scorn. To me it would not be more absurd if the shoemaker were to wait for inspiration, or the tallow-chandler for the divine moment of melting."

Eighty-three years later, Bellow made much the same point. Warning writers against "overcapitalizing the A in artist," he said, "Stravinsky says the composer should practice his trade exactly as a shoemaker does. . . . In the nineteenth century, the artist [not Trollope] loftily waited for Inspiration. Once you elevate yourself into the rank of a cultural institution, you're in for a lot of trouble."

"I think the best regimen is to get up early, insult yourself a bit in the shaving mirror, and then pretend you're cutting wood," said the Anglo-Irish novelist Lawrence Durrell, ". . . but all the Jungian guilt about the importance of one's message, and all that sort of thing – well, you get a nice corpulent ego standing in the way there, telling you that you're so damn clever that you're almost afraid to write it down, it's so wonderful. And the minute you get that, where are your cheques going to come from for next month's gas, light, and heat?"

With this down-to-earth, I-do-it-strictly-for-the-money attitude, Durrell completed each of the novels in *The Alexandria Quartet* (1962) in a matter of weeks. When an interviewer suggested he found writing "very easy," he replied, "Yes. I only pray that I can do it, and nothing else." He had discarded hundreds of his passages, but it took him only two days to bash out ten thousand words on his typewriter.

Among other British novelists to whom writing came without much trouble were the young Evelyn Waugh, who wrote and revised each of *Decline and Fall* (1928), *Vile Bodies* (1930), and *A Handful of Dust* (1934) in just six weeks; Somerset Maugham, who worked between 8 a.m. and 12:45 p.m. nearly every day for sixty-five years, and produced seventy-four books; Angus Wilson, who said, "When one starts writing it's natural for the stuff to come rolling off the stocks rather easily"; and Margaret Drabble, who told an interviewer she often wrote "terribly fast. And I don't rewrite very much either. I really just rattle along." For Booker Prize–winner Anita Brookner, who had a job at the Courtauld Institute of Art in London, writing a novel was little more than a pleasant thing to do during a summer vacation. She published her first when she was fifty-three and, for more than two decades after that, completed another nearly every year. Each was a first draft. "I feel well when I'm writing," she blithely explained. "I even put on a little weight."

Eugène Ionesco, the Rumanian-born French luminary of the Theatre of the Absurd, composed each of his plays in only three weeks or a month, and said, "They come out very quickly. A few tiny details I changed, but I wrote them like that. Then I read them over. And when I had a secretary, I dictated to her at the typewriter. I hardly ever change it."

Among American authors, none found writing more absorbing and pleasing than science-fiction ace Isaac Asimov. He was rarely *not* writing. While eating, bathing, shopping, and falling asleep, his mind worked on whatever he was writing, or about to write. When asked what rituals he performed to get in the proper mood for work, he cracked, "It is always necessary for me to turn on my electric typewriter and get close enough to it so that my fingers can reach the keys." At speeds of up to a hundred words a minute, he typed what he'd already written in his head. His concentration was so intense, he said, "you could put on an orgy in my office, and I wouldn't look up – well, maybe once." Fellow science-fiction writer Robert Heinlein said he "got it right the first time," and always sent his first draft to his publisher. "I'm not quite *that* good," Asimov said. "I do edit the first draft and make changes that usually amount to not more than five percent of the total, and *then* I send it out."

F. Scott Fitzgerald's notorious drunkenness overshadowed his record as a furiously hard worker. At twenty-four, he told an editor he'd written twelve thousand words of a story called "The Camel's Back" in twenty-one consecutive hours. His friend

Thomas Boyd reported, "Words come to his mind and they spill themselves in a riotous frenzy of song and colour all over the page. Some days he writes as many as 7,000 or 8,000 words; and then, with a small *Roget's Thesaurus*, he carefully goes over his work, substituting synonyms for any unusual words that appear more than once in seven or eight pages."

Then there was Jack Kerouac, surely an example of Trollope's "spasmodic Hercules." In 1951, "the king of the Beat generation" wrote the first draft of *On the Road* by typewriting "whatever came into [his] head – hopping freights, hitch-hiking, and working as a railroad brakeman, deckhand and scullion on merchant ships, government fire lookout, and hundreds of assorted jobs." He typed so fast that, in three weeks, he produced a single-spaced scroll of writing, with no margins or paragraph breaks, that stretched for 120 feet. It was an editor's nightmare. Kerouac believed in neither punctuation nor rewrites, but in fast, spontaneous work that was "confessional and pure and all excited with the life of it."

He said, "I spent my entire youth writing slowly with revisions and endless re-hashing speculation and deleting and got so I was writing one sentence a day and the sentence had no FEELING. Goddamn it, FEELING is what I like in art, not CRAFTINESS and the hiding of feelings."

Truman Capote sneered that *On the Road* "isn't writing at all, it's typing," but John Updike, whose work was anything but slapdash, felt Kerouac had a point. "There may be some reason to question the whole idea of fineness and care in writing," he said. "Maybe something can get into sloppy writing that would elude careful writing. I'm not terribly careful myself, actually. I write fairly rapidly if I get going, and don't change much, and have never been one for making outlines or taking out whole paragraphs or agonizing much. If a thing goes for me, it goes for me, and if it doesn't go, I eventually stop and get off."

Updike believed that, just as periods of rest and speed characterize the organic world, the act of writing should be organically varied. "But there's a kind of tautness you should feel within yourself," he added, "no matter how slow or fast you're spinning out the reel."

"I think I write much better if I'm flowing," Doris Lessing said. "You start something off, and at first it's a bit jagged, awkward, but then there's a click and you suddenly become quite fluent. That's when I'm writing well. I don't write well when I'm sitting there sweating about every single word." Raymond Chandler felt much the same way: "The faster I write, the better my output. If I'm going slow I'm in trouble. It means I'm pushing the words instead of being pulled by them."

Using an old manual Royal typewriter, novelist Kent Haruf, who took a year-long typing course in high school, wrote his first drafts while blind:

> It's the old notion of blinding yourself so you can see. So you can see differently, I mean. I remove my glasses, pull a stocking cap down over my eyes, and type the first draft single-spaced on yellow paper in the actual and metaphorical darkness behind my closed eyes, trying to avoid being distracted by syntax or diction or punctuation or grammar or spelling or word choice or anything else that would block the immediate delivery of the story. . . . I'm trying to avoid allowing the analytical part of my mind into the process too soon. Instead, I'm trying to stay in touch with subliminal, subconscious impulses and to get the story down in some spontaneous way. . . . It's important to me to maintain this impression of spontaneity . . . of freshness and vividness. Perhaps at times even a suggestion of awkwardness. Otherwise, to me prose sounds stilted and too polished, as if the life of it were perfected out of it.

The Unbearable Heaviness of Seeking Perfection

If D.H. Lawrence refused to revise while he worked but rewrote entire novels more than once, and if Durrell stormed ahead like a cavalry charge, many others toiled like builders of medieval cathedrals. Not until they'd installed one sentence as perfectly as possible did they start to wrestle another into place. They did what Lessing strove to avoid; they sat there sweating about every single word.

It took Günter Grass four or five years to write a novel. He sometimes worked for days on "just one period." He said, "I like periods. . . . I work and I work and it's all right. Everything's in there, but there's something heavy about it. Then I make a few changes, which I don't think are very important, and it works! This is what I understand happiness to be. It lasts for two or three seconds. Then I look ahead to the next period, and it's gone."

At last, the stone fits. Time to start shaping the next one.

"I think I'm very careful, maybe too careful," Nelson Algren said. "You can get too fussy. I do find myself getting bogged down wondering whether I should use a colon or a semicolon, and so on, and I keep trying each one out." Since Capote thought of himself as a stylist, he said, he was "notoriously obsessed with the placing of a comma, the weight of a semicolon. Obsessions of this sort, and the time I take over them, irritate me beyond endurance."

"I can't turn out slews of stuff each day," William Styron said. "I wish I could. I seem to have some neurotic need to perfect each paragraph – each sentence, even – as I go along." James Jones usually wrote three pages a day, but then, he said, "I often have to go back over it all the next day because I'm still dissatisfied. I guess I've got some neurotic compulsion to make everything as perfect as I can before I go on."

Gabriel García Márquez, working from 9 a.m. until mid-afternoon, often completed only one short paragraph, which he threw out the next day. Flaubert complained, "You don't know what it is to stay a whole day with your head in your hands trying to squeeze your unfortunate brain so as to find a word." Philip Roth knew what it was:

> I often have to write a hundred pages or more before there's a paragraph that's alive. Okay, I say to myself, that's your beginning, start there; that's the first paragraph of the book. I'll go over the first six months of work and underline in red a paragraph, a sentence, sometimes no more than a phrase, that has some life in it, and then I'll type all these out on one page. . . . If I'm lucky, that's the start of page one. I look for the liveliness to set the tone. After the awful beginning come the months of freewheeling play, and after the play come the crises, turning against your material and hating the book. . . . My page one can wind up a year later as page two hundred, if it's still even around. . . . I work all day, morning and afternoon, just about every day. If I sit there like that for two or three years, at the end I have a book.

"I don't write drafts," Anthony Burgess said. "I do page one many times, many times, and move on to page two. I pile up sheet after sheet, each in its final state, and at length I have a novel that doesn't – in my view – need any revision."

Far more than the speedsters like Durrell and Ionesco, the cathedral-builders tended to think their work was staggeringly hard to do, and sometimes impossibly so.

When starting a novel, Robertson Davies said, "I toil like a swimmer who feels himself about to sink beneath the waves."

"Conrad found imaginative writing a form of exquisite torture," his biographer Jeffrey Meyers wrote. "He converted nervous force into phrases, felt as if each page were wrenched from his very soul, and needed crisis and frenzy to complete his work." Conrad told a fellow novelist, "You must squeeze out of yourself every sensation, every thought, every image – mercilessly, without reserve and without remorse; you must search the darkest corners of your heart, the most remote recesses of your brain." While struggling with *Nostromo*, he said, "If I had written each page with my blood I could not feel more exhausted."

"Writing a book is a long, exhausting struggle, like a long bout of some painful illness," Orwell wrote. "One would never undertake such a thing if one were not driven by some demon one can neither resist nor understand." While working on a novel, Flannery O'Connor said, "I had to wade through tides of revulsion every day." Hemingway spoke of writers who committed themselves to "long, dull, unrelenting, no-quarter-given-and-no-quarter received fights . . . to do something as they believe it should be done before they die."

Simenon, whenever he wrote, saw no one and took no phone calls. He said he had to be "in the skin" of his main character and feel everything he felt. "And it's almost unbearable after five or six days," he said. "That is one of the reasons why my novels are so short; after eleven days I can't – it's impossible. I have to – it's physical. I am too tired." Before starting any novel, he asked his doctor to check his blood pressure "because I have to be sure that I am good for the eleven days." On the twelfth day, his blood pressure was "usually down."

"I find that in the course of the day while I'm writing," Edward Albee said, "after three or four hours of intense work, I have a splitting headache, and I have to stop."

Some writers made such a monumental commitment to writing a novel that, the moment a publisher accepted the manuscript, they plunged into a kind of post-partum depression. If they disliked their own creation, the feeling was even worse. "I never much liked *The Wapshot Scandal* [1959], and when it was done I was in a bad way," John Cheever said. "I wanted to burn the book. I'd wake up in the night and I would hear Hemingway's voice – I've never actually heard Hemingway's voice, but it was conspicuously his – saying, 'This is the small agony. The great agony comes later.' I'd get up and sit on the edge of the bathtub and chain-smoke until three or four in the morning."

MORNING GLORIES, AND NIGHT OWLS

"Writing is a nerve-flaying job," Joan Acocella wrote. Clichés came to mind much faster than anything exact or fresh, and "to hack one's way past them requires a huge, bleeding effort." That was why many seasoned writers, like Albee, could work no longer than three or four hours a day. Tolstoy, Hemingway, Dos Passos, Wharton, Mann, Katherine Anne Porter, Aldous Huxley, Flannery O'Connor, Alberto Moravia, Anthony Burgess, William Maxwell, Edna O'Brien, Robert Stone, John Barth, Anthony Powell, and C.S. Forester all chose to write in the morning. Peruvian novelist Mario Vargas Llosa called the morning hours in which he wrote "sacred to [him]." Less respectfully, Gore Vidal said, "First coffee, then a bowel movement. Then the muse joins me."

Proust, O'Hara, Tolkien, Algren, Kerouac, James Baldwin, Cynthia Ozick, and Paul West preferred night shifts, and Donald E. Westlake, the American author of more than a hundred books, most of them crime fiction, said, "I write from ten at night to four in the morning, about 7,000 words at a time. It's like being in the basket of a blimp, working at that hour. It's wonderful. There's just one little room with me in it, and I'm sailing through the night wherever the story will go. Just me, alone."

"Why do I write at night?" Dostoevsky wrote to a friend. "Well, as soon as I wake up around one [p.m.], there is a ring at the door: someone has come to ask me for something, someone else wants something else, a third person comes with some request or other, a fourth demands that I shall resolve some quite unresolvable 'accursed question' for him – otherwise I'll go and shoot myself, he says. (And this is the first time I have seen him.) Then delegates come from the students, from the gymnasium, from the Society of Noblemen – all wanting me to take part in evening readings. When will I get time to think, to work, to read, to live?"

Among literary history's noted insomniacs were Poe, Dickens, Dumas, Tolstoy, Twain, Proust, Kipling, Kafka, Nabokov, and Jorges Luis Borges, who spoke of "the atrocious lucidity of insomnia." Journalist Dennis Drabelle wondered if the affliction, even as it tormented its victims, weren't some sort of gift to creative writers. "As an insomniac myself," he wrote in the *Washington Post*, "I often go to bed with drooping eyelids, only to find a few minutes later that my brain is on the boil with ideas I might pitch to editors, or directions in which I might take the one I'm currently writing." Insomnia curses the nights of so many authors that one wonders if it doesn't make a writer's imagination shift into overdrive and race into territory it would not normally explore.

IF AT FIRST YOU DON'T SUCCEED, REPORT TO YOUR DESK ANYWAY

Even when some writers could not find the right words for the blank and intimidating page, they stubbornly faced it for a set number of hours per day. If Dickens couldn't write, he doodled or stared out a window. "But I always sit here for that certain time [from nine a.m. to two p.m.]," he said. "I work every day – or at least I force myself into office or room," Mordecai Richler said. "I may get nothing done, but you don't earn bonuses without putting in time. Nothing may come for three months, but you don't earn the fourth without it."

"The one ironclad rule is that I have to try," Anne Tyler said. "I have to walk into my writing room every weekday morning. If I waited till I felt like writing, I'd never write at all." Flannery

O'Connor sometimes threw out writing she'd worked on for months, but said, "I don't think any of that was time wasted. Something goes on that makes it easier when it does come well. And if you don't sit there every day [between eight and noon], the day it would come, well, you won't be sitting there." If poet John Ashbery was in the wrong mood for writing, he went to his desk as usual to try, because "even if you don't succeed, you'll be developing a muscle that may do it later on." Nadine Gordimer suffered "awful days" on which she could not get into the right frame of mind for work but, she said, "I don't stop and do something else. I sit in front of that paper for the normal time that I would be writing. And then, well, I break through."

"You have to show up at your desk, even though there's nothing in you, and sit there for hours, whatever number of hours you told yourself you were going to put in," Norman Mailer said. "Then, if nothing happens, you still show up the next day and the next and the next, until that recalcitrant presence, the unconscious, comes to decide you can finally be accepted. Such acceptance is crucial."

But obeying a rigid schedule every day struck some writers as futile, if not deadening. Jean Cocteau believed that creative artists, unlike mere cobblers, answered to a mysterious force, and that literature came into being only when the force chose to compel a writer to write. "When you speak of these things to one who works systematically – one such as Mauriac – they think you jest," he said. "Or that you are lazy and use this as an excuse. Put yourself at a desk and write! You are a writer, are you not? *Voilà!* I have tried this. What comes is no good. *Never any good.* [Paul] Claudel at his desk from nine to twelve. It is unthinkable to work like that!"

Henry Miller ate breakfast, sat before his typewriter, and then, he said, "if I find that I am not able to write, I quit." Novelist, biographer, and cultural critic Edmund White said, "If you're not writing well, why continue it? I just don't think this grinding away is useful."

FIVE HUNDRED WORDS A DAY? A THOUSAND?
JUST "GET THE MISERABLE THING DONE"

Without the decision to grind away for either a pre-set number of hours or a pre-set number of words, however, many writers would never have become writers at all. When Greene was twenty, he fought his belief that he had utterly no talent by vowing to complete five hundred words every day. To his future wife, he wrote, "Terrifying thought, 500 words [per day] for another, say, forty years. 7,300,000, not allowing for leap years. Darling!! I *should* get a cramp!" During the following half-century, he endured slumps, in which he managed only a few hundred words in a whole month, and surges, in which he wrote two thousand a day but on far more days than not, he simply met his goal. Five hundred words, on the button.

Jack London was twenty-two when he set a thousand words as his daily target. From then, until shortly before his death at forty, he stuck to his routine. "Every day, a thousand words before lunch," wrote his biographer Alex Kershaw, "whether caught in a gale rounding Cape Horn, waiting for cannibals to attack, or lying hung over in bed in an expensive hotel in New York. . . . If he fell behind his daily quota, he compensated the following morning."

Fans of C.S. Forester's novels about the adventures of the Royal Navy's Horatio Hornblower during the Napoleonic Wars found them anything but dull, but writing them, the author said, was such "a toilsome bore" that "the only way to get it done is to set your course for a given number of words every day." The number, "more or less a fixed minimum," was a thousand, and "you just have to get the miserable thing done." J.G. Ballard, who published more than forty novels and short-story collections, said, "Unless you're disciplined, all you'll end up with is a lot of empty wine bottles. All through my career I've written 1,000 words a day – even if I've got a hangover." He wrote his daily allotment in longhand, edited it painstakingly, then typed it out. "Self-discipline is enormously important," he continued. "You can't rely on inspiration or a novel would take ten years."

TWENTY-THREE

"And How I Get There Is God's Grace"

Many writers quit their day's work, sometimes in mid-sentence, when they were feeling so good about it they knew exactly what to write next. This increased the odds that, the next day, they'd be off to a quick, confident start. The first major writer to share this trade secret was Hemingway. In the 1930s, he gave it to Thomas Wolfe. Maxwell Perkins, the editor for both men, passed it on to his last discovery, James Jones. In 1946, when Jones was writing *From Here to Eternity* (1951), he told Perkins, "Incidentally, that bit of advice you gave me about quitting when I'm hot has proved invaluable. I hope some day to be able to thank Hemingway for it also."

Hemingway knew that the next day, you might not feel the slightest twinge of inspiration. "But if you stopped when you knew what would happen next, you can go on. As long as you can start, you are all right. The juice will come."

Robert Stone, Mario Vargas Llosa, Katherine Anne Porter, and countless others gratefully followed Hemingway's advice about quitting while you're ahead. Porter had another habit that helped her avoid blocks. In the real world, she said in 1963, an event was important only as it affected "your life and the lives of those around you." It wasn't the event that mattered, but its *consequences*, "and if I didn't know the ending of a story, I wouldn't begin. I always write my last lines, my last paragraph, my last page first, and then I go back and work towards it. I know where I'm going. I know what my goal is. And how I get there is God's grace."

Forty-two years later, John Irving said, "I build a novel from the back to the front. I know the end of the story before I write the first sentence. I try to write the last sentence first, even the last several paragraphs." When Bernard Malamud started to write a novel, he'd been making notes about it for months, if not years, and knew so much about it that he had "the ending in mind, usually the last paragraph almost verbatim."

Most writers, however, began at the beginning. After an interviewer reminded Joan Didion that, like Hemingway, she'd said, "Once you have your first sentence you've got your piece," she replied, "What's so hard about that first sentence is that you're stuck with it. Everything else is going to flow out of that sentence. And by the time you've laid down the first *two* sentences, your options are all gone. . . . I start a book and I want to make it perfect, want it to turn every colour, want it to *be the world*. Ten pages in, I've already blown it, limited it, made it less, marred it. That's very discouraging. I hate the book at that point."

"I know that many writers – Joyce Cary, for instance – compose the principal scenes of a novel before putting the connective work around it," Robertson Davies said. "Other people work backward and do all sorts of interesting things, but I don't. I just go from start to finish, and that's the first draft."

Ross MacDonald, writer of hard-boiled novels starring detective Lew Archer, wrote that one of his fictional district attorneys "prepared his cases as if he were laying the foundations of a society," and that's how Davies prepared to write a novel. "I make very, very careful plans and a great many notes – so many notes indeed that sometimes they are as long [as] or longer than the eventual book," he said. "And sketches of characters and suggestions and references to things that will be useful. All that takes a long time."

Before writing any novel, J.G. Ballard worked out his story and his cast in a detailed synopsis that might run to thirty thousand words and, in the case of *The Unlimited Dream Company* (1979), was longer than the published book. Sinclair Lewis's synopsis for *Babbitt* (1922) was sixty thousand words long. Nobel Prize laureate Naguib Mahfouz said that if he had not compiled files on each character in his three-thousand-page epic *The Cairo Trilogy* (1956–57) before starting to write it, he "would have gotten lost and forgotten something."

"I'm a great believer in outlines," Tom Wolfe said. "The outline for *The Right Stuff* [1979], for example, my nonfiction book about the astronauts, was three-hundred pages, cross-indexed. So I did a very thorough outline for *The Bonfire of the Vanities* [1987]."

Alberto Moravia had an entirely different kind of mind. He never worked from notes, or thought about his work while away from his desk, or, when he sat down with pen in hand, knew what he was about to write. "I trust in inspiration, which sometimes comes and sometimes doesn't," he said. "But I don't sit back waiting for it. I work *every* day."

Nor did Joseph Heller do any preparatory work for writing *Catch-22*:

> I was lying in bed in my four-room apartment on the West Side when suddenly this line came to me: "It was love at first sight. The first time he saw the chaplain, Someone fell madly in love with him." I didn't have the name Yossarian. The chaplain wasn't necessarily an army chaplain – he could have been a *prison* chaplain. But as soon as the opening sentence was available, the book began to evolve clearly in my mind – even most of the particulars . . . the tone, the form, many of the characters, including some I eventually couldn't use. All of this took place within an hour and a half.

It got me so excited that I did what the cliché says you're supposed to do: I jumped out of bed and paced the floor. That morning I went to my job at the advertising agency and wrote out the first chapter in longhand.

WRITING MEANS REWRITING. AND THEN? REWRITING

For many novelists, finishing a first draft was like merely crossing Mount Everest's foothills during an expedition to the peak. What made completing a book so formidable was the mountain of work they still faced. "I rewrite the whole thing anywhere from six to a dozen times," Erskine Caldwell said, "because I'm never satisfied." William Kennedy, who won a Pulitzer Prize for *Ironweed* (1983), wrote *Legs* (1975) eight times and said, "It was taller than my son when both he and the manuscript were six years old."

To avoid feeling discouraged, Gore Vidal raced through his first draft without rereading any of it. With the whole thing in front of him for the first time, and having forgotten much of it, he could see it afresh. "Rewriting, however, is a slow, grinding business," he said. "For me the main pleasure of having money is being able to afford as many completely retyped drafts as I like. When I was young and poor, I had to do my own typing, so I seldom did more than two drafts. Now I go through four, five, six. The more the better, since my style is very much one of afterthought."

Wallace Stegner said he knew his *Crossing to Safety* (1987) would be a novel, but not "*what* the book was. I've got piles of manuscripts over there, eight and ten inches high, of stuff written and tossed aside in the process of finding out. . . . Every morning you have to read over what you did yesterday, and if it doesn't persuade you, it has to be redone. Sometimes it takes me three hours in the morning to get over the feeling that I've been wasting my time for the past week, and that everything I've written up to that point is drivel."

E.L. Doctorow wrote his novels as many as eight times. As he began one, he had no idea how it would end. Writing it, he said, was like driving a car at night. You could finish an entire trip without ever seeing beyond your headlights. If you did happen to hit a dead end, you started all over again. After spending several months writing the first 150 pages of *The Book of Daniel* (1971), Doctorow threw them all away, but "the realization that I was doing a really bad book created the desperation that allowed me to find its true voice."

Once truly underway on your nocturnal drive, he said, "you may wander into culverts, through fences into fields, and so on. When you're off the road you don't always know it immediately. If you feel a bump on page one hundred, it may be you went off on page fifty. So you have to trace your way back, you see. It sounds like a hazardous way of working – and it is – but there is one terrific advantage to it: each book tends to have its own identity rather than the author's. It speaks from itself rather than you. Each book is unlike the others because you are not bringing the same voice to every book."

In the end, Doctorow said, Hemingway's bringing his own voice to every book "trapped him, restricted him, and defeated him. He was always Hemingway writing, you see. Of course, at his best that wasn't such a bad thing, was it? But if we're speaking of entry to the larger mind, his was not the way to find it."

Joan Didion wrote novels by retyping, retyping, retyping. "Every day I go back to page one and just retype what I have," she said. "It gets me into a rhythm. Once I get over maybe a hundred pages, I won't go back to page one, but I might go back to page fifty-five, or twenty, even. But then every once in a while I feel the need to go to page one again and start rewriting. At the end of the day, I mark up the pages I've done – pages or *page* – all the way back to page one. I mark them up so that I can retype them in the morning. It gets me past that blank terror." Was it any wonder that as she neared the end of her book, she slept in the same room with it? "Somehow," she said, "it doesn't leave you when you're asleep right next to it."

How to Turn Chaos into Order: Revise

In *My Miscellanies* (1863), Wilkie Collins marvelled over the fanatical busyness and thoroughness with which Balzac ripped into his own first drafts:

> In spite of all the preliminary studying and thinking, when his pen had scrambled its way straight through to the end of the book, the leaves were all turned back again, and the first manuscript was altered into a second with inconceivable patience and care. Innumerable corrections and interlinings, to begin with, led, in the end, to transpositions and expansions which metamorphosed the entire work. Happy thoughts were picked out of the beginning of the manuscript, and inserted where they might have better effect at the end. Others at the end would be moved to the beginning, or the middle. In one place, chapters would be expanded to three or four times their original length; in another, abridged to a few paragraphs; in a third, taken out altogether or shifted to new positions. With all this mass of alterations in every page, the manuscript was at last ready for the printer. Even to the experienced eyes in the printing office, it was now all but illegible.

Henry Miller, whose most famous novels (or, among those who saw them as obscene, most infamous novels) were *Tropic of Cancer* (1934) and *Tropic of Capricorn* (1939), reworked a first draft with similar zeal. A speedy typist, he raced through it "in any old way," just as it arrived in his mind. Then, after it "cooled off" for a month or two, he said, "I have a wonderful time of it. I just go to work on it with an axe. . . . I use a pen and ink to make changes, cross out, insert. The manuscript looks wonderful afterwards, like a Balzac." While retyping it, however, he made further changes. "I prefer to retype everything myself, because even when I think I've made all the changes I want, the mere mechanical business of touching the keys sharpens my thoughts, and I find myself revising while doing the finished thing."

Hemingway had such trouble "getting the words right" on the last page of *A Farewell to Arms* that he rewrote it thirty-nine times. "The first draft of anything," he said, "is shit." Short-story master Raymond Carver rewrote for up to fifteen hours a day and said, "There's not much that I like better than to take a story that I've had around the house for a while and work it over again. . . . I've done as many as thirty or forty drafts of a story." Robert Graves revised a manuscript "till I can't read it any longer, then I get somebody to type it, then I revise the typing. Then there's a third typing. Nothing should then remain that offends the eye."

Dismissing the theory that Colette wrote easily and thoughtlessly, Marie-Christine Bellosta, an expert on French literature, wrote, "One has only to examine the manuscripts . . . laden with corrections, to understand the price [Colette] paid, line after line, for the density of expression, the precision of detail, that transparency . . . that gives us the illusion of naturalness."

Owing to its pun-riddled and weirdly experimental prose, James Joyce's *Finnegans Wake* (1939) was notoriously incomprehensible, and Waugh saw it as proof that its creator had ended up "a lunatic," but American literary scholar David Stephen Calonne believed it was dazzling proof that revision was creative: "Joyce's astonishing manuscript is a maze of crossed-out words, bold scrawls, huge Xs splayed across the page, squiggly lines, scratches, a labyrinth, a massive, splendid, messy, outlandish display of genius. . . . Yet out of that chaos, Joyce made his own unique order."

In 1923, Sinclair Lewis showed the English novelist Arnold Bennett the manuscript of one of his novels, probably *Arrowsmith*

(1925), and Bennett showed Lewis the manuscript of his *Old Wives' Tale* (1908). To the American, the Englishman's document was "a strange MS, handwritten, in the most delicate script, legible as typing, with almost no changes in it, and decorated with colored initials by him, so that it's like a monkish scroll." To the Englishman, the American's first typescript of a work in progress was "a terrible sight." Indeed, it was "all blue and red with millions of alterations."

For some writers, revision meant having the courage to scrap tens of thousand of words they'd written. Lewis said he junked all but a few pages of the first thirty thousand words of *Main Street*. A young John Hersey spent a summer as his secretary and watched as he "endlessly" retyped drafts and "ruthlessly slashed out" thousands of words – "not scattered words and phrases but long passages, whole scenes."

William Gass, who created a character who wanted "to rise so high that when I shit I won't miss anybody," was sounding decidedly like himself when he defined "the real writing process" as "simply sitting there and typing the same old lines over and over and over and over and sheet after sheet after sheet gets filled with the same shit." That, perhaps, is why it took him twenty-six years to write *The Tunnel* (1995). That, perhaps, is also why *The Tunnel* was so good that critic Michael Silverblatt told readers of the *Los Angeles Times* it was "the most beautiful, most complex, most disturbing novel to be published in my lifetime."

"We Are Only Telephone Wires"

While trying to think, we often close our eyes. As cognitive neuroscientist Mark Jung-Beeman says, "Focus is all about blocking things out." He has spent fifteen years studying what happens inside your brain when you experience the kind of insight that might inspire you to cry, "Eureka!"

"This mental process will always be a little unknowable, which is why it's so interesting," he says. "At a certain point, you just have to admit that your brain knows more than you do." The brain contains a veritable Pacific of undiscovered knowledge, and perhaps creative writers – while blocking stuff out to achieve intense focus – have a rare if unwitting ability to extract what they need from that hidden ocean.

What, in the End, Was Reality?

The act of writing, Gore Vidal said, "obliterates time . . . Three hours seem like three minutes." John Hersey said he became "totally involved in the pictures and sounds" of passages he was writing and got "so lost in them that I'm unaware of my real surroundings." A young daughter of William Butler Yeats boarded a bus and found him there in a trance. He was humming, beating time with his hands, and staring straight ahead. Other passengers asked him if he was all right, but the little girl knew enough not to disturb him. After father and daughter got off the bus at their home, he turned to her, and murmured vaguely, "Oh, and who is it you wish to see?" When American poet Donald Hall was young, he remembered, his poems "arrived in a rush," and so captured his mind that he stumbled into furniture and could not recognize his children.

One of Tennessee Williams's landladies said he must have lost his mind because "he stalks about the room talking out loud," but a friend of his assured her he was "just writing." While Dickens wrote, he strode around his study, muttered to himself, yanked his beard, and made strange faces before a mirror. He saw and heard his characters, and laughed and wept with them. They were as real to him as his wife and children. "In the two or three or four months that it takes me to write a play," Edward Albee said, "I find that the reality of the play is a great deal more alive for me than what passes for reality. I'm infinitely more involved in the reality of the characters and their situation than I am in everyday life. The involvement is terribly intense."

"One can live so intensely with one's characters and the experience one creates or records," D.H. Lawrence wrote, "[that] it is a life in itself, far better than the vulgar thing people *call* life, jazzing and motoring and so on." Turkish novelist Orhan Pamuk said, "If I've been able to create even a tiny part of this miraculous world, I feel happy the moment I reach my desk. . . . In no time at all I can leave behind the familiar, boring world of the everyday, and step into this other, bigger place to wander freely, and most of the time I have no desire to return to real life."

When Flaubert was writing about Emma Bovary's suicide, he said, he could taste the arsenic she took. Michael Ondaatje remembered that, as he wrote the passage in his *In the Skin of the*

Lion (1987) about a man going through an underwater tunnel, "it was a bright, sunny day outside, the birds were twittering – and I was inside this damp tunnel, blackness all around me."

Salman Rushdie felt "completely possessed" by the people in *Shalimar the Clown* (2005), "to the extent that I found myself crying over my own characters. There's a moment in the book where Boonyi's father, the pandit Pyarelal, dies in his fruit orchard. I couldn't bear it. I found myself sitting at my desk weeping. I thought, what am I doing? This is somebody I've made up."

"James Jones greeted a laundryman with tears streaming down his face because of the punishment he was inflicting on his fictional offspring," author Ralph Keyes wrote. "Robert Stone, after killing a character he liked, couldn't write for a month."

"I really love the people I'm writing about," Canadian fiction writer Sandra Birdsell said. "I grew up with these women. I know what makes them cry, what makes them laugh. I could never be mean to them. And I have this really strong sense of loyalty to my family. You don't badmouth family. I wouldn't want to hurt them."

"I don't have a very clear idea of who the characters are until they start talking," Joan Didion explained. "Then I start to love them. By the time I finish the book, I love them so much that I want to stay with them. I don't want to leave them. Ever."

"Oh, the characters in my first novel [*The House of Breath*, 1950], haunt me to this day!" William Goyen said in 1975. "Actually *haunt* me. And characters like Oil King, who's been in my life a long, long time. I've lived with him and loved him and written about him for many, many years. They stay with me, yes, indeed they do. They stay. They not only enter my life, but I begin to see them in life, here, there."

Asked if writing *A Book of Jesus* (1973) was as exciting as writing fiction, Goyen said, "It was as though I were creating a character in this man. A marvellous experience. Astonishing. A very real man began to live with me, of flesh and blood. He did the same work on me that He did to the people of the New Testament that He walked among. He won me over, enchanted and captured me, finally possessed me. I went rather crazy with the love from Him that I felt."

To invent worlds that strike fiction writers as more real than the real one, they must enslave themselves to their work. Philip Roth said that, without something that totally engaged him, "life is hell for me." For some, it's the total engagement that amounts to torture. Whenever William Gass suffered one of his feverish urges to write, he could not help angrily pacing about his house. "My ulcer flourishes," he said. "I have to chew lots of pills. When my work is going well, I am usually sort of sick." Paul Auster described his writing of *The Music of Chance* (1990) as a tense and wrenching experience. "I felt pulverized by the end of it," he said, "and I couldn't do anything for about six months."

"When I get into a book, very rapidly I get into the story, and it becomes the real world for me," Isabel Allende wrote. "That is, when I'm driving the car, I'm not looking at the landscape, I'm in the landscape of the book. I try not to have any social life. I try not to travel. Because everything that distracts me from the world of the book annoys me, and bores me terribly."

Peruvian novelist Mario Vargas Llosa said that, once he reached the heart of a story he'd been working on for some time, "everything I experience exists only in relation to what I am writing. Everything I hear, see, read seems in one way or another to help my work. I become a kind of cannibal of reality. . . . I live a kind of permanent double life. I do a thousand different things, but I always have my mind on my work."

As Marguerite Young began *Miss MacIntosh, My Darling* (1965), she thought she'd finish it in two years but, after its characters took over the story, she said, "I worked from nine to five, for what was to be eighteen years of breathless writing. I never stopped. I was never bored. . . . I realized somewhere along the line, early, that it would take a long time. . . . I knew for sure that nothing else in life was going to interfere. I would not easily marry, I would not easily travel. I wanted to write this book – and I don't regret it."

Her engagement was total.

WHO'S WRITING THIS BOOK ANYWAY?

Following the instant success of Charlotte Brontë's *Jane Eyre* (1847), she confidently asserted, "When authors write best . . . an influence seems to waken in them which becomes their master, which will have its own way, putting out of view all behests but its own, dictating certain words, and insisting on their being used, whether vehement or measured in their nature; new-moulding characters, giving unthought-of turns to incidents, rejecting carefully elaborated old ideas, and suddenly creating and adopting new ones. Is it not so? And should we try to counteract this influence? Can we indeed counteract it?"

One hundred and forty-three years later, Isabel Allende said that, while writing for ten to twelve hours a day, she was "just a medium or an instrument of something that is happening beyond me, voices that talk through me. I'm creating a world that is fiction but doesn't belong to me. I'm not God. I'm just an instrument." Just a medium. "I feel the story I am writing existed before I existed," John Irving said. "I'm just the slob who finds it, and rather clumsily tries to do it, and the characters, justice. I think of writing fiction as doing justice to the people in the story, and doing justice to *their* story – it's not my story. It's entirely ghostly work. I'm just the medium."

About the unbidden invasion of Mavis Gallant's mind by bits of a story, she said, "It's almost as if it already existed and I was getting scraps of it. I don't sit down and think, now this man is going to do this. It just comes. And I don't know where from. I don't mean I'm a mystic. I don't mean it comes from the planet Venus or anything."

"Who writes the great books?" Henry Miller asked. "It isn't we who sign our names. What is an artist? He's a man who has antennae, who knows how to hook up to the currents which are in the atmosphere, in the cosmos. Who is original? Everything that we are doing, everything that we think, exists already, and we are only intermediaries, that's all, who make use of what's in the air." No matter how revered a writer might become, Miller continued, "he has nothing to be proud of, his name means nothing, his ego is nil, he's only an instrument in a long procession."

Rudyard's Kipling's closest friend, Rider Haggard, whose most famous novel was *She* (1887), in 1918 recorded in his diary Kipling's insisting "that anything any of us did *well* was no credit to us, that it came from somewhere else: 'We are only telephone wires. . . . You didn't write *She*, you know,' he said, 'something wrote it through you!'"

"When I feel I'm going to write something, then I just am quiet, and I try to listen," Jorges Luis Borges explained. "Then something comes through. And I do what I can in order not to tamper with it. And then, when I begin to hear what's coming through, I write it down. . . . So, I try to interfere as little as possible with the revelation. . . . I believe the author is actually one who receives."

A novel might jell in Robertson Davies's mind for years, and his preparatory notes might be longer than the eventual book, but it was only as he wrote it that he discovered its ending. In 1986, he told an audience in New York, "I shrink from saying this, but I've agreed to come here and talk about it, and it's true: I hear the story, I am told the story, I record the story. I don't pretend that some remarkable person somewhere else is whispering in my ear, or that a beautiful lady in a diaphanous gown is telling me what I should write. It is just a part of my own creative process that I am not immediately in touch with and certainly not in full control of."

"I feel myself inhabited by a force or being – very little known to me," Jean Cocteau said. "It *gives* the orders; I follow. . . . If the ideas come, one must hurry to set them down out of fear of forgetting them. They come once; once only." Cocteau did not use words like "sacred" or "divine," but he seemed to believe that any correcting, revising, or rewriting of whatever he wrote while obeying the force would be a sacrilege. At times, he felt that not even punctuation should intrude on what the force made him create. In his long poem, "Requiem," he blithely explained, "I leave repetitions, *maladresses*, words badly placed quite unchanged, and there is no punctuation. It would be artificial to impose punctuation on a black river of ink. A hundred and seventy pages – yes – and no punctuation."

Conrad, the most long-suffering of perfectionists, would have seen Cocteau's belief in the sanctity of unrevised, unpunctuated rivers of ink as ludicrous, but when his literary confidante, Edward Garnett, suggested he change certain paragraphs in the manuscript of *An Outcast of the Islands* (1896), he replied, "All my work is produced unconsciously (so to speak) and I cannot meddle to any purpose with what is within myself – I am sure you understand what I mean. – It isn't in me to improve what has got itself written."

Pulitzer-winning poet James Wright described "a force of life like the spring that mysteriously takes shape without your even having asked it to take shape." This had happened to him only a few times. It enabled him to finish certain poems "in almost nothing flat," but was "terribly frightening." Wright had no idea where those particular poems had come from. "Being a poet sometimes puts you at the mercy of life," he said, "and life is not always merciful."

The English novelist, writer of children's fiction, and defender of Christianity, C.S. Lewis, believed no mortal was ever a creative writer. "We rearrange elements He has provided," he insisted.

"There is not a vestige of real creativity *de novo* in any of us. Try to imagine a new primary colour, a third sex, a fourth dimension, or even a monster which does not consist of bits of existing animals stuck together. Nothing happens. And that surely is why our works never mean to others quite what we intended: because we are recombining elements made by Him and already containing *His* meanings."

"That's our function, to mix the elements He has given us," said Pamela Lyndon Travers, who wrote the *Mary Poppins* books. "See how wonderfully anonymous that leaves us? You can't say, '*I* did this; this gross matrix of flesh and blood and sinews and nerves did this.' What nonsense! I'm given these things to make a pattern out of. Something gave it to me."

Talking in 1975 about the experience of working on *The Gulag Archipelago* (1970), Aleksandr Solzhenitsyn revealed, "It seemed as if it was no longer I who was writing; rather, I was swept along, my hand was being moved by an outside force, and I was only the firing pin attached to a spring." He felt he was God's tool. "I had learned in my years of imprisonment to sense that guiding hand," he later wrote, "to glimpse that bright meaning beyond and above myself and my wishes."

American novelist John Gardner, who believed God might have put him on earth to write, said he'd have plots of several novels all boiling around in his head at the same time but, for reasons he did not understand, one would rise above all the others: "One of them catches you like a nightmare. Then you have no choice but to write it; you can't forget it. It's a weird thing. If it's the kind of plot you really don't want to do because it involves your mother too closely, or whatever, you can try to do something else. But the typewriter keeps hissing at you and shooting sparks, and the paper keeps wrinkling and the lamp goes off and nothing else works, so finally you do the one that God said you've got to do."

GET A GRIP ON YOURSELF, HEDKY. YOU'RE NOT EVEN REAL

An interviewer reminded Nabokov that Forster talked about his major characters having dictated the course of his novels, and asked, "Has this ever been a problem for you, or are you in complete command?"

"My knowledge of Mr. Forster's works is limited to one novel, which I disliked," Nabokov replied testily, "and anyway, it was not he who fathered that trite little whimsy about characters getting out of hand; it is as old as the quills, although of course one sympathizes with *his* people if they try to wriggle out of that trip to India or wherever he takes them. My characters are galley slaves."

Nor did the Canadian fiction writer Alistair MacLeod allow his characters to become so independent they took over his plots. "I'm too frugal a Scotsman," he said. "I say, 'You be careful, or I'll kill you before page twenty-six. This is *my* novel.'"

"The legend that characters run away from their authors – taking up drugs, having sex operations, and becoming president – implies that the writer is a fool with no knowledge or mastery of his craft," John Cheever said. "This is absurd. Of course, any estimable exercise of the imagination draws upon such a complex richness of memory that it truly enjoys the expansiveness – the surprising turns, the response to light and darkness – of any living thing. But the idea of authors running around helpless behind their cretinous inventions is contemptible."

If not exactly helpless, however, many writers find themselves in a clash of wills with a cretinous invention who demands to go not their way but his own. "For example, in *The Rat* [1987] I had never planned to reintroduce Mr. Matzerath as a sixty-year-old man," Günter Grass said. "But he presented himself to me, kept asking to be included, saying, I am still here; this is also my story. He wanted to get into the book. I have often found that . . . these invented people begin to make demands, contradict me, or even refuse to allow themselves to be used. One is well advised to take heed of these people now and then. Of course, one must listen to one's self. It becomes a kind of dialogue, sometimes a very heated one. It is cooperation."

Speaking of characters who "forge their own way," American playwright August Wilson said, "Hedky in *Seven Guitars* [1995], for example, assumed a much larger presence than I had originally imagined. He ended the first act, and I was surprised to find him on stage alone at the start of the second act. He *demanded* that I focus on him and what he had to say. He was a most unruly character. He threatened to knock down the set and remake the world to his liking. In times like that you have to reassert your authorial control."

When William Maxwell, fiction editor of *The New Yorker*, was writing his novel *Time Will Darken It* (1949), it wasn't just a Matzerath or Hedky who took charge. "A set of characters seized me, and ran off with me," Maxwell recalled. He failed to reassert his authorial control. "My function was simply to record what they said and did, rather than shape the goings on."

Joyce Carol Oates admitted her *The Assassins* (1975) was much too long because "it was impossible to shut Hugh Petrie up once he got going. . . . The problem with creating such highly conscious and intuitive characters is that they . . . try to guide or even to take over the direction of the narrative. Hugh did not want to die, and so his section went on and on, and it isn't an exaggeration to say that I felt real dismay in dealing with him."

As the most spectacular example of a fictional character who defied his creator by choosing his own fate and speaking his own dialogue, Robert Fulford nominated Shylock. For here was "a secondary character who grew like Frankenstein's monster until finally he swamped an otherwise neatly constructed comedy, which he was supposed to garnish with his exotic presence. . . . [Shylock is] so abrasive in his bitterness that audiences go home

thinking only of him and forgetting all the people around him."
The strange blossoming of the Jew who demanded his pound of
flesh, Fulford believed, startled even Shakespeare.

It's the "Unexpected Dividend"
That Makes It All Worthwhile

"One day around chapter two or three, I'll be slogging through
some dialogue and all of a sudden a character says something that
makes me laugh," American novelist Anne Tyler said. "Where did
that come from? *I'm* not funny. Then another will flatly refuse the
plot contrivance I've designed for him. I'll write a scene this way,
write a scene that way; it slows to a crawl and stops. Finally, I say,
'Oh, all right,' and I drop the contrivance and the scene falls into
place and I see a motive I'd never guessed and I understand where
we're going. It's as if someone else is telling the story."

Katherine Anne Porter told an interviewer, "By the time I write
my story my people are up and alive and walking around and
taking things into their own hands. They exist as independently
inside my head as you do before me now." Eudora Welty's characters were so real to her that she wrote scenes and dialogue for
them that she knew she'd never use. "Just to let them loose on
something," she laughed. "My private show."

"Of all my books [*Shalimar the Clown*] was the book that was
most completely written by its characters," Salman Rushdie said.
"Quite a lot of the original conception of the book had to be jet-
tisoned because the characters wanted to go another way."

Erskine Caldwell insisted that his characters "completely" controlled him. "I have no influence over them," he said. "I'm only an
observer, recording. The story is always being told by the characters themselves. In fact, I'm often critical, or maybe ashamed, of
what some of them say and do – their profanity or their immoral-
ity. . . . Some of them are reprehensible."

Sir Roy Vendervane, the fifty-four-year-old lover of a seventeen-year-old girl in Kingsley Amis's *Girl, 20* (1971) was certainly reprehensible. Amis, however, said, "Oh, I'm very fond of Roy," and then, as though Vendervane were as real as Philip Larkin, "One couldn't think of a better chap to have a boozy lunch with."

After Ray Bradbury's publishers asked him to add twenty-five thousand words to his novella, *The Fireman* (1951), to turn it into the novel *Fahrenheit 451* (1953), he called his characters back, "and asked them to speak to me, which is how I do all my writing. I listen to my characters, I watch them and I put down their reactions. I knew that Beatty, the Fire Captain, had more to offer about his history of book burning. I knew that Clarisse McClellan had something to say about her fancies and about the culture she survived in. . . . So I listened to them again."

"You have to be able to surprise yourself," Robert Stone said. "In *Dog Soldiers* [1974] I didn't know Hicks was going to shoot Dieter until the day I wrote it. I just began writing their dialogue until it became inevitable." William Kennedy believed a story "percolates" only when a character does something the writer never expected, and said, "If I knew at the beginning how the book was going to end, I would probably never finish." James Jones had written three hundred pages of *From Here to Eternity* (1951) before he realized that Sergeant Milt Warden was headed for a passionate affair with Karen Holmes, the wife of Captain Dana Holmes. "So I had to go back and bring that about," Jones said. "But even then I didn't know how it would end."

The surprise that awaited Styron, as he wrote *Sophie's Choice* (1979), was that Sophie Zawistowska had "an obsessive need to lie." While recalling her life for Stingo, the young narrator of the novel, she described her father as a Polish intellectual – and a brave saviour of Jews during World War II. Styron believed her. "But it began to dawn on me later on as I was writing the book that what she was saying was a lie," he said. "That she was deceiving Stingo for her own self-protection, her own self-image, to prevent her from telling the truth. Which was the fact that instead of being a man who helped save Jews, [her father] was in fact a rabid anti-Semite. Of course I reveal that later, but it's one of the interesting aspects of the creative process that I really believed her in the beginning."

Styron told this story as though Sophie were a woman whose voice he'd heard over cocktails, whose arm he'd held while crossing Fifth Avenue, whose fragrance he could still smell. It had taken him a while to discover the truth about her, but there it was. She was a liar.

"I'm always waiting for a character who's going to come in and confuse the plot a bit more," Michael Ondaatje said, "or make it more interesting, take it another way, try to kidnap it." That's what happened while Susan Sontag wrote *The Volcano Lover* (1992). She intended it to be the story of Sir William Hamilton but, she said, his twenty-year-old wife, Emma, the lover of Lord Nelson, "kidnapped the book. And that permitted the novel to open out . . . into a furor of storytelling and of reflections about justice, war and cruelty."

Truman Capote said he invariably had the illusion that the start, middle, and ending of a story all occurred in his mind simultaneously. "But in the working-out, the writing-out, infinite surprises happen," he said. "Thank God, because the surprise, the twist, the phrase that comes at the right moment out of nowhere, is the unexpected dividend, that joyful little push that keeps a writer going."

Anthony Burgess prepared to compose a novel by writing a list of names and rough synopses of chapters but, he said, "one daren't overplan; so many things are generated by the sheer act of writing." John Irving, however, believed that the authority of the storyteller's voice came "from knowing how it all comes out before you begin." There was nothing "divine" about the happy accidents that occurred while he wrote. "I believe you have constructive accidents en route through a novel only because you have mapped a clear way," he said. ". . . The more you know about a book, the freer you can be to fool around."

AND THE CREATION TEACHES THE CREATOR

In Margaret Atwood's *The Edible Woman* (1969), Marian McAlpin begins to feel that a steak her boyfriend is eating has human qualities and imagines it "knocked on the head as it stood in a queue like someone waiting for a streetcar." Soon, she can no longer eat anything "with bone or tendon or fibre." Atwood later allowed, "I've looked at steak differently since seeing it through the eyes of Marian – which was how I first learned that writing fiction is a two-way street. If the author gets too bossy, the characters may remind her that, though she is their creator, they are to some extent her creator as well."

TWENTY-FIVE

What's Worse Than Writing? *Not* Writing

Describing Colette in 1926, portrait painter André Dunoyer de Segonzac wrote, "Her fine and powerful arms served as buttresses on the lectern. She remained there, as if frozen, for hours. . . . Only the rustling page, as she threw it off with controlled rage, broke the silence from time to time." Half a century later, controlled rage was the engine behind the work of American essayist and fiction writer William Gass. "Usually, I am in my best working mood when I am, on the page, very combative, very hostile," he said. "That's true even when I write to praise. . . . If I write about Colette, as I am now, my appreciation will be shaped by the sap-tongued idiots who don't perceive her excellence."

It was authors like Gass that Cynthia Ozick had in mind when she said, "One reason writers write is out of revenge. Life hurts; certain ideas and experiences hurt; one wants to clarify, to set out illuminations, to replay the old bad scenes and [say] the words one didn't have the strength or ripeness to say when those words were necessary for one's dignity or survival." Life hurts. It began to hurt Gass in his childhood. His mother was a spineless drunkard, and his father, crippled and soured by arthritis, was bigoted and abusive.

Getting even, Gass believed, was "one great reason for writing," and "I write because I hate. A lot. Hard. . . . I wish to make my hatred acceptable because my hatred is much of me, if not the best part. Writing is a way of making the writer acceptable to the world – every cheap, dumb, nasty thought, every despicable desire, every noble sentiment, every expensive taste. There isn't very much satisfaction in getting the world to accept and praise you for things that the world is prepared to praise. The world is prepared to praise only shit. One wants to make sure that the complete self, with all its qualities, is not just accepted but approved . . . not just approved – whoopeed."

Another angry novelist, Robert Stone, admired *Caligula* (1944), a play by Albert Camus, because its plot spun round "a wonderful idea": Caligula revenged himself against the world for being "a murderous, bad place," by becoming a murderous, bad tyrant. Not only Stone but many of his characters felt "a kind of fundamentally childish rage against things for being so imperfect. For being so unsatisfactory. This brings forth a tremendous anger. And when you're making up stories . . . perhaps you're trying to make things come out right."

Poet Amy Clampitt believed every poet sometimes wrote out of rage, but women more than men. "Women have been given reason to recognize a lot of things that have been covered up for a long time," she said in 1993. "What preceded the rage was a lot of anxiety. When you get over the anxiety you discover you should have been mad a long time ago. Women are full of steam, and mostly they're making a lot of noise. I don't necessarily like it, but some very plausible stuff is being written by women in a way that most men are not doing."

If rage compelled some to write, boredom compelled others. For Graham Greene, boredom was not just a matter of stifling yawns when trapped by the tedious during weekends in the country; it was continuing psychological torture and a powerful ally of suicidal depression. Greene sought to escape the monster by taking opium; drinking heavily; hiring prostitutes; journeying to exotic, primitive, and dangerous corners of the world; and burying himself in his writing.

Boredom was Evelyn Waugh's "greatest enemy, and it haunted him throughout his days," his son, Alexander Waugh, wrote. "Fear of it and cravings for shock or excitement are classic symptoms of a depressive disorder. . . . The stark horrors of boredom terrified him." Waugh may have been the only major writer who ever suffered nightmares about being bored. He complained about "dreams of unendurable boredom – of reading page after page of dullness, of being told endless, pointless jokes, of sitting through cinema films devoid of interest." Not even foreign travel lifted the curse. The boredom Waugh endured during four days in Abyssinia was "as black and timeless as Damnation; a handful of ashes thrown into the eyes, a blanket over the face, a mass of soft clay, knee deep."

Turkish novelist Orhan Pamuk said he had to be "bored to distraction" in order to write, but this was tolerable because real life bored him to distraction: "It is when I am bombarded with noise, sitting in an office full of ringing phones, surrounded by friends and loved ones on a sunny seashore or at a rainy funeral . . . that I will suddenly feel I'm no longer there, but watching from the sidelines. I'll begin to daydream. If I'm feeling pessimistic, I can think about how bored I am. Either way, there will be a voice inside me, urging me to 'go back to the room and sit down at the table.'"

When an interviewer reminded Margaret Drabble that many of her characters were terrified of boredom, she said, "Well, so am I. I don't see why other people don't worry about it more." At the same time, "in some awful way," boredom was creative. "One's got to rise out of it in some way," she said. "And the way that I'm most familiar with is by writing."

"You have to use your imagination to invent something better than life," Erskine Caldwell said, "because life itself is dull and prosaic."

LIFE WITHOUT WRITING? NOT POSSIBLE

New York novelist and biographer Francine du Plessix Gray, whose parents had left her alone with a horrifying governess every night during her childhood, found in her writing "a mature way of exorcizing the fear of abandonment, the dread of annihilation which filled my early years. The text in progress is like a fire in the room, an animal, it speaks, hollers, barks, growls back at me, like a magical dog guarding my body from evils, guarding me against the threat of extinction."

Like her, many writers knew their work was essential to their sanity, if not their very existence. Peruvian novelist Mario Vargas Llosa vowed, "If I didn't write, I would blow my brains out, without a shadow of a doubt." Four years before Katherine Mansfield died of tuberculosis, she confided to her diary, "Life without *work* – I would commit suicide. Therefore work is more important than life." Pablo Neruda declared, "For me, writing is like breathing. I could not live without breathing and I could not live without writing." Canadian novelist Marian Engel asserted, "If writing ever deserts me, I shall have no life at all," and James Dickey said, "If I lose poetry, which is the centre of my creative wheel, I lose everything."

"Writing is something I cannot imagine living without," said poet and fiction writer William Goyen. "Not to live daily as a writing person is inconceivable to me." For John Irving, writing was an appetite he had no choice but to satisfy: "I am compulsive about writing. I need to do it the way I need sleep and exercise and food and sex; I can go without it for a while, but then I need it."

Philip Roth said that any illness that stopped him from writing but left him otherwise healthy would drive him clean out of his mind. His *only* interest was solving the problems that writing a book threw at him. That, he explained, was "what stops my brain spinning like a car wheel in the snow, obsessing about nothing."

Henry Vincent Yorke, the upper-class English gent who published nine novels under the pseudonym Henry Green, said in 1950, "The great thing in life is to get yourself right – not your health, but your brain. . . . And I found quite early that I can only get myself right by writing. In other words, a kind of mental diarrhea, do you see? And I found, and I believe, that the only happiness in life is by self-expression. Oh, yes, there's married life, and children, but there's something beyond that – and I've been married twenty-two years. The expression of one's self, which I still believe is writing. . . . And so I found my happiness in life not through earning my living or through gardening or fishing but through writing."

Green published nothing after 1952 and, long before he died twenty-one years later, spiralled into hopeless alcoholism. Describing him in his later years, Evelyn Waugh wrote, "Very long black hair, one brown tooth, pallid puffy face, trembling hands, stone deaf, smoking continuously throughout meals, picking up books in the middle of conversation & falling into maniac giggles, drinking a lot of raw spirits, hating the country and everything good." Green had found happiness through writing; having quit the writing, he lost the happiness.

THE CURSE THAT REWARDS ITS VICTIMS

Gish Jen, whose first novel, *Typical American* (1991), was a finalist for the National Book Critics' Circle Award, later doubted the worth of her work and, like a cigarette addict trying to quit smoking, applied the cold-turkey treatment to her habit. She busied herself with everything but writing. She gardened, lunched, contributed to worthy causes, chatted with dog owners and "leafleteers," and spent much good time with her children. None of this worked. "I went back [to writing] because life without prose was prosaic," she said. "It seemed as though the wind had stopped blowing. It seemed as though someone had disinvented music – such silence. I felt as though I had lost one of my senses."

Gore Vidal called Anthony Burgess "easily the most interesting English writer in the last half century," but when Burgess was fifty-six and had written eighteen novels, he said he disliked what he did for a living. "Establishing one's identity through an art form," he said, turned one into "a kind of Frankenstein creating a monster." While writing, he suffered "intolerable" anxiety. His income did not make up for "the expenditure of energy, the damage to health caused by stimulants and narcotics, the fear that one's work isn't good enough." If he only had enough money, he vowed, "[he'd] give up writing tomorrow."

When he died two decades later, he was a multimillionaire. For years, he'd had more than enough money to quit writing, but the tomorrow on which he'd promised to do it had never come. In his last five years, he wrote the second volume of an autobiography; a book about Mozart; "An Essay on Censorship," which was an open letter in verse to Salman Rushdie; introductions or prefaces to thirteen books by others; and four novels. He finished the last of these, *Byrne* (1995), on his deathbed, and critic Dana Gioia said it was "so fresh, funny and inventive that it ranks among his finest creations."

Why was it that Burgess, even while succumbing to lung cancer, could not lift his nose from the grindstone? "To some of us," he once wrote, "the wresting of beauty out of language is the only thing in the world that matters."

He was hardly the only author who both hated and loved to write.

"Writing is like a contact sport, like football," said the muscular and athletic Irwin Shaw. "You can get hurt, but you enjoy it."

In 1954, less than two minutes after Styron said, "Let's face it, writing is hell," he added, "I find that I'm simply the happiest, the placidest, when I'm writing. . . . It's the only time that I feel completely self-possessed, and I suppose that that, for me, is the final answer." Forty-five years later, after surviving a depression that shoved his mind into "deep stagnation" and threatened his very life, he said writing was "every bit as hard as it was [in 1954], if not harder."

But then: "How wonderful it's been to make these various breakthroughs and feel the power of creation, which is a great joy indeed."

For Walker Percy, whose six novels included the National Book Award winner *The Moviegoer* (1961), writing was "the worst and best of all possible worlds." While staring at a blank sheet of paper, first thing in the morning, he envied even "a guy selling Electroluxes, any salesman, anybody, a garbage collector. At least he's doing honest work, and here I'm looking at this stupid piece of paper and wondering what's going to happen, what am I doing here. This is a bad way to spend your life."

But then: "If I'm writing well, I'd rather write than anything else."

On any day that Orhan Pamuck's writing went poorly, he said, the world "becomes unbearable, abominable. . . . I feel as if there is no line between life and death. I don't want to speak to anyone, and anyone seeing me in this state has no desire to speak to me either."

But then: "The greatest source of happiness is to write a good half page every day," and "the thing that binds me to life is writing novels."

As far back as Ozick could remember, she believed she was born to write a novel, and at fifty-seven she said, "I think of·this given condition as a kind of curse, because there is no way out of it. What a relief it would be to have the freedom of other people!

Any inborn condition of this sort is, after all, a kind of slavery." In her twenties, she turned herself into "an unnatural writing beast." She read books so incessantly that she became "some kind of monster. I'm still that monster." The monster, however, now knew something inescapable: "The only thing more tormenting than writing is not writing."

A native of New York whose intense Jewishness influenced her work, Ozick hadn't much in common with Flannery O'Connor, a native of Georgia whose intense Catholicism influenced *her* work but, as writers, perhaps they were sisters under the skin. After finishing one novel, O'Connor confided to a friend, "Not writing is a good deal worse than writing."

Like Ozick, Pulitzer-winning poet James Wright saw his calling as "a kind of a curse." He often wondered, "Why the hell couldn't I have been a carpenter or a handyman?" Unwittingly, however, he soon answered that question with a passionate, ferry-across-the-Styx tribute to poetry that no carpenter or handyman could ever have uttered:

"Language is the element of definition, the defining and descriptive incantation. It puts the coin between our teeth. It whistles the boat up. It shows us the city of light across the water. Without language there is no poetry. Without poetry there's just talk. Talk is cheap and proves nothing. Poetry is dear and difficult to come by. But it poles us across the river and puts a music in our ears. It moves us to contemplation. And what we contemplate, what we sing our hymns to and offer our prayers to, is what will reincarnate us in the natural world, and what will be our hope for salvation in the What's-To-Come."

Now *That's* Happiness

Some authors wrote not out of rage or boredom, or to remain sane, or because a curse left them no choice, but simply because they *liked* to write. E.M. Forster actually found writing "pleasant," a word that made the work that tormented Philip Roth sound no more onerous than a stroll among the blossoms and swans in Regent's Park. Forster could not understand what other writers meant by "throes of creation." He "enjoyed" writing and believed that, "in some ways," his published work was good. "Whether it will last," he casually added, "I have no idea."

While writing was hard and exhausting, Aldous Huxley said, "I've always considered myself very lucky to be able to make a living at something I enjoy doing. So few people can." Erskine Caldwell supposed he wrote for the same reason that some people were "addicted to singing to themselves. . . . I write because it makes me feel good."

Did William Maxwell enjoy writing seven days a week? "An insane life, but what happiness!" he replied. "It's really self-indulgence." At seventy-six, Somerset Maugham, who had been writing novels, short stories, and plays for more than half a century, said, "Even when a thing is difficult, if you are a writer you are never so happy as when you are writing." Whenever Simenon's doctor diagnosed him as unhappy, he asked him when he had finished his last book. "And when I say, 'Six weeks ago,' Simenon recalled, the doctor invariably replied, 'Then I have one thing only to prescribe: Start a novel.'"

Early one Sunday afternoon, at a beach house in Southern California, E.L. Doctorow finished *The Book of Daniel* (1971) and asked his wife to read the manuscript. Beside the surf and under the wheeling gulls on the sunny beach, he walked by himself for hour after hour, worrying all the while if his "dark book, very much a New York City book," was any good. He returned home, with "the house in shadows now, and there was Helen sitting in the same chair and the manuscript was piled upside down on the table and she couldn't speak; she was crying, there were these enormous tears running down her cheeks, and it was the most incredible moment – never before had I known such happiness."

Asked if he felt godlike while writing, Cheever said, "No, the sense is of one's total usefulness. We all have power of control. . . . We have it in love, in work that we love doing. It's a sense of ecstasy, as simple as that. The sense is that 'this is my usefulness, and I can do it all the way through.' It always leaves you feeling great. In short, you've made sense of your life." He had never written anything that totally satisfied him but, he said, "When I write a story that I really like, it's . . . why, wonderful!"

A year before Katherine Mansfield succumbed to tuberculosis at thirty-four, she ended her short story "A Cup of Tea" and interrupted the morbid and deeply despairing tone of her diary to exult, "There is no feeling to be compared with the feeling of having written and finished a story. I did not go to sleep, but nothing mattered. There it was, *new* and complete."

To write well, said novelist and historian Shelby Foote, "is a huge pleasure, and you feel awfully good about it." Loneliness was a deadly enemy of happiness but, he continued, "when you're working very hard you're not lonely; you are the whole damn world." He deserved no credit for working hard, because he was doing exactly what he wanted to do. "Shakespeare said it best: 'The labour we delight in physics pain.'" At eighty-two, Foote asserted, "There's no better feeling in the world than to lay your head on the pillow at night looking forward to getting up in the morning and returning to that desk. That's real happiness."

NEVER SAY QUIT

In 1910, at thirty-nine, Marcel Proust – an eccentric, asthmatic semi-invalid, and unknown literary genius – holed up in his smelly, cork-lined apartment in Paris to write *À la recherche du temps perdu*, which would eventually run to nearly 1.5 million words. As year after year passed, his asthma attacks became more violent, and his

novel became his life. When the tortures of bronchitis and pneu-
monia succeeded those of asthma, Proust raced with death to
improve his manuscripts and correct his proofs. "He still wanted
the time to make *À la recherche* as perfect as he imagined it," C.P.
Snow wrote. "He was getting weaker, his lungs were failing at
last. One night [his right-hand woman, Céleste Albaret], sleepless
by the sickbed, copied in her firm strong hand passages from his
shaking one, adding them to the manuscript of [one of the novel's
several volumes]. He died the next day, November 18, 1922."

During the last two decades of Colette's eighty-one years, a
crippling form of arthritis gained on her, but it was only when she
could no longer hold her pen that she quit writing. William
Maxwell joined *The New Yorker* as an editor at twenty-eight and
kept right on contributing to it until he was ninety-one, when
death silenced his typewriter.

On May 30, 1990, Isaac Asimov, who knew he was dying of heart
and kidney failure, finished typing his third autobiography and
wrote, "It is now all ready to hand in, 125 days after I started it. Not
many can write 235,00 words in that time, while doing other things
as well." As he grew weaker he still wrote every day and, when he
could no longer type, dictated articles to his wife, Janet. In the last
of these, he said, "It has always been my ambition to die in harness
with my head face down on a keyboard and my nose caught
between two of the keys, but that's not the way it worked out."
At seventy-two, in April 1992, he died peacefully in hospital.

Even after V.S. Pritchett reached his eighties, he raced up four
flights of stairs to his study at 9 a.m. every day, lit his pipe, laid a
pastry board across the arms of his chair, and, using a pen and
paper, wrote reviews and short stories. Whole mornings, he said,
flashed by "in a few minutes." He often worked before and after
dinner as well, and there were nights when he wrote even in his
sleep, "in English mostly but often, out of vanity, in Spanish."
Pritchett was a journalist, biographer, autobiographer, travel

writer, novelist, and perhaps the best writer of both short stories and literary criticism that England produced in the twentieth century. In his mid-eighties, he remained a favourite critic of the *New York Review of Books*. At eighty-eight, he published his biography of Chekhov, and at eighty-nine, his *A Careless Widow and Other Stories* (1989). He slowed down in his nineties and, not long after suffering a stroke in 1997, died in a London hospital.

When Patrick O'Brian died at eighty-five in 2007, he left sixty-five handwritten pages of his twenty-first novel about the adventures during the Napoleonic Wars of British naval officer Jack Aubrey and his constant shipmate, the physician and naturalist Stephen Maturin. Readers bought more than two million copies of the Aubrey-Maturin yarns, and critics and writers compared O'Brian to Austen, Melville, Proust, and Conrad. For decades, he lived in a French fishing village near Spain, but his wife died before he tackled his last book, and on his own he could not manage the house in which he'd built the ideal hideout for his writing. He now worked by himself in quarters at Trinity College, Dublin.

For his diehard fans, HarperCollins of London published *The Final Unfinished Voyage of Jack Aubrey* (2004), which was also the final unfinished voyage of Patrick O'Brian, and in the foreword William Waldegrave wrote, "It is impossible not to be moved by the courage and anxiety of O'Brian, now an old man and alone . . . as he tries to keep his pages in order, writes notes about the need for more ink cartridges for his pen, and on one page writes, very small, 'I am absurdly sleepy,' in the way that medieval scribes sometimes wrote comments about the weather or their health in the margins of the illuminated manuscripts on which they were working.

"It is the courage that is most striking: the discipline, the will. He has no intention of retiring or throwing in the towel."

At ninety-one, P.G. Wodehouse, who had written nine novels in his eighties and had just finished another, whose title, *Bachelors Anonymous*, he called "wonderful," said he loved writing so much he could not stop, but he did not want to be like Bernard Shaw. "He turned out some awfully bad stuff in his nineties," Wodehouse said. "He knew the stuff was bad but he couldn't stop writing."

Shaw's last book was a collection of short pieces for the stage, and in the preface he admitted that, at ninety-four, "I can hardly walk through my garden without a tumble or two; and it seems out of all reason to believe that a man who cannot do a simple thing like that can practice the craft of Shakespeare. . . . Well, I grant all this; yet I cannot hold my tongue nor my pen. As long as I live I must write."

In April 2007, seven months before Mailer died at eighty-four, an interviewer asked him what he thought of a rumour that a senior American novelist had recently visited another senior American novelist – one who was much older, and at the twilight of his life – and told him, "Enough now, no more writing."

"No, I can't believe it," Mailer said. "I'll tell you, if anyone ever came to me with that, I'd say, kidding is kidding, but get your ass off my pillow."

From the Great French Hunter
of *"le Mot Juste"*: *le Mot Dernier*

W hen Gustave Flaubert started to write *Madame Bovary* in 1852, he was a thirty-year-old failure. He had achieved nothing, but he told his lover, Louise Colet, "I am a man of the quill. I feel through it, because of it, in relation to it, and much more with it." That same year, he wrote, "I love my work with a frenetic and perverted love, as the ascetic loves the hair shirt that scratches his belly."

He wrote in the white eighteenth-century mansion that his late father, a wealthy doctor, had bought in 1844 at Croisset, a hamlet on the Seine, just downriver from the heavy industries of Rouen in Normandy. Flaubert shared the house with his mother and orphaned niece but, for his writing, reserved the finest room for himself. A silent first-floor chamber with tall windows, it offered a splendid view of his garden, wooded islands in the curving river, and far-off meadows.

At work, Flaubert often wore not the professional man's clothing of the day – a tight, scratchy outfit made of black serge – but a burnoose, which was both comfortable and exotic. A long, white, hooded cloak that fitted his corpulent body loosely, it might have come from Arabia or North Africa. It was the sort of garment people would expect to see on the novelist soon to be known throughout France as "the hermit of Croisset," and he sometimes wore it while strolling in his garden.

On a big round writing table, he kept his quills in a brass bowl, his ink in a frog-shaped well, and his paper in a neat stack. A white bearskin rug lay before the fireplace, and a green carpet covered most of the floor. While writing, Flaubert sat in a green morocco armchair with ornate wooden trim and a tall back. His divan, also green leather, was essential to his creativity. "I think best lying on my back with my eyes closed," he said. Sometimes, however, he sprawled "in every possible position all over my room in search of what to say."

"Croisset was horribly damp," his biographer Geoffrey Wall wrote. "On the ground floor the moisture ran down the walls. Damp houses, damp souls. . . . We have to imagine the smell of the place, a rich, warm, damp, blend of riverbank, garden leaf-mould, ancient staircase, leather-bound folio, authorial pipe smoke, and *cuisine bourgeoisie*." Memories of the dead mingled with the smell; in 1846, Flaubert's younger sister and beloved father had died within three months of each other.

Flaubert regularly wrote all night, and men on the river used the lamplight from his windows as a beacon. As if this weren't enough to make him a local curiosity, he was one of the noisiest writers who ever lived. With quill in hand, he moaned, whispered, and repeated words again and again. Then, having found the ones that satisfied him for the moment, he marched around his study, chanting their syllables in time with his steps. He also tramped throughout the house, shouting, singing, and bursting into tears. He declaimed from one novel he was writing at such length and volume that he had to drink jugfuls of water. While writing *Un Coeur simple* in 1876, his health was collapsing – he had four more years to live – but that did not stop him from "bellowing like a fiend in the silence of [his] study." Twenty-four years before that, as he wrestled with *Madame Bovary*, he wrote, "Don't know why my chest hasn't caved in, I've been bellowing four hours without stopping."

When he finished *Madame Bovary*, he gave it a pre-publication tryout. "As he stomps up and down the avenue of lime trees in his garden, sometimes with his friend and mentor Louis Bouilhet," wrote Timothy Unwin, a British expert on French literature, "Flaubert bellows out the sentences of *Madame Bovary*, to the amazement or amusement of the folk in passing river craft. This is the legendary *gueuloir*, or 'yelling place,' where the novelist puts his writing through the test of sound, rhythm and vocal fluidity, subjecting it to the final quality control."

Flaubert loved to share with friends his yet-to-be-published manuscripts. Eyes bulging, face red, arms thrashing, and shouting at the top of his lungs for ten hours, he joyfully delivered all of his second novel, *Salammbô*, to a handful of fellow writers. Jules and Edmond de Goncourt described this performance as "fierce, resonant, roaring . . . droning out dramatically like the voice of an actor." Two of Flaubert's closest friends, Bouilhet and Maxime Du Camp, endured his reading an early version of *La Tentation de Sainte Antoine* for no fewer than thirty-two hours. After the hermit of Croisset worked all one night in 1876, wrote Frederick Brown, another of his biographers, early risers among his neighbours may well have heard passages from *Un Coeur simple*, "for in the absence of friends, he recited what he had written to the tulip tree, the moon and the river."

Diseased, Bloated, and Furious

Flaubert tried to keep his affliction a secret, but he was an epileptic and, throughout his writing life, suffered both partial and full-scale convulsive seizures. He was twenty-two when the first of his "nervous attacks" struck him. Remembering, he said it was "like being swept away in a torrent of flames . . . sudden as lightning . . . an instantaneous irruption of memory. . . . You feel the images pouring out of you like a stream of blood. It seems as if everything in your head is going off at once, like a thousand fireworks." He fell down, unconscious. In 1852, during a rendezvous with Louise Colet in a Paris hotel, he suffered a seizure that terrified her. She recalled, "He begs me not to call for help; his convulsions, the noises in his throat, the foam coming out of his throat, the marks his nails left in my arm. He came round after about ten minutes, vomiting." Some believe that what killed him in 1880, at fifty-eight, was another such seizure, but for decades he'd been making himself old before his time.

When he visited North Africa and the Middle East in 1850 he was only twenty-eight, but so fat it took several Egyptian guides to help him reach the top of the Great Pyramid. By the time he returned to Croisset, he was thirty. "Wearing baggy Turkish pants, a smock of Indian inspiration, a yellow cravat with silver and gold thread, he looked noticeably older," Brown wrote. "His hair had thinned – had in fact fallen out in clumps. His face showed a redness that could be taken for roseola. We know he was drinking syrup of mercury and would do so again whenever chancres reappeared, fearing with good reason that he had con-tracted syphilis. It cost him some teeth, though not as many as his eternal pipe would."

The treatment Flaubert endured may well have tortured him more than the syphilis: "For a whole week [when he was thirty-two], his tongue was too big to fit into his mouth, swollen to 'nearly the size of an ox's tongue.' Salivating uncontrollably, unable to eat or speak or sleep, he feverishly dribbled and sweated. He endured various remedies – leeches, ice, bleedings – then he took huge doses of mercury, which turned his penis the colour of slate."

Describing the "prematurely decrepit" Flaubert when he was thirty-five, American author Judith Thurman wrote, "He would always tower above his contemporaries – he was over six feet tall – but he had lost the striking Apollonian beauty of his youth to the Nubian desert sun; to a sedentary life; to his venereal souvenirs from the dives of Esneh [Egypt's notorious capital of prostitution, 450 miles downriver from Cairo]; to an excessive fondness for his pipe; and to the periodic attacks of epilepsy that, with syphilis, probably killed him. He had become a nearly bald and paunchy giant with a heavy, saturnine countenance chronically plagued, as was his body, by eczema and boils – the sort of man, he once joked, 'that whores wince at when it comes to the shagging.'"

As though Flaubert's physical afflictions weren't punishing enough, he endured devastating bouts of depression and self-disgust. When *"la maladie noire"* struck him in 1858, he said, "My heart gives off a sickening smell. Sometimes I feel sad enough to drop dead."

"Where do they come from, these waves of black depression that engulf one from time to time to time?" he asked George Sand in 1866. "It's like a rising tide. You feel you're drowning, you have to flee." In 1874, he told her, "I'm mortally depressed. When I'm not fretting about my work I moan about myself. In my leisure hours I think only of the dead." In 1875, he felt "old, stale, and disgusted with everything," and suffered from "roving twinges of gout, pains everywhere, an invincible melancholia, a sense of 'universal futility'. . . ."

"My *me* bores me to death," he complained in 1867. Two years later, his boredom was "hideous." He was "bored, bored, bored." Boredom was a curse, a threat, a poison. Having crept inside Emma Bovary, it grew insidiously until it helped make adultery irresistible to her. After she and her dull husband returned home from a great ball, where she sniffed the life of glamour she craved, he chirped, "How nice it is to be back home again!" Not for her. "This life of hers," Flaubert wrote, "was as cold as an attic that looks north; and boredom, quiet as the spider, was spinning its web in the shadowy places of the heart." As he said later, *"Emma, c'est moi."*

If he was only sometimes "horribly bored" or wallowing in "bottomless melancholy," he was constantly angry. He saw the French bourgeoisie as unbearably obtuse. After witnessing a political rally in 1847, he sneered at the "delirious asininity on display." A quarter-century later, he raged, "Never have hatred of everything that is great, contempt for all that is beautiful, abhorrence for literature been so manifest. I have always tried to live in an ivory tower; but a sea of shit is beating up against its walls, it's enough to bring it down. . . ."

To research *Bouvard et Pécuchet*, the novel he called his "encyclopedia of human stupidity," he ploughed through 1,500 books and, while anticipating this Herculean task, complained to Léonnie Braine, a beautiful widow and journalist, "All this for the sole purpose of spitting out on my contemporaries the disgust they inspire in me. I shall proclaim my way of thinking, exhale my resentment, vomit my hatred, expectorate my bile, ejaculate my anger, sluice out my indignation."

The Manuscript Looked Like a Battlefield, and So It Was

Fuelled by his passionate belief that a novelist, like God, must "create and keep quiet," and be "present everywhere, yet visible nowhere," Flaubert became fiction's first master of realism. As Harvard professor James Wood wrote in 2006, "He is the originator of the modern novel; indeed, you could say that he is the originator of modern narrative – that the war reporter and the thriller writer owe as much to him as the avant-garde fictionist. The great bear of Croisset, the monkish aesthete who spent much of his life in one house, and a great deal of that time in one room, has sired thousands of successors."

Unlike, say, Dickens or Hugo, Flaubert refused to let his emotions, convictions, personality, or any odour of romanticism infect his fiction. While writing *Bovary*, he told Louise Colet he had said goodbye to "the personal, the intimate, to everything connected with me." (In 1854, he icily said goodbye to her, too; his being more addicted to his writing than to her had long irritated her.) A dozen years later, he told George Sand, "I feel an unconquerable aversion to putting anything of my heart on paper. I even think that a novelist *hasn't the right to express his opinion* on anything whatsoever. Has God ever expressed his opinion?"

While striving to create what Wall called "the private, fastidious magic of style," Flaubert set for himself impossibly high standards. Since he believed the very language he used was "like a cracked cauldron upon which we beat out melodies fit for making bears dance when we are trying to move the stars to pity," how could he ever achieve the perfection he sought?

He became an excruciatingly slow writer. "May I die like a dog," he wrote, "rather than try to rush through even one sentence before it is ripe." Having studied the draft of Flaubert's *L'Éducation sentimentale* in the French National Library, Judith Thurman had rare insight into his all-night struggles to find *le mot juste*, that one precise word, and to make everything he wrote supremely right. "The draft runs to 2,500 [leather-bound] folio pages – a fortune in stationery," she wrote. "The writer so wary of self-indulgence was profligate with ink and paper. He covered his leaves minutely, on both sides, with wiry black script. Almost every line is altered or crossed out, then recopied dozens of times. The manuscript has the aspect of a battlefield on which each inch of forward momentum has been wrested at exorbitant human cost from an implacable enemy."

The Goncourt brothers figured that Flaubert, while writing *Bovary*, managed all of five words an hour. Biographer Wall called this estimate "scurrilous," but Flaubert himself said he wrote his masterpiece at a rate of five hundred "irreproachable" words a week. That meant maybe seventy per day or, in each ten-hour day, seven per hour. It took him four and a half years to complete *Madame Bovary*. He began to write *La Tentation de Saint Antoine* in 1847, messed with it fitfully for more than a quarter-century, and finally saw it published in 1874. He was twenty-one when he started work on his first version of *L'Éducation sentimentale* and forty-seven when the final version was published. His collected works amount to little more than three novels (one unfinished), three short stories, and *La Tentation*, the novel he structured in the form of a play script.

FROM WHERE DID THIS TERRIBLE ANGUISH COME?

If Flaubert kept himself out of his fiction, he did no such thing in his tens of thousands of letters to friends. "His novels are objective constructions which unfold in authorial absence," British novelist Julian Barnes wrote. "His letters are a place of riotous opinion-giving and frank emotional unbuttoning." They were "an outlet, which purged the intrusive self and helped liberate the fiction into its desired impersonality." In many of them, Flaubert cursed the misery his work imposed on him.

At twenty-four, unknown and unpublished, he confessed, "I'm still afraid of writing." He described "a sort of religious terror that comes upon me just before I begin." Not for the rest of his life would the terror leave him for long. "I hesitate, I worry, I vex myself," he wrote in 1847. "I lose my nerve, my taste becomes more exacting as my verve decreases." Mocking himself, he complained about "the humiliations that adjectives inflict on me," and "the cruel ravages of the relative pronoun." Nineteen years later, even after *Madame Bovary* and *Salammbô* had earned him fame and adulation, he told George Sand his violent spells of literary anguish still baffled him: "At such times I no longer know how to

go about writing, and after infinite fumbling I succeed in express-
ing a hundredth part of my ideas. . . . These last two days, for
example, I've been casting and recasting a paragraph, and still
haven't solved it. At times I want to weep." Three years later, after
rereading his outline for *L'Éducation sentimentale*, he confided,
again to Sand, "The amount I still have to write . . . makes me
almost vomit from discouragement. It's always like this when I get
back to work."

He knew that, to write a novel, he had to "drink up an ocean
and then piss it all out again." A novel was "something essentially
organic, a part of ourselves. We tear out a length of gut from our
bellies and serve it up to the bourgeois." Thus, in letters to friends
throughout much of his life, he compared his work to the sweati-
est kinds of manual labour. He ceaselessly hammered at an anvil,
ploughed a furrow, mended a road. His writing was "like drag-
ging a heavy cartload of stones." He toiled not only "like an ox"
and "an old post horse," but like "a convict breaking stones," like
"umpteen million negroes," and "five hundred devils."

While wrestling in 1861 with his sprawling, lurid historical
novel *Salammbô*, which took place during a bloody revolt by mercenaries in ancient Carthage, he told fellow writer Ernest Feydeau,
"The *writing* is becoming more and more impossible. In short,
I'm like a toad squashed by a paving stone, like a dog with its guts
crushed out by a shit-wagon, like a clot of snot under a police-
man's boot, etc. The military art of the ancients makes my head
swim; I'm stuffed with it; I vomit catapults, have hoisting
machines up my ass. . . ."

To another friend, he complained that, while his fictional poisoning of Emma Bovary had made him spew real vomit into a
chamber pot, his fictional assault on Carthage gave him real
"aches and pains in my arms." To Jules de Goncourt, he wrote,
"War machines are sawing my back in half, I'm sweating blood,
pissing boiling water, shitting catapults and farting slingsmen's

stones. . . . I've succeeded in introducing, into the same chapter, a shower of shit and a procession of pederasts. I've stopped there. Am I being too sober?"

In 1863, he felt "as limp as a dog's dick after coitus." He was "red, breathless, and moist, wilting and incapable of any new spurt." In July 1867, he felt "as old as a pyramid, and as tired as a donkey." Six months later, he wrote, "There are days like today when I feel utterly fagged out. I can scarcely stand on my feet, and I have choking fits when I can scarcely breathe." A year after that, "My bugger of a novel is draining the very marrow of my bones." In 1880, just two weeks before he died, he confided to his niece Caroline, "I think I'm liquefying like an old Camembert, I feel so weary."

Ah, Yes, to Drown in Work

Flaubert remains famous for his astounding devotion to his work. His bodily ailments, violent moods, self-loathing, and seemingly unattainable artistic goals never kept him from his writing table for long. Nor did his grief over the deaths of his parents and most beloved friends; his stormy eight-year affair with Louise Colet; the Revolution of 1848 that set up a French republic; the *coup d'état* in 1851 that swept it aside to install Napoleon III as emperor and dictator; or the heavy hand of state censorship during the Second French Empire. Even while Flaubert faced courtroom prosecution for insulting public morality, offending decency, and glorifying adultery in *Madame Bovary*, even during the crushing humiliation of France in the Prussian-Franco War of 1870–71, even as Prussian soldiers occupied his house on the Seine, and even as a family financial crisis in his later years threatened his very possession of the place, he continued to hammer at his anvil and break his stones.

Although this performance appeared heroic, the truth was he could not *not* write. It was his writing that enabled him, from time to time, to escape himself, to banish his self-disgust, tame his hysterical contempt for the human race, and come to grips with what he saw as the meaninglessness of life. In 1872, he informed Sand, "I'm working again. Because existence is tolerable only if one forgets one's wretched self." That same year, he told Turgenev, "If I didn't work there would be nothing for it but to throw myself into the river with a stone round my neck."

If Flaubert moaned endlessly about the tortures he endured while writing, he occasionally acknowledged that, when his work was going well, life was actually good. While struggling with *Salammbô*, he wrote to Ernest Feydeau, "At every line, every word, language fails me. . . . It will kill me, my friend, it will kill me. No matter: it begins to be tremendous fun."

"People don't sufficiently realize the trouble it takes to produce a well-made sentence," he told an actress friend in Paris. "But what a joy when everything turns out. I mean colour, relief, harmony. You were speaking to me the other day about the Banquet of Mercenaries [in *Salammbô*]. I can tell you I sweated over that chapter, but when I finished reading it to you, you gave a cry of satisfaction that I can still hear. Ah, that little flat in the Boulevard du Temple was the scene of some great literary feasts!"

At 2 a.m. on December 24, 1853, after twelve hours of working on *Bovary*, Flaubert described in a letter how he felt while composing the crucial scene in which the wealthy Rodolphe seduces Emma Bovary in a forest:

> I've reached the Big Fuck, I'm right in the middle of it. We are in a sweat and our heart is nearly in our mouth. This has been one of the rare days of my life which I have spent in a state of complete Enchantment, from beginning to end. Just now . . . at the

moment when I wrote the phrase "nervous attack," I was so carried away, I was making such a racket, and feeling so intensely what my little woman was feeling that I began to fear I was about to have one myself. I stood up from my writing table and I opened the window to calm myself down. My head was spinning. . . . I am like a man who has just come too much (if you will forgive me the expression). I mean a sort of lassitude which is full of exhilaration. It is a delectable thing, writing, not having to be yourself, being able to circulate in amongst the whole creation that you are describing. Today . . . as a man and as a woman, as lover and mistress both, I have been out riding in a forest on an autumn afternoon, and it was the horses, the leaves, the wind, the words that they spoke to each other and the red sunlight that made them half-close their eyes, eyes that were brimming with love.

Flaubert once compared his writing compulsion to a rash: "I keep scratching myself, and yelling as I scratch. It's pleasure and torture combined." One day, during the early stages of his work on *Bovary*, he lay in despair on his leather divan for five hours. He felt only "imbecile inertia" but then, with no warning, a flash of creativity rushed him to his writing table. "I had to go and get my handkerchief," he told Colet. "The tears were running down my face. I had written myself into a state, and it was immensely enjoyable . . . a state of the soul so far above ordinary life, a state in which fame counts for nothing and even happiness is irrelevant."

Surely it was while he recalled such moments that the hermit of Croisset decided something important:

"Writing is a dog's life, but the only life worth living."

Acknowledgments

I have known Robert Fulford for almost half a century and, though we have met only a dozen times since I left Toronto for Halifax in 1971, our friendship, and my respect for his judgment, have remained strong. Thus, his enthusiasm for my ideas about this book helped me decide to write it. When my own enthusiasm flagged, Bob reacted so favourably to the two unfinished chapters I imposed on him, that he recharged me. I actually jumped back into the work with pleasure.

Thank you, Bob.

When he and I worked at *Maclean's* magazine in the early 1960s, our boss was its editor, Ken Lefolii. In the past four decades, I saw Ken even fewer times than Bob and, between 1988 and 2008, lost track of him entirely. Since he was the best magazine editor I ever had, however, I tracked him down in London, England, and eagerly burdened him, too, with rough chunks of prose from my work-in-progress. He responded with not only meaty research tips, but the same mixture of encouragement and critical intelligence that, back in 1963, made me feel I might just become a writer.

Thank you, Ken.

A generous interest in what I was writing inspired several others to tell me good stories, lend me useful books and, in one way or another, fan the flames of my obsession. I am therefore grateful to publisher and television producer Neil Patterson of Hillsborough, North Carolina; novelist and short-story writer Alistair MacLeod, whom I interviewed at his ancestral home on Cape Breton Island; writers Silver Donald Cameron and Marjorie Simmins in Halifax; Robert Patzelt, a vice-president at Scotia Investments Ltd., also in Halifax; and to the following on the West Coast: writers Paul and Audrey Grescoe; writer Leslie Millin and librarian Elsie Wollaston; writer and teacher of creative non-fiction Andreas Schroeder; writer and publisher Alan Twigg; the poet, English professor, and author of *The History of Canadian Literature,* William (Bill) New; and Ann Cowan, executive director of the Vancouver Campus at Simon Fraser University, and founding director of its Writing and Publishing Program.

I am also most grateful to copy editor Wendy Thomas of Toronto. While applying her thoroughly professional services to my manuscript, she cleansed it of bungles on my part that, if left uncorrected, would have endlessly embarrassed me. And then there was my editor-in-chief, Douglas Gibson. He understood and applauded what I was trying to pull together, gave me a list of writers whose memories I might pick, and sent me clippings about how others worked. After I submitted the manuscript to him, he did not butcher my prose, which I naturally saw as untouchable, but did suggest – oh, so gently – certain changes that I'd have been a fool to reject. Doug keeps his editing shrewdness and diplomatic manner in perfect balance, and I count myself extremely lucky to have had him apply his deft touches to my prose about "the wond'rous mystic art."

Harry Bruce

Bibliography

BIBLIOGRAPHICAL NOTE

While friends sent me clippings of useful magazine and newspaper pieces, and I happened upon a few myself, it was with the Google search engine that I retrieved perhaps ninety percent of the research I gained from periodicals. My Internet sources included not only articles, interviews, and reviews that had previously appeared in *The Guardian*, *The New Yorker*, *The New York Times*, *The Paris Review*, and other print media, but also websites for online magazines and a variety of blogs that individuals, organizations, and institutions maintain to share information on the making of literature.

From the Halifax and Vancouver public libraries, I borrowed most of the books I consulted, but it was to Google that I owed my discovery of several others. Notable among these were Wilkie Collins's *My Miscellanies* (1863) and Amelia Edwards's *Egypt and Its Monuments: Pharaohs, Fellahs and Explorers* (1891).

– Harry Bruce

(Abbreviations: *The Guardian – G; The New Yorker – NY; The New York Times – NYT; The Paris Review – PR.*)

"The Achievement of Isaac Bashevis Singer: A Roundtable Discussion." Moderator, Max Rudin. *Library of America.*

Ackerman, Diane. "O Muse! You do make things difficult!" *NYT*, Nov. 12, 1989.

Ackroyd, Peter. *Dickens.* London: Sinclair-Stevenson Limited, 1990.

————. *Shakespeare: The Biography.* London: Chatto & Windus, 2005.

Acocella, Joan. "Blocked." *NY*, June 14 and 21, 2004.

————. "A Fire in the Brain." *NY*, Dec. 8, 2003.

————. "The Typing Life." *NY*, April 9, 2007.

————. "Waugh Stories." *NY*, July 2, 2007.

Adelman, Gary. *Retelling Dostoevsky: Literary Responses and Other Observations.* Lewisburg, Penn.: Bucknell University Press, 2001.

"Alethea Hayter." Telegraph.co.uk, Jan. 11, 2006.

Alexander, Caroline. "The other Wordsworth, in England's Lake District." *NYT*, Feb. 28, 1999.

Allemang, John. "The write place to work." *Globe and Mail*, Nov. 2, 2002.

Allen, Brooke. "The House on Middagh Street." *The New Criterion*, online, June, 2005.

————. "Reading Henry Greene." *The New Criterion*, online, March, 1993.

Allende, Isabel, and John Redden. *Conversations with Isabel Allende.* Austin: University of Texas Press, 2004.

Alvarez, Al. "The long road home." *G*, Sept. 11, 2004.

Amis, Martin. *Experience.* Toronto: Alfred A. Knopf Canada, 2000.

"Anne Tyler Interview." failbetter.com, Spring, 2006.

"Art and Healing: Conversation with Kenzaburo Oe." Institute of International Studies, UC Berkeley, April 16, 1999.

"The Art of Criticism No. 2: George Steiner." Interviewer, Ronald A. Sharp. *PR*, Winter, 1995.

"The Art of Fiction No. 4., continued: Irwin Shaw." Interviewers, Willie Morris, Lucas Matthiessen. *PR*, Spring, 1979.

"———— No. 11: Nelson Algren." Interviewers, Alston Anderson, Terry Southern. *PR*, Winter, 1955.

"———— No. 35: Simone de Beauvoir." Interviewers, Bernard Frechtman, Madeleine Gobeil. *PR*, Spring-Summer, 1965.

"———— No. 36: William S. Burroughs." Interviewer, Conrad Knickerbocker. *PR*, Fall, 1965.

"———— No. 48: Anthony Burgess." Interviewer, John Cullinan. *PR*, Spring, 1973.

"———— No. 53: J.P. Donleavy." Interviewers, Molly McKaughan, Fayette Hickox. *PR*, Fall, 1975.

"———— No. 59: Kingsley Amis." Interviewer, Michael Barber. *PR*, Winter, 1975.

"———— No. 62: Erskine Caldwell." Interviewers, Elizabeth Pell Broadwell, Ronald Wesley Hoag. *PR*, Winter, 1982.

"———— No. 65: William Gass." *PR*, Summer, 1970.

"———— No. 67: Paul Bowles." Interviewer, Jeffrey Bailey. *PR*, Fall, 1981.

"———— No. 68: Anthony Powell." Interviewer, Michael Barber. *PR*, Spring-Summer, 1978.

"———— No. 70: Margaret Drabble." Interviewer, Barbara Milton, *PR*, Fall-Winter, 1978.

"———— No. 107: Robertson Davies." Interviewer, Elisabeth Sifton, *PR*, Spring, 1989.

"———— No. 109: John Fowles." Interviewer, James R. Baker. *PR*, Summer, 1989.

"———— No. 124: Günter Grass." Interviewer, Elizabeth Gaffney. *PR*, Summer, 1991.

"———— No. 129: Naguib Mahfouz." Interviewer, Charlotte El Shabrawy. *PR*, Summer, 1992.

"———— No. 132: Mark Helprin." Interviewer, James Linville. *PR*, Spring, 1993.

"———— No. 135: Don DeLillo." Interviewer, Adam Begley. *PR*, Fall, 1993.

"———— No. 139: Chinua Achebe." Interviewer, Jerome Brooks. *PR*, Winter, 1994.

"———— No. 143: Susan Sontag." Interviewer, Edward Hirsch. *PR*, Winter, 1995.

"———— No. 151: Martin Amis." Interviewer, Francesca Riviere. *PR*, Spring, 1998.

"———— No. 156: William Styron." Interviewer, George Plimpton. *PR*, Spring, 1999.

"———— No. 158: Shelby Foote." Interviewers, Carter Coleman, Donald Faulkner, William Kennedy. *PR*, Summer, 1999.

"———— No. 178: Paul Auster." Interviewer, Michael Wood. *PR*, Fall, 2003.

"———— No. 184: Barry Hannah." Interviewer, Lacey Galbraith. *PR*, Winter, 2004.

"———— No. 186: Salman Rushdie." Interviewer, Jack Livings. *PR*, Summer, 2005.

"———— No. 195: Kenzaburo Oe." *PR*, Winter, 2007.

"The Art of Journalism No. 1: Hunter S. Thompson." Interviewers, Douglas Brinkley, Terry McDonell. *PR*, Fall, 2000.

"The Art of Poetry No. 8: Allen Ginsberg." Interviewer, Thomas Clarke. *PR*, Spring, 1966.

"———— No. 10: Robert Creeley." Interviewers, Lewis MacAdams, Linda Wagner-Martin. *PR*, Fall, 1968.

"———— No. 19: James Wright." Interviewer, Peter A. Stitt. *PR*, Summer, 1975.

"———— No. 20: James Dickey." Interviewer, Franklin Ashley. *PR*, Spring, 1976.

"————. Richard Wilbur." Interviewers, Helen McCloy Ellison, Elessa Clay High, Peter A. Stitt. *PR*, Winter, 1977.

"———— No. 40: Anthony Hecht." Interviewer, J.D. McClatchy. *PR*, Fall, 1988.

"———— No. 41: Charles Wright." Interviewer, J.D. McClatchy. *PR*, Winter II, 1989.

"———— No. 43: Donald Hall." Interviewer, Peter A. Stitt. *PR*, Fall, 1991.

"———— No. 45: Amy Clampitt." Interviewer, Robert E. Hosmer. *PR*, Spring, 1993.

"The Art of Theatre No. 10: Neil Simon." Interviewer, James Lipton. *PR*, Winter, 1992.

"—— No. 14: August Wilson." Interviewers, Bonnie Lyons, George Plimpton. *PR*, Winter, 1999.

"Arthur Hailey." Telegraph.co.uk., Nov. 27, 2004.

Ascherson, Neil. "A Far-Flung Correspondent." *New York Review of Books*, Dec. 21, 2006.

Ashton, Rosemary. *George Eliot: A Life*. London: Hamish Hamilton, 1996.

Asimov, Isaac. *I. Asimov: A Memoir*. New York: Doubleday, 1994.

Astle, Thomas. *The Origin and Progress of Writing [etc.]*. London: J. White, 1803.

Atwood, Margaret. *Moving Targets: Writing With Intent, 1982–2004*. Toronto: House of Anansi Press Inc., 2004.

Auden, W.H. *The Dyer's Hand and Other Essays*. New York: Random House, 1948.

Austen-Leigh, J.E. *A Memoir of Jane Austen by Her Nephew*. London: The Folio Society, 1989.

The Author Speaks: Selected PW Interviews, 1967–1976, by Publishers Weekly *Editors and Contributors*. New York & London: R.R. Bowker Company, 1977.

Bachelor, John. *The Life of Joseph Conrad: A Critical Biography*. Oxford (U.K.) & Cambridge (U.S.): Blackwell, 1994.

Bailey, Mark. *Hemingway & Bailey's Bartending Guide: Great American Writers*. Chapel Hill, N. Carolina: Algonquin Books of Chapel Hill, 2006.

Baker, Russell. "Just like Jolson." *NYT*, August 3, 1985.

——. "Let them play guitars." *NYT*, April 8, 1989.

——. "The processing process." *NYT*, Feb. 10, 1985.

Balakrishnan, Anima. "The vanishing manuscript." *The Hindu*. Dec. 4, 2006.

Ballard, J.G. "How I write." Times Online. Sept. 19, 2000.

——. "Writers' rooms: J.G. Ballard." guardian.co.uk, March 9, 2007.

"Balzac – The Pleasures and Pains of Coffee." Translator, Robert Onopa. *The New Partisan*, March 7, 2005. Website article.

Banville, John. "Homage to Philip Larkin." *New York Review of Books*, Feb. 23, 2006.

Barker, Juliet. *The Brontës*. London: Weidenfeld and Nicolson, 1994.

Barnes, Julian. "Lost fragments from the life of Flaubert." Times Online, Feb. 1, 2006.

———. "Flaubert, C'est Moi." *New York Review of Books*. May 25, 2006.

Batchelor, John. *The Life of Joseph Conrad: A Critical Biography*. Oxford (U.K.) and Cambridge, (U.S.): Blackwell, 1994.

Bayles, David, and Ted Orland. *Art and Fear: Observations on the Perils (and Rewards) of Artmaking*. Santa Cruz, California, and Eugene, Oregon: The Image Continuum, 2001.

Bell, Quentin. *Virginia Woolf: A Biography*. New York: Harcourt Brace Jovanovitch, 1972.

Bellis, Mary. "The Battle of the Ballpoint Pens." Website article.

———. "A Brief History of Writing Instruments." Website article.

Bellow, Saul. "Man Underground." *Commentary*, June, 1952.

Bennett, Arnold. *Essays of To-Day and Yesterday*. London: George G. Harrap & Co. Ltd., 1926.

Benstock, Shari. *No Gifts from Chance: A Biography of Edith Wharton*. New York: Charles Scribner's Sons, 1994.

Berg, A. Scott. *Max Perkins: Editor of Genius*. New York: E.P. Dutton, 1978.

Bierce, Ambrose. *The Devil's Dictionary*. Oxford: Oxford University Press, 1999.

Bigelow, Albert. *Mark Twain: A Biography* (in three volumes). New York: Harper and Brothers, 1912.

"The Biro Story." Museum of Berkshire Aviation. Website article.

Bloom, Harold. "They have the numbers; we, the heights." *Boston Review*, April/May, 1998. Website article.

———. "On first looking into Gates's Crichton." *NYT*, June 4, 2000.

Bose, Sudip. "A Complicated Business." newcriterion.com, May, 2001.

Bourque, Joseph. "History of the Waterman Pen." Website article.

Bradbury, Ray. "Fahrenheit Revisited." *UCLA Magazine*, Summer, 2002.

Breit, Harvey. *The Writer Observed*. New York: Collier Books, 1961.

"British novelist Muriel Spark dies at 88." *USA Today*, April 15, 2006.

Brontë, Charlotte. *Villette*. London: J.M. Dent & Sons, 1993.

"A Brooklyn identity – Paul Auster interview." Interviewer, Charles Bremner. *The Times*, March 16, 1991.

Bryk, William. "Dr. Feelgood. Past and Present." *New York Sun*, Sept. 20, 2005.

Burroughs, William S. *Last Words: The Final Journals of William S. Burroughs*. Edited and with an introduction by James Grauerholz. New York: Grove Press, 2000.

Calonne, David. *Revision: History, Theory, and Practice*. West Lafayette, Indiana: Parlor Press, 2006.

The Cambridge Companion to Flaubert. Edited by Timothy Unwin. Cambridge (U.K.): Cambridge University Press, 2004.

Campbell, B.G. *Human Evolution: An Introduction to Man's Adaptations*. London: Heinemann, 1967.

Campbell, James. "Bill and Dot and Sam and Sara." *NYT*, March 18, 2007.

"Carlyle's soundproof room." *NYT*, February 24, 1886.

Carpenter, Humphrey. *Geniuses Together: American Writers in Paris in the 1920s*. Boston: Houghton Mifflin Company, 1988.

Carr, David. "Leaving out what will be skipped." *NYT*, May 13, 2005.

Carr, Nicholas. "Is Google Making Us Stupid?" *The Atlantic*, July / August, 2008.

Carter, Humphrey. *Tolkien: A Biography*. London: Allen and Unwin, 1977.

Chambers, Robert. *The Picture of Scotland*. Edinburgh: William Tait, 1827.

Chandler, Daniel. *The Act of Writing: A Media Theory Approach*. Aberystwyth: University of Wales, 1995.

Charlton, James, and Lisbeth Mark. *The Writer's Home Companion*. New York: Penguin Books, 1989.

Cheever, Susan. *Home Before Dark*. New York: Houghton Mifflin, 1984.

Cheminki, Rudi. "After 500 Novels and 10,000 Women, Georges Simenon Has Earned His Retirement." *People* magazine, Jan. 28, 1980.

Cohen, Matt. *Typing: A Life in 26 Keys*. Toronto: Random House Canada, 2000.

Cohen, Morton C. "Children's books; Curiouser and curiouser! The endurance of Little Alice." *NYT*, Nov. 11, 1990.

Collins, Wilkie. *My Miscellanies*. London: Samson Low, Son & Co., 1863. Available on the Web.

Conrad, Jessie. *Joseph Conrad as I Knew Him*. London: William Heinemann Ltd., 1926.

Conrad, John. *Joseph Conrad: Times Remembered*. Cambridge (U.K.): Cambridge University Press, 1981.

Cooke, Nathalie. *Margaret Atwood: A Biography*. Toronto: ECW Press, 1998.

Coren, Michael. *J.R.R. Tolkien: The Man Who Created* The Lord of the Rings. Toronto: Stoddart, 2001.

D.H. Lawrence: Selected Letters. Selected by Richard Aldington, with an introduction by Aldous Huxley. London: Penguin Books in association with William Heinemann Ltd., 1954.

Dalsimer, Katherine. "Images in Psychiatry: Virginia Woolf (1882–1941)." *The American Journal of Psychiatry*, May, 2004.

DeLillo, Don, interviewed by Peter Henning. Translated from German by Julia Apitsch. *Frankfurter Rundschau* magazine, Nov. 20, 2003.

Dostoevsky, Anna. *Dostoevsky: Reminiscences*. Translated and edited by Beatrice Stillman, with an introduction by Helen Muchnic. New York: Liverwright, 1975.

Drabelle, Dennis. "To sleep, perchance to lose your edge." *Washington Post*, March 6, 2007.

Duchene, Lisa. "Is Writer's Block Real?" Pennsylvania State University. Website article.

Encyclopedia Britannica. Cambridge (U.K.): Cambridge University Press, 1910.

Eder, Richard. "Coleridge was Wordsworth's albatross." *NYT*, March 15, 2007.

Edwards, Amelia. *Egypt and Its Monuments: Pharaohs, Fellahs and Explorers*. New York: Harper & Brothers, 1891. Available on the Web.

Epel, Naomi. *Writers Dreaming: Twenty-Six Writers Talk About Their Dreams and the Creative Process*. New York: Carol Southern Books, 1993.

Epstein, Joseph. *In a Cardboard Belt!* Boston and New York: Houghton Mifflin Company, 2007.

———. *Life Sentences: Literary Essays.* New York and London: W.W. Norton & Company, 1997.

———. *Partial Payments: Essays on Writers and Their Lives.* New York and London: W.W. Norton & Company, 1989.

———. *Pertinent Players: Essays on the Literary Life.* New York and London: W.W. Norton & Company, 1993.

———. *Plausible Prejudices: Essays on American Writing.* New York and London: W.W. Norton & Company, 1985.

Ernest Hemingway on Writing. Edited by Larry W. Phillips. New York: Charles Scribner's Sons, 1984.

"Exhibition on History of Papermaking at New York Public Library." *Alkaline Paper Advocate*, May, 1990.

Fairbanks, Alfred J. *The Story of Handwriting: Origins and Development.* New York: Watson-Guptill, 1970.

Fein, Esther B. "Talking history with: David McCullough; Immersed in facts, the better to imagine Harry Truman's Life." *NYT*, Aug. 12, 1992.

Ferguson, Brian. "J.K. Rowling's fame spoils her café culture." *Edinburgh Evening News*, Feb. 6, 2003.

First Chapter: The Canadian Writers Photography Project. Photographer, Don Denton. Editor, Richard Harrison. Banff: Banff Centre Press, 2001.

Flaherty, Alice W. *The Midnight Disease.* Boston and New York: Houghton Mifflin, 2004.

Flaubert and Turgenev: A Friendship in Letters. Editor, Barbara Beaumont. New York and London: W.W. Norton & Company, 1985.

Flaubert–Sand: The Correspondence. Translators, Francis Steegmuller, Barbara Bray. Foreword by Francis Steegmuller. New York: Alfred A. Knopf, 1993.

"Flu blamed for death of Scottish author." BBC News, Jan. 10, 2000.

Frank, Joseph. *Dostoevsky: The Mantle of the Prophet, 1871–1881.* Princeton, N.J.: Princeton University Press, 2002.

Friedell, Deborah. "Desk Job." *New York Review of Books*, Nov. 15, 2007.

F. Scott Fitzgerald On Writing. Edited by Larry W. Phillips. New York: Charles Scribner's Sons, 1985.

Fulford, Robert. "Hall's measure of a life in metre." *National Post*, June 20, 2007.

———. "A new key to Shylock." *National Post*, Dec. 12, 2006.

Garis, Leslie. "Simenon's last case." *NYT*, April 22, 1984.

Gascoigne, Bamber. "Catherine Cookson (1906–1998)."

Gasson, Andrew. "Wilkie Collins and Laudanum (Opium)."

Gogol, Nikolai. *Dead Souls*. New York: Vintage Books, 1997.

Goodwin, Jason. "Ottoman of his time." Times Online, U.K. April 2, 2005.

Goodwin, Karin. "Drug took Stevenson face to face with Hyde." *Sunday Times*, Scotland, March 20, 2005.

Gopnik, Adam. "Blows Against the Empire: The Return of Philip J. Dick." *NY*, Aug. 20, 2007.

Gorra, Michael. "'V.S. Pritchett': Wizard of the Lower Middle." *NYT*, Jan. 23, 2005.

Grace, Sherrill E. *The Voyage That Never Ends: Malcolm Lowry's Fiction*. Vancouver: University of British Columbia Press, 1982.

Grimes, William. "Exploring the links between depression, writers and suicide." *NYT*, Nov. 14, 1994.

Gurko, Leo. *Joseph Conrad: Giant in Exile*. New York: The Macmillan Company, 1962.

Hall, Donald. *Life Work*. Boston: Beacon Press, 1992.

Handley, Elaine. "Writer's Block." Empire State College. Website article.

Hard, Jane. "Some Personal Memories of My Uncle Rud." *The Kipling Journal*, September, 2007.

Hastings, Selina. *Evelyn Waugh: A Biography*. London: Sinclair-Stevenson, 1994.

"Hawthorn in Salem – Images Related to the Wayside in Concord." Website article.

Hayward, Malcolm. "William Wordsworth Working: Art, Leisure, and a Curious Form of Consumption." Website article.

Hazlitt, William. "On the Conversation of Authors." *London Magazine*, September, 1820.

———. "My First Acquaintance with Poets." First published in *The Liberal*, April, 1823.

Heath, Jeffrey. *The Picturesque Prison: Evelyn Waugh and His Writing*. Kingston, Ont.: McGill-Queen's University Press, 1982.

Heidegger, Martin. "Hands." From *The Body*, edited and introduced by Donn Welton. Oxford: Blackwell Publishing, 1999. Available on the Web.

Heighton, Steven, "Jogging with Joyce." *Geist*, Summer, 2006.

Hendrickson, Robert. *American Literary Anecdotes*. New York: Facts on File, 1990.

———. *British Literary Anecdotes*. New York: Facts on File, 1990

———. *World Literary Anecdotes*. New York: Facts On File, 1990.

Herschma, Jablow, and Julien Lieb. *The Key to Genius: Manic Depression and the Creative Life*. Buffalo, N.Y.: Prometheus Books, 1988.

"History of the Lead Pencil." EarlyOfficeMuseum.com.

How I Write: The Secret Lives of Authors. Edited by Dan Crowe, with Philip Oltermann. New York: Rizzoli International Publications, 2007.

Howe, Irving. "Ralph Ellison's *Invisible Man*." *The Nation*, May 10, 1952.

Howse, Christopher. "Noise is bad manners – not raw decibels." *Daily Telegraph*, Nov. 3, 2007.

"A hunger to write." *NYT*, March 5, 1946.

Interview with Isabel Allende. "Questions & Answers." isabelallende.com. Website article.

Interview with John Irving. Bookreporter.com, July, 2005. Website article.

Italie, Hillel. "'Sophie's Choice' author dies at 81." *Globe and Mail*, Nov. 2, 2006.

James, Henry. *The Portrait of a Lady, Volume 1*. 1908 New York Edition. Available on the Web.

Jamison, Kay Redfield. *Touched with Fire: Manic-Depressive Illness and the Artistic Temperament*. New York: Free Press, Macmillan, 1993.

"JK Rowling Says She Contemplated Suicide." The Huffington Post, March 24, 2008. Website article.

"John Keats: Letters: To George and Georgiana Keats, September, 1819." Website article.

Jong, Erica. *Seducing the Demon: Writing for My Life*. New York: Jeremy P. Tarcher/Penguin, 2006.

Joseph Conrad: Interviews and Recollections. Edited by Martin Ray. Iowa City: University of Iowa Press, 1990.

Journal of Katherine Mansfield. Editor, J. Middleton Murry. New York: Alfred A. Knopf, 1927.

Kakutani, Michiko. "Kafka's Kafkaesque love letters." *NYT*, April 2, 1998.

Keates, Jonathan. *Stendhal*. New York: Carroll & Graf Publishers, 1997.

Kenyon, Frederic G. *The Story of the Bible: A Popular Account of How It Came to Us*. London: J. Murray, 1936. Available on the Web.

Kershaw, Alexander. *Jack London: A Life*. New York: St. Martin's Press, 1997.

Keyes, Ralph. *The Courage to Write: How Writers Transcend Fear*. New York: Henry Holt and Company, 1995.

Kirsch, Adam. "The Mystic Word: The Life and Work of Hart Crane." *NY*, Oct. 9, 2006.

Kjetsaa, Geir. *Fyodor Dostoevsky: A Writer's Life*. New York: Viking, 1987.

Knoche, Grace F. "Two-Thirds God, One-Third Human." *Sunrise* magazine, November, 1980.

Knox, Malcolm. "Panic after a first successful novel is perfectly natural, but what if it never passes?" *Sydney Morning Herald*, Jan. 5, 2006.

Kochanski, John. "9 Top Baseball Superstitions." ezinearticles.com. Sept. 24, 2008.

Kramer, Hilton. "Art view; Beguiling tools of the writer's craft." *NYT*, Nov. 22, 1981.

Krebs, Albin. "James Dickey, two-fisted poet and the author of 'Deliverance,' is dead at 73." *NYT*, Jan. 21, 1997.

Lahr, John. "Write, stop, pivot, punch." *G*, April 7, 2008.

Lamott, Anne. *Bird by Bird: Some Instructions on Writing and Life*. New York: Anchor Books, 1994.

Lanchester, John. "High Style: Writing under the Influence." *NY*, Jan. 6, 2003.

Langworth, Richard M. "Churchill and the Art of the Statesman-Writer." An address at the Boston Atheneum, May 6, 1999.

LaPlante, Eve. *Seized*. New York: HarperCollinsPublishers, 1993.

"Larkin is nation's top poet." BBC News, Oct. 15, 2003.

"Last of the Leftists?" *Time*, May 28, 1951.

Lawrence, D.H. *Selected Letters*. Selected by Richard Aldington. Introduction by Aldous Huxley. London: Penguin Books in association with William Heinemann Ltd., 1954.

Leader, Zachary. *The Life of Kingsley Amis*. London: Jonathan Cape, 2006.

Lefebure, Molly. *A Bondage of Opium*. New York: Stein & Day, 1974.

Lehmann-Haupt, Christopher. "Odd angles on alcoholism and American writers." *NYT*, Nov. 7, 1988.

Lehrer, Jonah. "The Eureka Hunt: Why Do Good Ideas Come to Us When They Do?" *NY*, July 28, 2008.

Leonard, Linda Schierse. *Witness to the Fire: Creativity and the Veil of Addiction*. Boston and London: Shambhala, 2001.

The Letters of Gustave Flaubert, 1857–1880. Selected, edited, and translated by Francis Steegmuller. Cambridge (U.S.): The Belknap Press of Harvard University Press, 1982.

The Letters of Virginia Woolf, Vol. 6. Edited by Nigel Nicolson and Joanne Trautmann. Fort Washington, Pa.: Harvest Books, 1982.

Lévy-Bruhl, Lucien. *How Natives Think*. Translated from French by L.A. Clare. London: George Allen and Unwin, 1926.

Lewis, Peter H. "Computer words: Less perfect?" *NYT*, Nov. 1, 1992.

Lindquist, Evan. "Old Writing and Drawing Inks." Website article.

Long, Jean. *The Art of Chinese Calligraphy*. Mineola, New York: Dover Publications, 2001.

"Louis Charles Alfred de Musset." *Encyclopedia of World Biography*, 2003.

Lucas, A., and J.R. Harris. *Ancient Egyptian Materials and Industries*. London: Edward Arnold (Publishers) Ltd., 1962.

Lyall, Sarah. "A Chinese-born writer is winner of the Nobel." *NYT*, Oct. 13, 2000.

Lyons, Richard D. "Ralph Ellison, author of 'Invisible Man,' is dead at 80." *NYT*, April 17, 1994.

Macfarlane, Alan. "The Conditions of Creativity in the Lives of Major Thinkers; Some Case Studies." www.alanmacfarlane.com/savage/MILK2.PDF. 2002.

MacFarquhar, Larissa. "East Side Story: Louis Auchincloss's Class Chronicle." *NY*, Feb. 25, 2008.

Madden, David. "An Interview with Paul West." Dalkey Archive Press.

Mailer, Norman. "The Mary McCarthy Case." *New York Review of Books*, Oct. 17, 1963.

———. *The Spooky Art: Some Thoughts on Writing*. New York: Random House, 2003.

Mallon, Thomas. "Lincoln at Two Hundred." *NY*, Oct. 13, 2008.

Mansnerus, Laura. "Here's puffing at you, kid." *NYT*, Jan. 12, 1994.

Maslin, Janet. "Under any name, a novelist gone and forgotten." *NYT*, March 22, 2001.

Maurois, André. *Olympio: The Life of Victor Hugo*. Translated from French by Gerard Hopkins. New York: Harper & Brothers, 1956.

———. *The World of Marcel Proust*. New York: Harper & Row, Publishers Inc., 1974.

Max, D.T. "Day of the Dead: The Mysterious Demise of Malcolm Lowry." *NY*, Dec. 17, 2007.

McBain, Jeremy. "Stepson of C.S. Lewis Speaks at College." *Petoskey News-Review*, Nov. 2, 2005.

McCall, Bruce. "The dog wrote it." *NYT*, Nov. 14, 1999.

Mehta, Ved Parkash. "Ved Mehta – een introductie." Autobiographical Essay. *Contemporary Author*, Vol. 212. Farmington Hills, MI: The Gale Group, 2004.

Menand, Louis. "Acid Redux: The Life and High Times of Timothy Leary." *NY*, June 26, 2008.

———. "Drive, He Wrote: What the Beats Were About." *NY*, Oct. 1, 2007.

―――. "Saved from Drowning." *NY*, Feb. 23, 2009.

Meyers, Jeffrey. *Joseph Conrad: A Biography*. New York: Charles Scribner's Sons, 1991.

―――. *Scott Fitzgerald: A Biography*. New York: HarperCollins, 1994.

―――. *Somerset Maugham: A Life*. New York: Alfred A. Knopf, 2004.

Michener, James A. *James A. Michener's Writer's Handbook*. New York: Random House, 1992.

Monroe, Russell R. *Creative Brainstorms: The Relationship Between Madness and Genius*. New York: Irvington Publishers, Inc., 1992.

Munro, Sheila. *Lives of Mothers and Daughters: Growing Up with Alice Munro*. Toronto: A Douglas Gibson Book, McClelland and Stewart, 2001.

Murdoch, Jason. "Superstitious Athletes." CBC sports online. May 10, 2005.

Murry, J. Middleton. *Pencillings*. London: W. Collins Sons and Company Limited, 1925. Available on the Web.

Nelson, Victoria. *On Writer's Block: A New Approach to Creativity*. New York: Houghton Mifflin Company, 1993.

Nichol, John. *Thomas Carlyle*. New York: Harper & Brothers, 1892. Available on the Web.

"Nigel Tranter: Scotland's Storyteller, 1909 to 2000." Website article.

Nolan, Tom. *Ross MacDonald: A Biography*. New York: Scribner, 1999.

Norman Mailer: Pontifications. Interviews. Edited by Michael Lennon. Boston and Toronto: Little Brown and Company, 1982.

O'Brian, Patrick. *The Final Unfinished Voyage of Jack Aubrey*. London: HarperCollinsPublishers. 2004.

O'Connor, Flannery. *The Habit of Being*. Letters edited and with an introduction by Sally Fitzgerald. New York: Farrar, Strauss, Giroux, 1979.

Ogle, Jane. "Beauty: Exploring scent therapy." *NYT*, Nov. 17, 1985.

Oishi, K. "Celeste Langan, *Romantic Vagrancy*." Romanticism On the Net 4, November, 1996.

Olsen, Tillie. *Silences*. New York: Delacorte Press/Seymour Lawrence, 1978.

"Ondaatje: The Q & A." Interviewer, Johanna Schneller. *Globe and Mail*, April 14, 2007.

Orwell, George. *It Is What I Think: 1947–48.* Edited by Peter Davison, assisted by Ian Angus and Sheila Davison. London: Secker & Warburg, 1998.

Owen, James. "Papyrus Reveals New Clues to Ancient World." *National Geographic News,* April 25, 2005.

The Oxford Dictionary of Literary Quotations. Edited by Peter Kemp. Oxford: Oxford University Press, 1997.

Palm, Christine. "The Enigma of Wallace Stevens." West Hartford, CT: *Hog River Journal,* Winter 2004/2005.

Pamuk, Orhan. "My Father's Suitcase." *NY,* Oct. 12, 2006.

The Paris Review Interviews, vol. I. Introduction by Philip Gourevitch. New York: Picador, 2006.

Parsons, Marie. "The History of Ancient Egyptian Writing." Website article.

Pauli, Michelle. "Harper Lee tops librarians' must-read list." guardian.co.uk, March 2, 2006.

"Penspotters: History of the Pen." Website article.

The Personal Papers of Anton Chekhov. Introduction by Matthew Josephson. New York: Lear, 1948.

Petroski, Henry. *The Pencil: A History of Design and Circumstance.* New York: Alfred A. Knopf, 1992.

Pierpont, Claudia Roth. "The Player Kings: How the Rivalry of Orson Welles and Laurence Olivier Made Shakespeare Modern." *NY,* Nov. 19, 2007.

"*Playboy* Interview: Vladimir Nabokov." Interviewer, Alvin Toffler. *Playboy,* January, 1964.

"Poetry Landmark: Wallace Stevens's Hometown of Hartford, CT." poets.org, The Academy of American Poets. Website article.

Powers, Richard. "How to speak a book." *NYT,* Jan. 7. 2007.

Pringle, Mary Beth. *John Grisham: A Critical Companion.* Westport, Conn.: Greenwood Press, 1997.

Pritchett, V.S. *Balzac.* Toronto: Clarke, Irwin & Co. Ltd., 1973.

———. "The Disconcerting Sybil." *New York Review of Books,* Aug. 17, 1978.

————. *The Pritchett Century*. Foreword and selections by Oliver Pritchett. New York: The Modern Library, Random House, 1997.

The Quotable Lewis. Editors, Wayne Martindale, Jerry Root. Carol Stream, Ill.: Tyndale Publishers, 1990.

Rae, John. *Life of Adam Smith*. London: Macmillan and Co., 1895.

Rafael, George. "Polite Literature." salon.com, Sept. 2, 1999.

Rehman, Bushra. "Rituals and Routines: How to Find Inspiration – or Help Inspiration Find You." articlearchives.com, Feb. 1, 2005.

Rekdal, Paisely. "The way we live now: 12-10-00: Questions for Gao Xingjian; Found in translation." *NYT*, Dec. 10, 2000.

Ricketts, Harry. *Rudyard Kipling: A Life*. New York: Carroll & Graf Publishers, Inc., 1999.

Rincon, Paul. "'Earliest writing' found in China." BBC News, April 17, 2003.

Rogers, Bruce Holland. "The Myth of Writer's Block." Website article.

Rosen, Jonathan. "Writer Interrupted: The Resurrection of Henry Roth." *NY*, Aug. 1, 2005.

Rousseau, Jean-Jacques. *The Confessions of Jean-Jacques Rousseau, Book IV*. (1792). Translated by W. Conyngham Mallory. Ebooks@Adelaide, University of Adelaide Library.

Rowley, Hazel. *Tête-à-Tête: Simone de Beauvoir and Jean-Paul Sartre*. New York: HarperCollinsPublishers, 2005.

Rudyard Kipling: The Critical Heritage. Edited by Roger Lancelyn Green. London and New York: Routledge, 1971.

Rudyard Kipling to Rider Haggard, the Record of a Friendship. Edited by M. Cohen. London: Hutchinson, 1965.

"Samford University conferred honorary doctorates on Wendell E. Berry," etc. *Seasons*, the magazine of Samford University, Summer, 2000.

Scott, A.O. "The Old Devil." *NYT*, June 3, 2007.

Selected Letters of Fyodor Dostoevsky. Editors, Joseph Frank and David I. Goldstein. Translator, Andrew R. MacAndrew. Piscataway, N.J.: Rutgers University Press, 1987.

Selected Letters of James Thurber. Editors, Helen Thurber, Edward Weeks. Atlantic-Little, Brown, 1981.

Sheinman, Mort. "A Chic in Wolfe's Clothing." Poynter Online, The Poynter Institute, August 5, 2003.

"Shelby Foote Interview." American Academy of Achievement, June 18, 1999.

Shelden, Michael. *Orwell: The Authorized Biography*. New York: HarperCollinsPublishers, 1991.

Sherry, Norman. *The Life of Graham Greene, Volume I: 1904–1939*. London: Penguin Books, 1989.

———. *The Life of Graham Greene, Volume II: 1939–1955*. London: Penguin Books, 1995.

Sillitoe, Alan. "Writer's rooms: Alan Sillitoe." guardian.co.uk, 2008.

Silverblatt, Michael. "The Tunnel: A Small Apartment in Hell." *Review of Contemporary Fiction*, Fall, 2004.

Smith, Sydney. *The Wit and Wisdom of Sydney Smith*. New York: Evert Augustus Duyckink, 1856.

Smoluchowski, Louise. *Lev and Sonya: The Story of the Tolstoy Marriage*. New York: G.P. Putnam Sons, 1987.

Snider, Suzanne. "Old Yeller: The Illustrious History of the Yellow Legal Pad." *Legal Affairs*, June, 2005.

Snow, C.P. *The Realists*. New York: Charles Scribner's Sons, 1978.

"Stanley Cup Playoff Beards." transugar.com. April 16, 2008.

Stephen, Sir Leslie. "Gibbon, Edward (1737–1794)." *Dictionary of National Biography, Vol. 7*. Oxford: Oxford University Press, 1921.

Stevens, William Bacon. "The Library of Alexander A. Smets, esq. Savannah." *The Magnolia*, vols. 1–4, Jan., 1840–June, 1842.

Stewart, Wayne. *Big-League Sluggers Reveal the Tricks of Their Trade*. New York: McGraw-Hill, 2004.

Strathern, Paul. *Dostoevsky in 90 Minutes*. Chicago: Ivan R. Dee, 2004.

Styron, William. *Darkness Visible: A Memoir of Madness*. New York: Random House, 1990.

Sursum Corda! The Collected Letters of Malcolm Lowry, Volume I: 1926–1946. Editor, Sherrill E. Grace. London: Jonathan Cape, 1995.

Swanberg, W.A. *Dreiser*. New York: Charles Scribner's Sons, 1965.

Swinging the Maelstrom: New Perspectives on Malcolm Lowry. Editor, Sherrill E. Grace. Kingston: McGill-Queen's University Press, 1972.

Tartakovsky, Joseph. "The spirits behind the writers." *Los Angeles Times,* Feb. 27, 2008.

Taylor, D.J. *Thackeray.* London: Pimlico, 2000.

Thacker, Robert. *Alice Munro: Writing Her Lives.* Toronto: A Douglas Gibson Book, McClelland and Stewart, 2005.

Thompson, James Westfall. *Ancient Libraries.* Berkeley, Calif.: University of California Press, 1940.

Thurman, Judith. *Secrets of the Flesh: A Life of Colette.* New York: Ballantine Publishing Group, 1999.

———. "An Unsimple Heart: A New Biography of Flaubert Distills His Life." *NY,* May 6, 2002.

Tierney, John. "You type. I type. Why bother with handwriting?" *NYT,* Jan. 19, 2007.

"Today's honorary subscriber is Oliver Wendell Holmes Jr. . . ." *Edupage,* Sept. 22, 1998.

Tolstoy's Dictaphone: Technology and the Muse. Edited by Sven Birkerts. St. Paul, Minn.: Graywolf Press, 1996.

Trollope, Anthony. *The Autobiography of Anthony Trollope.* Boston: IndyPublish.com, 2003.

Trubek, Anne. "Old Writing Technologies and New Histories of Writing: What Happens When the Materiality of Writing Surfaces." www.case.edu/affil/sce/MMLA_2003.htm.

Twigg, Alan. *For Openers: Conversations with 24 Canadian Writers.* Madeira Park, British Columbia: Harbour Publishing, 1981.

———. *Strong Voices: Conversations with Fifty Canadian Authors.* Madeira Park, British Columbia: Harbour Publishing Co. Ltd., 1988.

Tyler, Natalie. *The Friendly Jane Austen: A Well-Mannered Introduction to a Lady of Sense & Sensibility.* A Winokur/Boates Book, Viking, 1999.

"Typewriter History at a Glance." MyTypewriter.com.

Unholy Ghosts: Writers on Depression. Edited by Nell Casey. New York: HarperCollinsPublishers, 2001.

"Unmasking the Bourgeoise: Bella Juliette." The France of Victor Hugo. Website article.

Updike, John. "The Changeling: A New Biography of Edith Wharton." *NY*, April 16, 2007.

———. "Imperishable Maxwell: The Library of America Celebrates the Novelist's Centennial." *NY*, Sept. 8, 2008.

———. "Late Works: Writers Confronting the End." *NY*, Aug. 7 and 14, 2006.

———. "No Brakes: A New Biography of Sinclair Lewis." *NY*, Feb. 4, 2002.

Wagner, Erica. "Philip Larkin: The 50 greatest postwar writers: 1." Times Online, Jan. 5, 2008.

Waldron, Ann. "Writers and alcohol." *Washington Post*, March 14, 1989.

Wall, Geoffrey. *Flaubert: A Life*. London: Faber and Faber Limited, 2001.

Wallace, Anne. "'Inhabited Solitudes': Dorothy Wordsworth's Domesticating Walkers." www.hum.uit.no/nord.lit/1/wallace.html.

Watt, Ian. *Conrad in the Nineteenth Century*. Berkeley, Calif.: University of California Press, 1979.

Waugh, Alexander. *Father and Sons: The Autobiography of a Family*. New York: Nan Talese/Doubleday, 2007.

Wershler-Henry, Darren. *A Fragmented History of Typewriting*. Toronto: McClelland & Stewart, 2005.

Whalley, Joyce Irene. *Writing Implements and Accessories from the Roman Stylus to the Typewriter*. Detroit: Gale Research Company, 1975.

White, Edmund. *Marcel Proust*. New York: A Lipper/Viking Book, 1999.

White, Michael. *Tolkien: A Biography*. London: Little, Brown and Company, 2001.

Whitfield, Kit. "Depression and Children's Fiction." Kit Whitfield's Blog, Sept. 22, 2008.

"Why I Write." Interview with Tracey Chevalier. guardian.co.uk, Nov. 24, 2006.

"Why I Write." Interview with Wendy Holden. guardian.co.uk, Aug. 22, 2007.

Wilford, John Noble. "Discovery of Egyptian inscriptions indicates an earlier date for origin of the alphabet." *NYT*, Nov. 13, 1999.

Willett, Edward. *J.R.R. Tolkien: Master of Imaginary Worlds*. Berkeley Heights, N.J.: Enslow Publishers, Inc., 2004.

"William Cooper: Author of 'Scenes from Provincial Life.'" *The Independent*, online edition, Sept. 6, 2002.

Williams, Deb. "The Writing [Implement] of Jane Austen – the Quill Pen." Website article.

Williams, William Carlos. *Autobiography*. New York: Random House, 1951.

Wilson, Frances. "Wordsworths in love." Times Online, Feb. 23, 2008.

Winter, Bill. "Nelson DeMille – Libertarian." Advocates for Self-Government. www.theadvocate.org/celebrities/nelson-demille.html.

"'Wireless,' (notes edited by John McGivering)." kipling.org, June 11, 2008.

Wood, James. "The man behind Bovary." *NYT*, April 16, 2006.

Woolf, Virginia. *The Death of the Moth and Other Essays*. ebooks@ Adelaide, the University of Adelaide Library, 2004.

———. *A Room of One's Own*. London: Penguin Books – Great Ideas, 2004.

"The Work Habits of Highly Successful Writers." postscripts, online magazine, May 23, 2006.

Worthen, John. *D.H. Lawrence: A Literary Life*. Basingstoke (U.K.): Palgrave Macmillan, 1989.

Wright, S. Fowler. *The Life of Sir Walter Scott, Part II*. London: The Poetry League, 1832.

"Write stuff." *Cumberland News*, June 21, 2007.

"Writer craved booze, babes." *New York Post*. April 8, 2007.

Writers at Work: The Paris Review *Interviews*. First series, paperback. Edited by Malcolm Cowley. New York: Penguin, 1977.

———. Second series. Edited by George Plimpton. Introduction by Van Wyck Brooks. New York: Viking Press, c1963.

———. Third series. Edited by George Plimpton. Introduction by Alfred Kazin. New York: Viking Press, 1967.

———. Fourth series. Edited by George Plimpton. Introduction by Wilfrid Sheed. New York: The Viking Press, 1976.

———. Fifth series. Edited by George Plimpton. Introduction by Francine du Plessix Gray. New York: Penguin Books, 1981.

———. Sixth series. Edited by George Plimpton. Introduction by Frank Kermode. New York: The Viking Press, 1984.

———. Seventh series. Edited by George Plimpton. Introduction by John Updike. New York: Viking, 1986.

———. Eighth series. Edited by George Plimpton. Introduction by Joyce Carol Oates. New York: Viking Penguin, 1988.

———. Ninth series. Edited by George Plimpton. Introduction by William Styron. New York: Viking Penguin, 1992.

The Writer's Chapbook: A Compendium of Facts, Opinion, Wit, and Advice from the 20th Century's Preeminent Writers. Edited from The Paris Review interviews and with an introduction by George Plimpton. New York: Viking, 1989.

Writers on Writing. Selected and introduced by Walter Allen. London: J.M. Dent & Sons Ltd., 1971.

Writers on Writing: Collected Essays from The New York Times. Introduction by John Darnton. New York: Times Books, Henry Holt and Company, 2001.

Writers on Writing, Volume II: More Collected Essays from The New York Times. Introduction by Jane Smiley. New York: Times Books, Henry Holt and Company, 2003.

The Writer's Quotation Book: A Literary Companion. Edited by James Charlton. New York: Pushcart, 1985.

Zeringue, Marshal. "The Jane Austen of South Alabama." Campaign for the American Reader, June 5, 2006. Website article.

Zinsser, William. On Writing Well: An Informal Guide to Writing Nonfiction (fourth edition). New York: HarperCollinsPublishers, 1990.

———. Writing with a Word Processor. New York: Harper & Row, Publishers, 1983.

Index